Star Wars:
The Essential Guide to
Weapons and Technology

Star Wars:
The Essential Guide to Weapons and Technology

by Bill Smith

Original Illustrations by David Nakabayashi
Schematics by Troy Vigil

DEL REY

The Ballantine Publishing Group • New York

A Del Rey® Book
Published by The Ballantine Publishing Group

STAR WARS ® and copyright © 1997 by Lucasfilm Ltd. Title and character and place names protected by all applicable trademark laws. All Rights Reserved. Used Under Authorization.

All rights reserved under International and Pan-American Copyright Conventions. Published in the United States by The Ballantine Publishing Group, a division of Random House, Inc., New York, and simultaneously in Canada by Random House of Canada Limited, Toronto.

http://www.randomhouse.com/delrey/

Library of Congress Catalog Card Number: 97-97009

ISBN: 0-345-41413-6

Interior and cover design by Michaelis/Carpelis Design Associates, Inc.
Cover art by David Nakabayashi

Edited by Allan Kausch (Lucasfilm) and Steve Saffel (Del Rey)

Manufactured in the United States of America

First Edition: November 1997

10 9 8 7 6 5 4 3

Author's Dedication

To Amy, who knew what she was getting herself into and married me anyway…
thanks for being there during those late nights and working weekends.
To Allan Kausch and Steve Saffel, who made this book possible…
it has been a privilege, gentlemen.

Artists' Dedication

My work is dedicated to my family: Stacey, Dad, Mom, Stephie, Elvie, and Toby.

—Troy Vigil

To Stan "The Man" Fleming. One of the guys who always kept the ball rolling.

—David Nakabayashi

Table of Contents

Author's Acknowledgments

This book draws on virtually every *Star Wars* movie, novel, reference work, comic, and game book
that has been published. I have been fortunate enough to be able to draw from the work of dozens of writers and artists, and I would be
remiss in not thanking all of them for their contributions.

Artists' Acknowledgments

I extend my deepest appreciation to Lucasfilm Licensing, especially to Allan Kausch and Lucy Wilson,
for their guidance and generosity; Steve Saffel of Ballantine/Del Rey; and George Lucas for his timeless tale that has given
me my happiest childhood memories and continues to create more.

—Troy Vigil

To the artists who had the vision and discipline to push some boundaries and
create these inspired objects, and to…Doug Chiang & co., the Bells, the Elliots, the Ramirezes, Qris Yamashita,
and the rest of my great friends and family who have always delivered too much love and support. Major Domos!

—David Nakabayashi

Introduction

"Adventure. Heh! Excitement. Heh! A Jedi craves not these things."

... Ah, but millions of us do—and *Star Wars* delivers.

We feel the excitement of the moment when Luke Skywalker first grabs a blaster and starts firing away at stormtroopers. When I first saw *Star Wars,* at the impressionable age of eight, I wondered what it would be like to wield a lightsaber in battle or to challenge Chewbacca to a game of "holochess" aboard the *Falcon.* (Incidentally, I *still* think blasters and lightsabers are pretty cool.)

That's part of the magic of *Star Wars.* These gadgets are not merely movie props—they are the keys to adventure. They immediately let us know that *Star Wars* isn't set on Earth. Instead, we've been transported to another time and another place. These tools are exotic yet familiar enough that we can relate to them.

Still, how does a blaster work? Why did the Rebel snowspeeders carry harpoon guns? How do vaporators pull water from Tatooine's parched desert air? That's where *The Essential Guide to Weapons and Technology* comes in. This handbook to the wondrous tech of the *Star Wars* universe describes 100 different devices, ranging from thermal detonators and Wookiee bowcasters to Lobot's cyborg implant and the Empire's top-secret cloaking devices.

The book's six sections cover ranged weapons, melee weapons, starship and planetary weapons and defenses, communications and sensors, security devices, and finally, a catchall category devoted to general equipment. Every section offers an overview of the given category, grounding us in the basics. Each entry describes the specific item, covering its function and operation.

Of course, *Star Wars* is about a lot more than tools and weapons. One of the main messages to be found, beginning with the movies, is that reliance on technology only limits us. Luke Skywalker was able to destroy the first Death Star because he used his own skills rather than depending on his X-wing's targeting computer. The movies remind us that we can succeed at our chosen paths regardless of the obstacles that block our way, as long as we have the courage and determination of the human spirit. Technology can never replace our intelligence and ingenuity.

But it never hurts to have the right tool handy. You know...just in case.

Bill Smith
June 16, 1997

Introduction

"Adventure. Heh! Excitement. Heh! A Jedi craves not these things."

… Ah, but millions of us do—and *Star Wars* delivers.

We feel the excitement of the moment when Luke Skywalker first grabs a blaster and starts firing away at stormtroopers. When I first saw *Star Wars*, at the impressionable age of eight, I wondered what it would be like to wield a lightsaber in battle or to challenge Chewbacca to a game of "holochess" aboard the *Falcon*. (Incidentally, I *still* think blasters and lightsabers are pretty cool.)

That's part of the magic of *Star Wars*. These gadgets are not merely movie props—they are the keys to adventure. They immediately let us know that *Star Wars* isn't set on Earth. Instead, we've been transported to another time and another place. These tools are exotic yet familiar enough that we can relate to them.

Still, how does a blaster work? Why did the Rebel snowspeeders carry harpoon guns? How do vaporators pull water from Tatooine's parched desert air? That's where *The Essential Guide to Weapons and Technology* comes in. This handbook to the wondrous tech of the *Star Wars* universe describes 100 different devices, ranging from thermal detonators and Wookiee bowcasters to Lobot's cyborg implant and the Empire's top-secret cloaking devices.

The book's six sections cover ranged weapons, melee weapons, starship and planetary weapons and defenses, communications and sensors, security devices, and finally, a catchall category devoted to general equipment. Every section offers an overview of the given category, grounding us in the basics. Each entry describes the specific item, covering its function and operation.

Of course, *Star Wars* is about a lot more than tools and weapons. One of the main messages to be found, beginning with the movies, is that reliance on technology only limits us. Luke Skywalker was able to destroy the first Death Star because he used his own skills rather than depending on his X-wing's targeting computer. The movies remind us that we can succeed at our chosen paths regardless of the obstacles that block our way, as long as we have the courage and determination of the human spirit. Technology can never replace our intelligence and ingenuity.

But it never hurts to have the right tool handy. You know…just in case.

Bill Smith
June 16, 1997

A Guide to Major Manufacturers

Dozens of manufacturers are represented in these pages, ranging from massive conglomerates such as the Tagge Company and the SoroSuub Corporation to relatively small companies such as Plescinia Entertainments, which may manufacture only a few products and cater to specialized fields. These key manufacturers, arranged according to their areas of expertise, are as follows.

SECTION ONE: RANGED WEAPONS

BlasTech Industries

- Blaster Rifle (BlasTech E-11 blaster rifle)
- Blasters (BlasTech DH-17 blaster pistol)
- E-Web Repeating Blaster (BlasTech E-Web repeating blaster)
- Heavy Blaster Pistol (BlasTech DL-44 heavy blaster pistol)
- Light Repeating Blaster (BlasTech T-21 light repeating blaster)

One of the galaxy's top arms manufacturers, BlasTech Industries is a market leader in the production of personal energy weapons and light artillery. BlasTech also manufactures an extensive line of starship weaponry, including laser and ion cannons and various types of missiles. During the Galactic Civil War BlasTech refused to sign an exclusive sales agreement with the Empire, instead selling its products to any and all buyers. Many of its weapons reached Rebel forces.

Drearian Defense Conglomerate

- Sporting Blaster (Drearian Defense Conglomerate Defender)

The Drearian Defense Conglomerate (DDC) is a medium-size weapons manufacturer with a strong presence in the Inner Rim planets and the Expansion Region. The company manufactures a wide range of weapons, including blasters, grenades, and missiles. DDC supplies blasters for Arakyd Industries' and Cybot Galactica's security droid lines.

Golan Arms

- Anti-Infantry Battery (Golan Arms DF.9 anti-infantry battery)
- Flechette Launcher (Golan Arms FC1 flechette launcher)

Once a leader in military weapons sales, Golan Arms was a top artillery manufacturer until bickering within the Imperial Army's bureaucracy resulted in the loss of most of its contracts. When the opportunity came, Golan allied itself with the New Republic. This led to a steady flow of new weapons contracts. Golan does very little of its own research and development, instead copying and refining designs from BlasTech, Czerka, and Merr-Sonn Munitions.

Loronar Defense Industries

- Blaster Artillery (Loronar MAS-2xB)

Loronar is a diversified conglomerate that may soon challenge the supremacy of BlasTech, Czerka, and Merr-Sonn in the arms markets. The company has had a commanding presence in weapons production for decades—its Turbolaser System I emplacements were the Empire's main heavy artillery pieces—and the introduction of newer designs such as the System IV and the mobile MAS-2xB has cemented the company's dominant position. Loronar also has been a very successful starship manufacturer; its designs include Imperial *Strike*-class cruisers and torpedo spheres.

Merr-Sonn Munitions, Inc.

- Heavy Blaster Pistol (Merr-Sonn "Power" 5)
- Flame Projector (Merr-Sonn C-22 flame carbine)
- Flame Projector (Merr-Sonn CR-24 flame rifle)
- Grenade Mortar (Merr-Sonn MobileMortar-3)
- Grenades (Merr-Sonn C-22 fragmentation grenade)
- Grenades (Merr-Sonn glop grenade)
- Grenades (Merr-Sonn WW-41 CryoBan grenade)
- Missile Tube (Merr-Sonn Munitions PLX-2M)
- Thermal Detonator (Merr-Sonn Munitions Class-A thermal detonator)

Merr-Sonn Munitions is one of the galaxy's top three weapons manufacturers, lagging only slightly behind BlasTech in total sales. The company produces an extensive line of personal and vehicle blasters as well as artillery and starship turbolasers. Merr-Sonn also manufactures top-selling missile, grenade, projectile, and melee weapons. Other product lines include enhanced electronic sights, targeting systems, and personal defenses and armor. Subsidiaries include Merr-Sonn Mil/Sci, which produces heavy artillery and siege weapons.

Minor Manufacturers

There are a number of medium-size and small companies whose products are presented in this section. Atgar SpaceDefense produces the 1.4 FD P-Tower antivehicle artillery piece, while Kelvarek Consolidated Arms manufactures the MM9 wrist rocket system used by Boba Fett. Malaxan Firepower Incorporated's extensive weaponry line includes the FWG-5 flechette launcher and several other projectile and energy weapon designs. Oriolanis Defense Systems produces many low-tech weapons, including magnetic accelerator guns and the Striker projectile pistol. Pacnorval Defense Systems, Limited, manufactures a full range of sonic weapons, including the Sd-77 sonic pistol and the Sg-82 sonic rifle. Prax Arms builds various projectile weapons, such as the Stealth-2VX palm shooter and the Protector PRP-502 hold-out shooter dart pistols. The Tenloss Syndicate is a powerful criminal organization that manufactures many contraband goods, including the DX-2 disruptor pistol and the DXR-6 disruptor rifle. Timms UniStar Armaments long ago ceased operations, but it had the distinction of building the first beam tube energy weapons.

Various alien cultures have produced notable technological applications. The Dresselians managed to drive the Empire from their world, using only simple projectile rifles. The Jawas of the planet Tatooine developed ionization blasters for capturing droids. The alien Ssi-ruuk use ion paddle beamers to stun and disable their victims. The Stokhli people created spray sticks to down large beasts on their world's vast savannas. The Wookiees developed their formidable bowcasters to deal with the dangerous predators in Kashyyyk's jungles.

SECTION TWO: MELEE WEAPONS

Czerka

- Vibroblade (Czerka vibroknuckler)

The galaxy's third largest arms manufacturer, Czerka produces blasters, artillery, melee weapons, starship weapons, and starship defense systems. During the Galactic Civil War, Czerka reluctantly agreed to establish an exclusive distribution agreement with the Empire, although it has been a strong supporter of the New Republic in recent years.

Jedi Knights

- Exar Kun's Lightsaber (Double-bladed lightsaber)
- Lightsaber (Darth Vader's lightsaber)
- Lightsaber (Luke Skywalker's lightsaber)

The Jedi Knights guarded the Old Republic from threats for over a thousand generations, using their incredible lightsabers to battle against the forces of evil. Before the Jedi were nearly exterminated by Emperor Palpatine, they developed the designs and skills needed to craft lightsabers. These skills have been mastered by Luke Skywalker, who has established his own Jedi academy on Yavin Four.

SoroSuub Corporation

- Force Pike (SoroSuub Controller FP)
- Vibro-Ax (SoroSuub BD-1 Cutter vibro-ax)

SoroSuub Corporation is one of the galaxy's most diverse corporations, with interests in starships, weapons, communications and sensors, and droids. During the Galactic Civil War SoroSuub secretly supplied weapons and goods to the Rebel Alliance; the company remains a key ally of the New Republic.

Minor Manufacturers

Aeramaxis Technologies is a small manufacturer that produces the Evasive-13 individual field disruptor. The Gamorreans and the Tusken Raiders of the planet Tatooine are also notable for their development of melee weapons.

SECTION THREE: STARSHIP AND PLANETARY WEAPONS AND DEFENSES

Arakyd Industries

- Concussion Missiles (Arakyd ST2 concussion missile rack)

Arakyd Industries is still a large droid, weapons, and starship manufacturer despite its prior Imperial-loyalist position. Arakyd has a highly successful line of droid-brain-enhanced automated weapons systems and designs many prisoner control devices, including nerve disrupters and interrogation droids. It also manufactures highly advanced droids for the security market, using technology developed for its lethal probots and seekers.

Borstel Galactic Defense

- Ion Cannons (Borstel NK-7 ion cannon)

Borstel produces a wide range of starship weapons and defenses, including turbolasers, ion cannons, deflector shield generators, and missiles manufactured for the civilian and military markets.

Chempat Engineered Defenses

- Deflector Shield Generator (Chempat shield generator)

Chempat is a top developer of deflector shield and sensors technology. The company is jointly owned by Corellian Engineering Corporation and Kuat Drive Yards.

CoMar Weapons

- Planetary Shields (CoMar SLD-26 planetary shield generator)

A fierce competitor in the planetary defense market, CoMar is known for its large-scale shield generators and low-orbit blaster artillery weapons.

cyborg implants, also manufactures communications and sensor gear for starship, industrial, and personal use.

Cryoncorp.
- Portable Scanner (Cryoncorp. EnhanceScan general-purpose scanner)

Cryoncorp. produces a wide array of portable sensor units as well as sensor packs found in various New Republic combat vehicles.

Fabritech
- Comlinks (Fabritech PAC20 visual wrist comm)
- Starship Sensor Array (Fabritech ANq-51 sensor array computer)
- Sensor Beacon (Fabritech SE-Vigilant automated sensor beacon)

Fabritech has been a leader in starship sensor technology for nearly five decades, and its sensor systems are used in many warships, including all the New Republic's main fighters.

MicroThrust Processors
- Com-Scan (MicroThrust OrC-19 com-scan integrator console)

MicroThrust Processors specializes in communications integrations systems. Military contracts account for over two-thirds of its business, although it also develops routing systems for subspace networks and other transmission systems.

Neuro-Saav Technologies
- Electrotelescope (Neuro-Saav VXI-3 electrotelescope)
- Homing Beacon (Neuro-Saav XXt-26 S-Thread Tracker)

Neuro-Saav is a major electronics and technologies firm with divisions dedicated to imaging systems, sensors, communications, medical biotechnology, and military encryption. It is also one of the galaxy's top cybernetics manufacturers.

Minor Manufacturers
Miradyne Limited produces sensor and jamming systems, including the 4x-Phantom short-range jammer used in the New Republic's A-wing. Rhinsome Tracking Corporation manufactures portable tracking and detection systems.

Section Five: Security Devices

Athakam MedTech/RSMA
- Bioscan (Athakam/RSMA bioscan unit)

Athakam MedTech maintains a strategic partnership with Rhinnal State Medical Academy to produce high-technology medical equipment, including microsurgery computers, cybernetic controllers, and hyperbaric medical chambers.

Corporate Sector Authority (CSA)
- Anticoncussion Field (CSA *Rampart*-Class anticoncussion generator)
- Molecularly Bonded Armor (CSA molecular-bond armor sheath)

The Corporate Sector Authority (CSA) was established by the Empire as a quasi-independent company set up to rule over a vast tract of space and supply raw materials and finished goods to the Imperial war machine. After the Empire collapsed, the CSA closed its borders and internal power struggles exploded into open conflict. The CSA has since resumed trade, but key New Republic officials—including Han Solo—harbor considerable mistrust toward it. Like SoroSuub and the Tagge Company, the CSA is highly diversified.

Ubrikkian Transports
- Man Trap (Ubrikkian R-TechApp man trap)

Ubrikkian Transports is known primarily for its airspeeders and landspeeders, but the company manufactures a number of repulsorlift-equipped goods for industrial and military use.

Minor Manufacturers
Other security manufacturers include Corellidyne Visuals, maker of imaging systems and the CQ-3.9x holographic image disguiser. Locris Syndicated Securities manufactures stun cuffs, mobile prisoner cages, and other goods aimed at the security industry. OutlawTech is the fanciful name for a group of criminal slicers who build electronic lock breakers and other security intrusion systems. The Thalassian Slavers Guild—maker of slaving collars—was once one of the galaxy's most infamous slaving groups. It has been disbanded by the New Republic.

Section Six: General Equipment

BioTech Industries
- Cyborg Unit (BioTech Borg Construct Aj^6)
- Medpac (BioTech FastFlesh medpac)

BioTech Industries is one of the galaxy's top cybernetics manufacturers, particularly in the area of cyborg biocomputer implants. The company is jointly owned by Neuro-Saav and the Tagge Company.

Chiewab Amalgamated Pharmaceuticals Company
- Medpac (Chiewab GLiS emergency medpac)

Chiewab is a medical, pharmaceuticals, and chemicals conglomerate. It owns over six hundred planetary systems and devotes considerable resources to exploring planets to find plants that can be synthesized into valuable biotech goods. These products are spun off to subsidiaries such as Geentech Laboratories and Chiewab Nutrition for development and marketing.

Corellian Engineering Corporation

- Laser Cannons (Corellian Engineering Corporation AG-2G quad laser cannon)

Corellian Engineering Corporation (CEC) is best known for its fast starships, but it also maintains a top-flight staff of weapons design engineers. Its laser cannons have top-notch targeting computers, are easy to repair, and are popular with smugglers since they can be upgraded easily.

Frei-Tek, Inc.

- Cluster Bomb (Frei-Tek CL-3 Antistarfighter cluster bomb)

Frei-Tek first came to prominence as a starfighter design firm, but after its E-wing fighter was nearly grounded because of its ineffective laser cannons, the company moved into the designing of weapons and targeting computers. Frei-Tek now has a line of high-yield laser cannons as well as cluster bombs and EchoBurst concussion missiles with advanced homing computers.

Imperial Department of Military Research

- Cloaking Device (Imperial Cloaking Device)
- Galaxy Gun (Custom Imperial Superweapon)
- Orbital Nightcloak (Imperial Department of Military Research orbital nightcloak)
- Superlaser (Custom Imperial Superweapon)
- Sun Crusher (Custom Imperial Superweapon)

After seizing power, one of the Empire's top priorities was the development of weapons that could be used to terrify worlds into submission. While the Empire's top weapon designers developed horrifying siege weapons, such as the superlaser and the Sun Crusher, Rebel Alliance and New Republic forces destroyed those weapons before they could be used against the free worlds on a mass scale.

Kuat Drive Yards

- Deflector Shield Generator (KDY ISD-72x deflector shield generator domes)
- Planetary Ion Cannons (Kuat Drive Yards v-150 Planet Defender)
- Planetary Turbolaser (Kuat Drive Yards w-165 planetary turbolaser)

While Kuat Drive Yards is recognized as a starship designer, the company also has a planetary weapons department that produces laser and ion cannons used to drive off orbiting enemy fleets. Kuat's old-guard executives were quite loyal to the Empire, but a new generation of leaders has worked very hard to earn the trust of the New Republic government.

Sienar Fleet Systems

- Diamond Boron Missile (Sienar Fleet Systems MS-15 diamond boron missile)

Sienar Fleet Systems remains one of the galaxy's dominant starship design firms, and expansion into combat vehicles, weapon design, and planetary defenses has strengthened Sienar during the periods of uncertainty and conflict that have plagued the New Republic's rule. While Sienar built ships for the Empire until Grand Admiral Thrawn's defeat, the company now supplies vessels to all buyers, including the New Republic.

Taim & Bak

- Laser Cannons (Taim & Bak KX9 laser cannon)
- Turbolasers (Taim & Bak XX-9 turbolasers)

Taim & Bak is a smaller weapons company that has a high profile because its designs have been used in many starships, including X-wings, Corellian Corvettes, and Imperial Star Destroyers. The company is still owned by the Taim and Bak families, although it shares research and development facilities with Borstel Galactic Defense.

Minor Manufacturers

Some of the smaller manufacturers include Conner Ship Systems, a maker of specialty starship weapons such as capture nets and space mines. Krupx Munitions is a starship weapons supplier and makes MG7-A proton torpedoes and various concussion missile designs. Phylon Transport produces a wide range of tractor beam projectors for industrial and starship yard applications; its Q7 military-grade tractor beam was designed for use aboard Imperial Star Destroyers.

SECTION FOUR: SENSORS AND COMMUNICATIONS

Carbanti United Electronics

- Starship Sensor Array (Carbanti Universal Transceiver Package and Bertriak "Screamer" Active Jammer)

Carbanti is a top sensor manufacturer whose units are used by many of the largest starship manufacturers, including Koensayr and the Corellian Engineering Corporation.

Chedak Communications

- Subspace Transceivers (Chedak Frequency Agile subspace transceiver)

Chedak is a diversified communications company that produces comlink and subspace transmitters and owns several subspace broadcast networks and holographic entertainment studios.

Crozo Industrial Products

- Comlinks (Crozo Industrial Products 3-MAL personal comlink)
- Cybernetic Implant Comlink/Pager (Crozo Industrial Products At-cyb husher mike)

Crozo Industrial Products, an industry leader in biocomp

A Guide to Major Manufacturers

Dozens of manufacturers are represented in these pages, ranging from massive conglomerates such as the Tagge Company and the SoroSuub Corporation to relatively small companies such as Plescinia Entertainments, which may manufacture only a few products and cater to specialized fields. These key manufacturers, arranged according to their areas of expertise, are as follows.

Section One: Ranged Weapons

BlasTech Industries

- Blaster Rifle (BlasTech E-11 blaster rifle)
- Blasters (BlasTech DH-17 blaster pistol)
- E-Web Repeating Blaster (BlasTech E-Web repeating blaster)
- Heavy Blaster Pistol (BlasTech DL-44 heavy blaster pistol)
- Light Repeating Blaster (BlasTech T-21 light repeating blaster)

One of the galaxy's top arms manufacturers, BlasTech Industries is a market leader in the production of personal energy weapons and light artillery. BlasTech also manufactures an extensive line of starship weaponry, including laser and ion cannons and various types of missiles. During the Galactic Civil War BlasTech refused to sign an exclusive sales agreement with the Empire, instead selling its products to any and all buyers. Many of its weapons reached Rebel forces.

Drearian Defense Conglomerate

- Sporting Blaster (Drearian Defense Conglomerate Defender)

The Drearian Defense Conglomerate (DDC) is a medium-size weapons manufacturer with a strong presence in the Inner Rim planets and the Expansion Region. The company manufactures a wide range of weapons, including blasters, grenades, and missiles. DDC supplies blasters for Arakyd Industries' and Cybot Galactica's security droid lines.

Golan Arms

- Anti-Infantry Battery (Golan Arms DF.9 anti-infantry battery)
- Flechette Launcher (Golan Arms FC1 flechette launcher)

Once a leader in military weapons sales, Golan Arms was a top artillery manufacturer until bickering within the Imperial Army's bureaucracy resulted in the loss of most of its contracts. When the opportunity came, Golan allied itself with the New Republic. This led to a steady flow of new weapons contracts. Golan does very little of its own research and development, instead copying and refining designs from BlasTech, Czerka, and Merr-Sonn Munitions.

Loronar Defense Industries

- Blaster Artillery (Loronar MAS-2xB)

Loronar is a diversified conglomerate that may soon challenge the supremacy of BlasTech, Czerka, and Merr-Sonn in the arms markets. The company has had a commanding presence in weapons production for decades—its Turbolaser System I emplacements were the Empire's main heavy artillery pieces—and the introduction of newer designs such as the System IV and the mobile MAS-2xB has cemented the company's dominant position. Loronar also has been a very successful starship manufacturer; its designs include Imperial Strike-class cruisers and torpedo spheres.

Merr-Sonn Munitions, Inc.

- Heavy Blaster Pistol (Merr-Sonn "Power" 5)
- Flame Projector (Merr-Sonn C-22 flame carbine)
- Flame Projector (Merr-Sonn CR-24 flame rifle)
- Grenade Mortar (Merr-Sonn MobileMortar-3)
- Grenades (Merr-Sonn C-22 fragmentation grenade)
- Grenades (Merr-Sonn glop grenade)
- Grenades (Merr-Sonn WW-41 CryoBan grenade)
- Missile Tube (Merr-Sonn Munitions PLX-2M)
- Thermal Detonator (Merr-Sonn Munitions Class-A thermal detonator)

Merr-Sonn Munitions is one of the galaxy's top three weapons manufacturers, lagging only slightly behind BlasTech in total sales. The company produces an extensive line of personal and vehicle blasters as well as artillery and starship turbolasers. Merr-Sonn also manufactures top-selling missile, grenade, projectile, and melee weapons. Other product lines include enhanced electronic sights, targeting systems, and personal defenses and armor. Subsidiaries include Merr-Sonn Mil/Sci, which produces heavy artillery and siege weapons.

Minor Manufacturers

There are a number of medium-size and small companies whose products are presented in this section. Atgar SpaceDefense produces the 1.4 FD P-Tower antivehicle artillery piece, while Kelvarek Consolidated Arms manufactures the MM9 wrist rocket system used by Boba Fett. Malaxan Firepower Incorporated's extensive weaponry line includes the FWG-5 flechette launcher and several other projectile and energy weapon designs. Oriolanis Defense Systems produces many low-tech weapons, including magnetic accelerator guns and the Striker projectile pistol. Pacnorval Defense Systems, Limited, manufactures a full range of sonic weapons, including the Sd-77 sonic pistol and the Sg-82 sonic rifle. Prax Arms builds various projectile weapons, such as the Stealth-2VX palm shooter and the Protector PRP-502 hold-out shooter dart pistols. The Tenloss Syndicate is a powerful criminal organization that manufactures many contraband goods, including the DX-2 disruptor pistol and the DXR-6 disruptor rifle. Timms UniStar Armaments long ago ceased operations, but it had the distinction of building the first beam tube energy weapons.

Various alien cultures have produced notable technological applications. The Dresselians managed to drive the Empire from their world, using only simple projectile rifles. The Jawas of the planet Tatooine developed ionization blasters for capturing droids. The alien Ssi-ruuk use ion paddle beamers to stun and disable their victims. The Stokhli people created spray sticks to down large beasts on their world's vast savannas. The Wookiees developed their formidable bowcasters to deal with the dangerous predators in Kashyyyk's jungles.

Section Two: Melee Weapons

Czerka

- Vibroblade (Czerka vibroknuckler)

The galaxy's third largest arms manufacturer, Czerka produces blasters, artillery, melee weapons, starship weapons, and starship defense systems. During the Galactic Civil War, Czerka reluctantly agreed to establish an exclusive distribution agreement with the Empire, although it has been a strong supporter of the New Republic in recent years.

Jedi Knights

- Exar Kun's Lightsaber (Double-bladed lightsaber)
- Lightsaber (Darth Vader's lightsaber)
- Lightsaber (Luke Skywalker's lightsaber)

The Jedi Knights guarded the Old Republic from threats for over a thousand generations, using their incredible lightsabers to battle against the forces of evil. Before the Jedi were nearly exterminated by Emperor Palpatine, they developed the designs and skills needed to craft lightsabers. These skills have been mastered by Luke Skywalker, who has established his own Jedi academy on Yavin Four.

SoroSuub Corporation

- Force Pike (SoroSuub Controller FP)
- Vibro-Ax (SoroSuub BD-1 Cutter vibro-ax)

SoroSuub Corporation is one of the galaxy's most diverse corporations, with interests in starships, weapons, communications and sensors, and droids. During the Galactic Civil War SoroSuub secretly supplied weapons and goods to the Rebel Alliance; the company remains a key ally of the New Republic.

Minor Manufacturers

Aeramaxis Technologies is a small manufacturer that produces the Evasive-13 individual field disruptor. The Gamorreans and the Tusken Raiders of the planet Tatooine are also notable for their development of melee weapons.

Section Three: Starship and Planetary Weapons and Defenses

Arakyd Industries

- Concussion Missiles (Arakyd ST2 concussion missile rack)

Arakyd Industries is still a large droid, weapons, and starship manufacturer despite its prior Imperial-loyalist position. Arakyd has a highly successful line of droid-brain-enhanced automated weapons systems and designs many prisoner control devices, including nerve disrupters and interrogation droids. It also manufactures highly advanced droids for the security market, using technology developed for its lethal probots and seekers.

Borstel Galactic Defense

- Ion Cannons (Borstel NK-7 ion cannon)

Borstel produces a wide range of starship weapons and defenses, including turbolasers, ion cannons, deflector shield generators, and missiles manufactured for the civilian and military markets.

Chempat Engineered Defenses

- Deflector Shield Generator (Chempat shield generator)

Chempat is a top developer of deflector shield and sensors technology. The company is jointly owned by Corellian Engineering Corporation and Kuat Drive Yards.

CoMar Weapons

- Planetary Shields (CoMar SLD-26 planetary shield generator)

A fierce competitor in the planetary defense market, CoMar is known for its large-scale shield generators and low-orbit blaster artillery weapons.

Industrial Automaton

- Remote (Industrial Automaton Marksman-H combat remote)

Industrial Automaton, one of the galaxy's largest droid companies, also produces drones, computers, and automated machinery.

The Tagge Company (TaggeCo.)

- Recording Rod (TaggeCo. PersonalAssistant-4x recording rod)

The Tagge Company is one of the galaxy's largest and most influential corporations. It is also one of the few large, privately held companies, with sixty-five percent ownership by the Tagge family. TaggeCo. owns hundreds of subsidiaries, extending its reach into just about every conceivable market, and it was also the primary sponsor of the Corporate Sector Authority. TaggeCo.'s executive board was populated by staunch Imperial loyalists throughout the Galactic Civil War, although the company's operations are now supervised by New Republic observers.

Minor Manufacturers

Figg and Associates, Ltd., maintains substantial mining interests on Cloud City and manufactures carbon-freezing chambers. Gandorthal Atmospherics, maker of the Roamer-6 breath mask, specializes in survival and atmospheric processing equipment. Karflo Corporation is a mining, exploration, and xenobiotechnology company; its G2-GE beamdrill is one of dozens of heavy industry products. Lerrimore Contracting Co. has over three hundred subsidiaries and manufactures a wide range of household goods, appliances, and furniture. MicroData Technologies, maker of the Companion2000 datapad, is a mainstream computer and droid components manufacturer. Mitrinomon Transports is a personal transportation firm with a wide range of jet and rocket packs. Plescinia Entertainments is a holographic imaging company. Pretormin Environmental is a small company with interests in the fields of environmental control, exploration, and survival gear; its GX-8 water vaporators are very popular. Regallis Engineering and Udrane Galactic Electronics both produce computerized tools for mechanics and other technical professionals. Zaltin Bacta Corporation, based on the planet Thyferra, is one of the galaxy's top two bacta producers and controls over four hundred different planets for the cultivation of alazhi, a critical raw material used in bacta production. Zaltin also manufactures bacta tanks.

Star Wars:
The Essential Guide to
Weapons and Technology

RANGED WEAPONS

THE SOCIOLOGY OF WEAPONRY

Through thousands of years of galactic civilization, one constant is the ever-present struggle to resolve disputes peacefully. In the end, however, factors such as political turmoil, economic competition, misunderstanding, and greed have motivated societies to take up arms and settle their differences through the use of violence.

Each society devises its own values system when it comes to weaponry and warfare. The Wookiees of Kashyyyk developed weapons as tools for hunting and fending off dangerous predators but soon adapted them to combat after Imperial stormtroopers occupied their world. Similarly, the Mon Calamari had never known warfare on their peaceful ocean world, but when the Empire enslaved them, they also changed, using violence to cast out the attackers.

Other cultures are far more aggressive and use weapons to defeat and conquer. Rodians are among the galaxy's most warlike species, and in the early days of their civilization, wars between their clans caused immense devastation on their homeworld. In time they turned their aggression against other creatures and evolved into a culture in which hunting skills were prized above all others. Upon encountering the Old Republic, the Rodians learned about another type of hunt and embraced the heartless ways of bounty hunters.

EVOLUTION OF RANGED WEAPONS

Ranged weapons were developed when warriors realized it would be advantageous to be able to strike at opponents from a relatively safe distance. The first such weapons were primitive—crude spears, dart shooters, and bows and arrows—but they soon proved superior in battle.

Over thousands of years of civilization technological advances have been applied continually to achieve greater range, higher rates of fire, and more deadly results. As species have increased their knowledge, their weapons have incorporated more complex mechanisms and other innovations.

Many species experimented with new technologies, developing their own versions of slug throwers, missiles, flame projectors, magnetic accelerators, and sonic weapons. Each of these weapons enjoyed a period of supremacy on the battlefield, only to be rendered obsolete by new and improved defensive counterparts.

Many millennia ago, before the founding of the Old Republic, the invention of the portable power cell and the discovery of high-energy gases led to the development of the first energy weapons, known as beam tubes. Subsequent advancement produced higher-yield power cells and miniaturized components, and weapons became smaller—yet more deadly—and evolved into modern blasters.

Blaster technology now dominates all types of combat, from ground-level infantry battles to fleet battles conducted in the vastness of space, where banks of turbolasers hurl blasts of unbelievable power to devastate enemy vessels thousands of kilometers away.

High technology also has been applied to so-called archaic weapons, resulting in miniaturized wrist rockets, grenades with powerful thermite explosive cores, and missiles with sophisticated targeting computers. These weapons offer advantages in particular types of engagements and situations. For example, an old-fashioned projectile rifle may be practical, since the slug thrower can be silenced and has no visible energy beam, and its simple mechanical firing mechanism is easy to repair.

UNIQUE TECHNOLOGICAL APPLICATIONS

Many alien species have developed many weapons uniquely crafted to suit their needs. For example, the Wookiee bowcaster is almost unusable by many other species because a user must have incredible strength just to cock the weapon and contain its recoil. Yet its short-range explosive projectiles are perfectly suited to combat in the dense jungles of Kashyyyk.

In the same vein, most beings might consider an ionization blaster, used to disable droids, to be of marginal value, but this weapon sustains the Jawas of Tatooine, whose entire culture centers on scavenging, repairing, and selling droids and other machinery. Likewise, the Stokhli people of the planet Manress developed their spray sticks to capture and stun large game; the fact that the weapon has military applications is incidental as far as they are concerned.

WEAPON TERMINOLOGY

The ranged weapon category covers any tool that delivers an attack over a distance. This category also encompasses vehicle weapons and long-range artillery pieces, although it does not include starship weapons. This category's subsections are personal weapons, light artillery pieces, and artillery.

Personal weapons are those that can be carried and used easily by an individual soldier, including blaster pistols and rifles, projectile rifles, and dart shooters.

Light artillery pieces—also known as heavy weapons—are those that require more than one crew member. Most of them use portable power generators and tripod mounts; some are transported on repulsorlift trailers. The smallest of these weapons include BlasTech's T-21 light repeating blaster and the E-Web heavy repeating blaster. They are also known as infantry support weapons because each squad of soldiers normally carries a repeating blaster. Light artillery also includes vehicle weapons such as mounted repeating blasters, blaster cannons, missile racks, and grenade launchers.

Artillery weapons are designed for attacking fortified targets such as buildings, shield generators, and bunkers. Some medium-size artillery pieces also can be targeted

against vehicles and infantry squads. Most artillery pieces are stationary, with high-output power generators, large crews, and armored housings, although some are mounted on a repulsorlift chassis and used as mobile siege weapons. The largest artillery pieces are employed for long-range attacks against enemy bases and cities. This category does not include immense turbolasers that are used to attack orbiting starships. Those are classified as planetary weapons.

A weapon's optimal range is the distance at which a reasonably skilled gunner can expect to hit a target. Its maximum range is the upper end of the weapon's targeting distance: A hit at maximum range is possible but unlikely. Many factors affect a weapon's range, including its targeting/sighting system, energy output, and overall accuracy. For example, a blaster's range is determined by how much galven circuitry is used to keep the beam coherent over long distances.

A weapon's ammunition capacity indicates how many times it can be fired before more ammunition must be loaded. Its rate of fire indicates how often it can be fired. Limiting factors may include the amount of time a blaster's actuator needs to cool between shots and how quickly power cells can deliver an adequate charge. For projectile weapons, fire rate is based largely on how fast the mechanical feeder can load new ammunition into the firing chamber.

Line-of-sight (LOS) weapons are those that fire in a straight line, directly at the target. Blasters and slug throwers are LOS weapons. While their ranges are limited compared with those of other types of weapons, most LOS weapons deliver attacks so quickly that a target has almost no chance of avoiding an accurate shot.

Guided weapons, such as missiles, are capable of making midflight course corrections to home in on a target. While they tend to have longer ranges than do LOS weapons, their homing systems can be fooled by countermeasures systems and they can be shot down by antimissile defenses.

Unguided weapons include missiles and shells that can be used for indirect fire. They may be fired with an arcing trajectory in order to hit targets located beyond the horizon or behind cover. These weapons cannot be fooled by countermeasures since they have no guidance systems, although they may be destroyed by antimissile measures.

BLASTERS

BlasTech DH-17 Blaster Pistol

In a galaxy consumed by conflict, weapons are a dangerous but necessary fact of life. The most common sidearm is the high-energy laser/particle beam weapon commonly called a blaster.

The three main blaster manufacturers—BlasTech Industries, Merr-Sonn Munitions, Inc., and SoroSuub Corporation—produce many different blaster models that vary widely in size and energy output, ranging from palm-sized "hold-out blasters" to incredibly powerful E-Web heavy repeating blasters. Vehicles and starships often wield powerful blaster or laser cannons. Blasters offer many advantages, including reliability, portability, ease of maintenance and repair, and the ability to deliver a great deal of damage.

When a blaster is fired, a small amount of high-energy blaster gas moves from the gas chamber to the gas conversion enabler (commonly called an XCiter). There the gas is excited by energy from the weapon's power source, which is a small power pack for hand weapons and a reactor or a power generator for a larger weapon. The excited gas passes into the actuating blaster module, where it is processed into a beam comprised of intense energy particles coupled with light. The prismatic crystal housing focuses the beam, which is further focused, or "galvenned," as it passes down the blaster's barrel. The final particle beam, or "bolt," contains high-energy particles that cause tremendous damage to anything they hit; the bolt's visible light is a harmless by-product of this reaction.

The BlasTech DH-17 blaster pistol is a standard-issue military sidearm used by both Imperial Navy and Rebel soldiers. With its sturdy and reliable design, it remains a popular weapon with New Republic personnel. The DH-17 is designed for short-range combat, with an optimum range of 30 meters and a maximum range of 120 meters. Its blasts can pierce stormtrooper armor or penetrate a low-level force field but won't puncture the hull of a starship. It is a perfect weapon for shipboard troopers, and on the low-power "stun" setting a blast can knock a human unconscious for up to ten minutes.

The DH-17's blaster gas chamber carries enough blaster gas for over five hundred shots, while its power pack supplies sufficient energy for one hundred shots. An experienced trooper can change packs in about five seconds, and drained packs can be recharged via a generator in about fifteen minutes.

Like most sidearms, the DH-17 is semiautomatic, firing once each time the trigger is pulled. The weapon can be modified for fully automatic fire, although this mode drains the power pack in less than twenty seconds and excess heat may melt the internal components or cause an explosive overload. It has long been illegal for non-military personnel to possess blaster pistols on many Imperial and New Republic worlds, although they are widely available through black market channels.

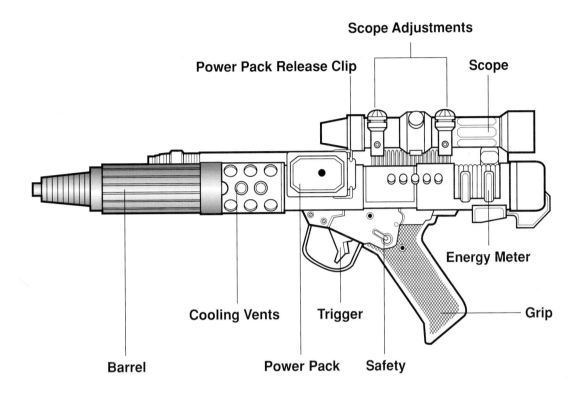

Scope Adjustments

Power Pack Release Clip

Scope

Energy Meter

Cooling Vents

Trigger

Grip

Barrel

Power Pack

Safety

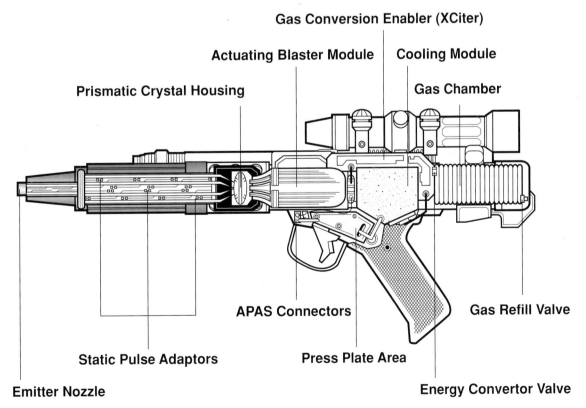

Gas Conversion Enabler (XCiter)

Actuating Blaster Module

Cooling Module

Prismatic Crystal Housing

Gas Chamber

APAS Connectors

Gas Refill Valve

Static Pulse Adaptors

Press Plate Area

Emitter Nozzle

Energy Convertor Valve

BLASTER RIFLE

BLASTECH E-11 BLASTER RIFLE

The BlasTech E-11 blaster rifle was declared the standard sidearm for Imperial stormtroopers because it offered the great range and heavy damage of a traditional long-barreled rifle in a compact, easy-to-wield weapon. The E-11 has a light, well-balanced design that permits accurate one-handed fire, allowing soldiers to move unencumbered and use the weapon in close quarters almost as easily as one wields a pistol. This rifle has good long-range targeting because of the extendable sighting stock, the barrel's advanced galven circuitry, and the computer-enhanced scope, which filters out smoke and haze and enhances vision in low-light conditions.

The E-11 blaster rifle has a maximum range of three hundred meters and an optimum range of one hundred meters, nearly three times the reach of a blaster pistol. This range is achieved because the barrel runs almost the entire length of the weapon, producing a tightly focused and very powerful particle beam.

To accommodate this barrel design, only the actuating blaster module and the prismatic crystal housing are placed behind the barrel. Other components are mounted to the side or underneath the galven circuitry, while the gas chamber has a unique tubular design that wraps around the back of the barrel. These components are mounted on a single module that slides out of the back of the weapon for repair or replacement.

To prevent dangerous heat buildup, the E-11's

cooling coils force-feed a liquid cooling agent called freelol through an intricate capillary system that carries heat away from vital components and into the forward vent capacitator.

The side-mounted power pack supplies enough energy for one hundred shots. The E-11 can be set for a variety of power levels, from stun to full blast. Because of its large quarter-centimeter bore, the E-11 is quite lethal at full power. Although both Imperial and New Republic soldiers normally use the semiautomatic setting in order to conserve ammunition and allow adequate cooling, the weapon has full automatic and pulse fire settings. Extended automatic fire may throw the barrel out of alignment.

While the E-11 was sold exclusively to the Empire during the Galactic Civil War, the Rebel Alliance managed to acquire thousands of these weapons through black market purchases and outright theft. The E-11 and its technological "clone," a SoroSuub-manufactured blaster rifle called the Stormtrooper One (later renamed the Freedom One), remained favorites of both Imperial and New Republic forces.

Other blaster rifle models frequently used by military forces include the SoroSuub Heavy Tracker 16, the Merr-Sonn G8, and the very powerful BlasTech A280, but none of these weapons matches the versatility or reliability of the E-11.

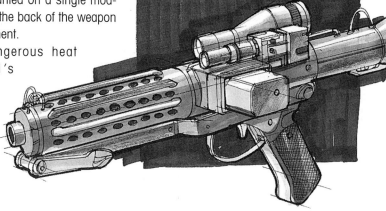

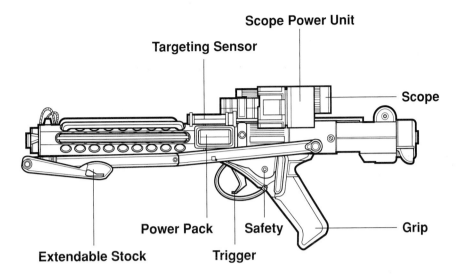

Scope Power Unit

Targeting Sensor

Scope

Power Pack   Safety   Grip

Extendable Stock   Trigger

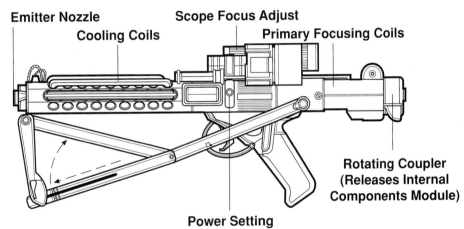

Emitter Nozzle   Scope Focus Adjust

Cooling Coils   Primary Focusing Coils

Rotating Coupler
(Releases Internal
Components Module)

Power Setting

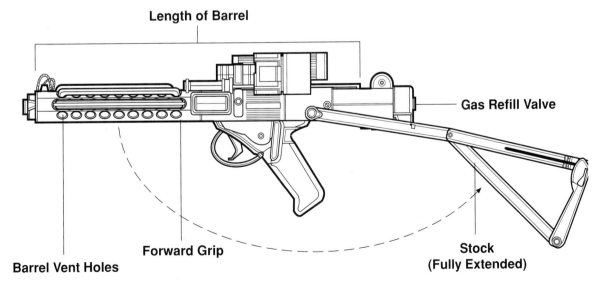

Length of Barrel

Gas Refill Valve

Barrel Vent Holes

Forward Grip

Stock
(Fully Extended)

HEAVY BLASTER PISTOL

BLASTECH DL-44 HEAVY BLASTER PISTOL

A weapon made famous by the smuggler turned diplomat Han Solo, the BlasTech DL-44 heavy blaster pistol packs the formidable punch of a high-powered rifle into a small sidearm not much bigger than a standard pistol. Favored by gunmen and smugglers—dangerous people with quick reflexes, keen peripheral vision, and a willingness to do whatever it takes to survive—it causes even the bravest to duck for cover when they find themselves staring down its barrel.

Designed for close-quarters combat, this portable and very lethal blaster was often carried by Rebel soldiers because it reliably punched through stormtrooper armor. In addition to the DL-44 (top schematic), two popular heavy blaster pistols are the Merr-Sonn "Flash" 4 (a knockoff of BlasTech's design) and the more compact Merr-Sonn "Power" 5.

A weapon favoring brute force over finesse, the DL-44 delivers tremendous damage, yet is small enough to be fired one-handed; its range is twenty-five meters with a maximum of fifty meters, however. The DL-44's XCiter consumes energy at four times the rate of a blaster pistol, draining a power pack after only twenty-five shots. The user must carefully target shots instead of "filling the air with energy"(indiscriminately firing in the general direction of a target). Because of the excessive power consumption, the DL-44's grip has a vibrating "cautionary pulser" that silently alerts the user when the

pack is down to five shots or less. A quick release lever and the power pack's convenient location—immediately in front of the trigger—allow very quick replacement of drained packs. Soldiers bringing heavy blaster pistols into battle normally carry at least a dozen power packs.

Just as the *Millennium Falcon* is far from being a "stock" freighter, Han Solo's DL-44 is custom-crafted and greatly enhanced. Solo added a scope with motion sensor software and computer-enhanced low-light sighting. The galven circuitry is extensively modified to deliver increased damage without draining additional power. Solo carries the blaster in a quick-draw holster, giving him an added edge when speed counts.

In his younger days Han Solo was as famous for his blindingly fast draw as for his outrageous smuggling exploits. Time and again he outdrew—and outsmarted—some of the galaxy's most ruthless individuals, including the bounty hunter Greedo, the Tiss'shar assassin Uul-Rha-Shan, and the infamous gunman Gallandro.

While Solo has retired from the smuggling game—or "gone almost respectable," as he would put it—he insists on keeping his customized DL-44 close by. Often he is the last person standing in harm's way, protecting the New Republic's chief of state, Leia Organa Solo. His still-sharp reflexes, combined with this deadly weapon, have repeatedly shielded her and their children from injury.

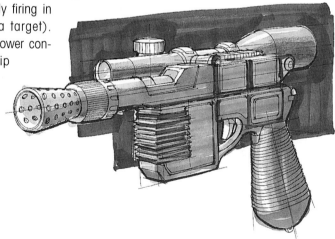

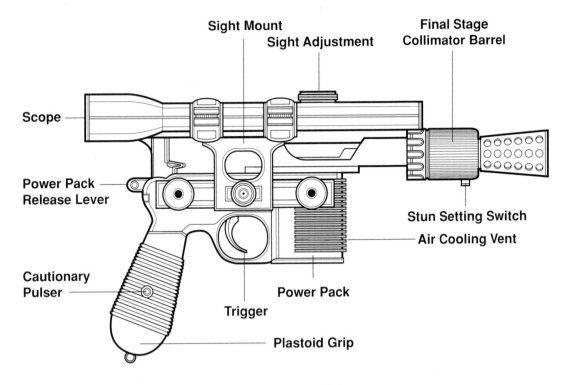

Sight Mount

Sight Adjustment

Final Stage
Collimator Barrel

Scope

Power Pack
Release Lever

Stun Setting Switch

Air Cooling Vent

Cautionary
Pulser

Power Pack

Trigger

Plastoid Grip

BlasTech DL-44

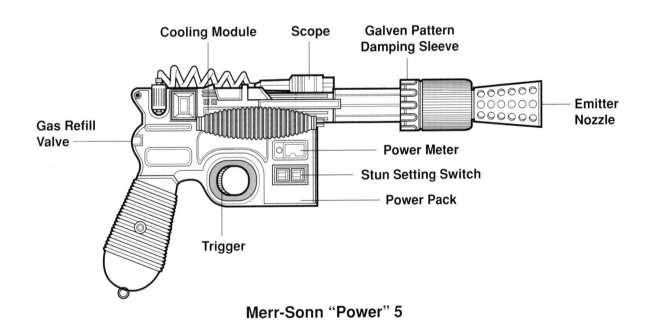

Cooling Module

Scope

Galven Pattern
Damping Sleeve

Gas Refill
Valve

Emitter
Nozzle

Power Meter

Stun Setting Switch

Power Pack

Trigger

Merr-Sonn "Power" 5

SPORTING BLASTER

DREARIAN DEFENSE CONGLOMERATE DEFENDER

Among the most diminutive and least powerful blasters, sporting blasters are short-range pistols often used for small-game hunting or as personal defense weapons. When she was a member of the Imperial Senate, Princess Leia Organa of Alderaan often carried a Drearian Defense Conglomerate Defender sporting blaster under the pretext that her humanitarian assistance missions involved a considerable amount of danger. In truth, Leia was using her status as a senator to allow her to spy for the outlaw Rebel resistance, and her unerring marksmanship with this weapon allowed her to permanently silence many Imperial soldiers before they could report her Rebel activities.

Sporting blasters are marketed to the civilian population, and because of their low-power blasts, they are often legal on worlds with otherwise stringent weapons control laws. The two top-selling models are the Defender and Merr-Sonn's "Quick 6." As a result of their relatively nonlethal nature, sporting blasters are the preferred weapons for the archaic "honor duels" that are still prevalent in some cultures. Considered something of an aristocratic weapon and widely regarded as more ceremonial than practical, sporting blasters are socially acceptable sidearms for nobles, diplomats, and ambassadors.

The Defender has relatively unsophisticated components and costs only 350 credits. (Many blaster pistols cost over five hundred credits.) It uses a minimum of blaster gas, instead relying on its small power pack to supply energy for each blast. The blaster bolt produces very little destructive energy, and only a direct hit is capable of killing a human. A simple

sight replaces the sophisticated electronic targeting scope found on most larger blasters.

The Defender's reliance on its power pack leads to several design limitations. The weapon has an optimal range of thirty meters, with a maximum range of sixty meters. A power surge dampener is needed to protect the delicate actuating blaster module, and several sophisticated components are needed to maintain the blaster bolt's cohesion. These include enhanced galven circuitry modules (in the barrel), focusing coils (in the final stage collimator barrel), and the galven ring in the emitter nozzle. An extended cooling coil sleeve protects these electronic components from intense waste heat.

In spite of these limitations, the Defender exhibits a number of advantages. Power packs can be changed quickly, and the internal computer automatically repairs minor malfunctions. The weapon's slim design is perfect for concealment, and many nobles order clothing with special pockets to hide the weapon from view. For added discretion, a three-digit code can be entered into the access panel (above the trigger), releasing the locking clamps and magnetic fasteners and causing the weapon to snap into three parts: the handle (with power pack), the main body (with main blaster components), and the barrel. The Defender can be reassembled in less than ten seconds.

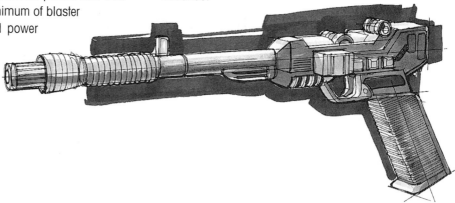

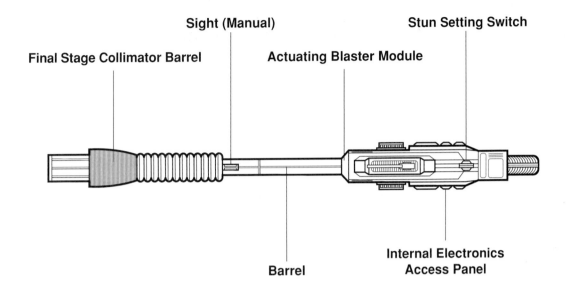

Sight (Manual)

Stun Setting Switch

Final Stage Collimator Barrel

Actuating Blaster Module

Internal Electronics
Access Panel

Barrel

Top View

Side View

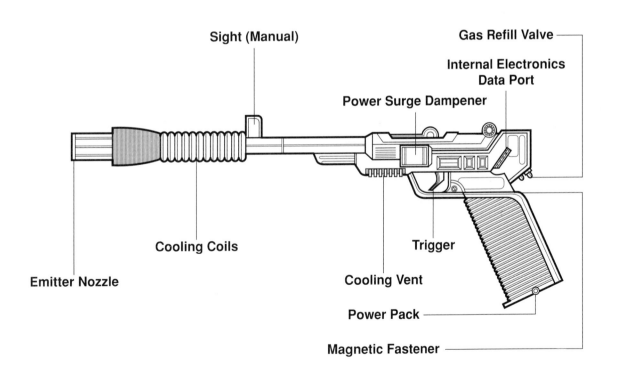

Sight (Manual)

Gas Refill Valve

Internal Electronics
Data Port

Power Surge Dampener

Cooling Coils

Trigger

Emitter Nozzle

Cooling Vent

Power Pack

Magnetic Fastener

LIGHT REPEATING BLASTER

BlasTech T-21 Light Repeating Blaster

Significantly more powerful than the standard blaster rifle, the BlasTech T-21 light repeating blaster is the most deadly Imperial blaster that can be transported and fired by one soldier. The T-21 proved a common support weapon for army and stormtrooper squads. For example, the Burning Sands sandtrooper squads sent to Tatooine to recover the droids Artoo-Detoo and See-Threepio used T-21s as their primary support weapons. Imperial artillery sections normally include at least one soldier with a T-21 who will provide cover for other crewmen while they are setting up artillery pieces and heavy repeating blasters such as the E-Web. Because of its portability, the T-21 also proved to be a popular weapon among Rebel squads during the Civil War and is still issued to some New Republic units.

While medium and heavy repeating blasters provide significantly more firepower than does the T-21, they are also bulkier and require crews of two to three soldiers. They take several minutes to set up or break down, and far too often military units don't have the luxury of waiting around for heavy support weapons.

By contrast, the T-21 package is designed for use by a soldier on the move. The weapon, its belt-carried tripod, and the twenty-kilogram backpack generator can be set up and made operational in less than thirty seconds. While the blaster can be fired

two-handed by a moving soldier, the light tripod offers improved accuracy. The tripod can be fully extended for instances when the T-21 is to be used as a weapon emplacement, but a partially extended position is superb for sniper attacks, allowing the gunner to take advantage of the T-21's maximum range of three hundred meters. Rebel squads often used the T-21, which has an optimum range of one hundred and fifty meters, to eliminate Imperial weapon emplacements and cover advancing Alliance infantry.

While the T-21's standard power packs supply only enough energy for twenty-five shots, its separate continuous-feed power generator gives the weapon potentially unlimited fire capability, although the generator's low cooling capacity in turn limits the fire rate to once per second.

This weapon is devastating against infantry, wielding enough power output to slice easily through personal armor suits or break down force fields. The T-21 also can cut through the armor plating used on many light combat vehicles, such as armored landspeeders. In the hands of a skilled operator, the T-21 can eliminate an entire enemy squad in a matter of seconds.

Some military units pair the T-21 with an even larger power generator for full autofire, but this tactic requires a second crew member to carry and maintain the bulkier generator. Gunners must use carefully controlled bursts, since heat buildup from sustained autofire has been known to melt the T-21's.

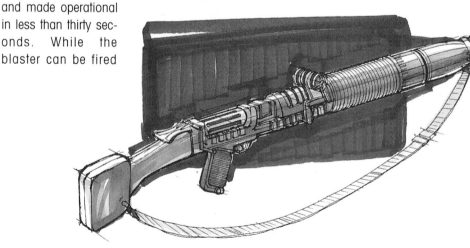

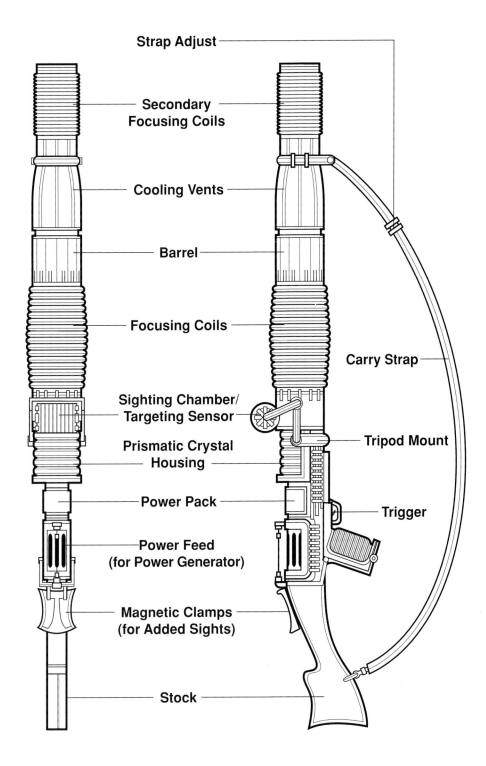

Strap Adjust

Secondary
Focusing Coils

Cooling Vents

Barrel

Focusing Coils

Carry Strap

Sighting Chamber/
Targeting Sensor

Prismatic Crystal
Housing

Tripod Mount

Power Pack

Trigger

Power Feed
(for Power Generator)

Magnetic Clamps
(for Added Sights)

Stock

Top View

Side View

E-WEB REPEATING BLASTER

BlasTech E-Web Repeating Blaster

Among the most powerful heavy repeating blasters in the Imperial arsenal, the BlasTech E-Web has proved highly effective against vehicles and infantry units alike. The E-Web ("Emplacement Weapon, Heavy Blaster") has an optimum range of two hundred meters with a maximum range of half a kilometer and offers enough firepower to punch through a snowspeeder's armor plating. Imperial snowtroopers tried to use an E-Web against the *Millennium Falcon* on Hoth—a lucky shot could have damaged the hyperdrive components or other critical systems—but its lengthy setup time gave Han Solo enough time to destroy the weapon with the *Falcon*'s autoblaster cannon.

For optimal effectiveness, the E-Web requires both a gunner and a second crew member who monitors and adjusts the Eksoan Class-4T3 power generator. Like many high-yield generators, the 4T3 is prone to overheating—and potentially explosive overload—despite its advanced Gk3 Cryocooler cooling unit. Power is fed into the E-Web via a three-meter-long conduit that connects to the base of the BlasTech TR-62 autocushion tripod. The E-Web's built-in long-range comlink includes an automatic encryption module for secured communications with other units. The computerized fire control and targeting system includes Starvision and IR (infrared) low-light enhancement modules for use in night combat.

Extended setup time is the E-Web's greatest limitation. If the 4T3 generator is "cold," it takes nearly fifteen minutes for personnel to deploy the weapon, calibrate the generator's power flow, and configure the targeting software. Some Imperial crews precharged the generator for faster setups, but this makes it prone to power surges. Thus, the second crew member must carefully adjust power flow to prevent an overload.

A single soldier can operate an E-Web, but at greatly reduced efficiency. In such instances, a gunner chooses the power generator's "preset" mode, which dramatically reduces the rate of fire but keeps both the generator and the E-Web well within safe operating temperatures.

The E-Web was designed as a joint venture by BlasTech and Merr-Sonn Munitions; Merr-Sonn dubbed its version the EWHB-10. While the E-Web design is far from new, the weapon is still in common use across the galaxy. Several E-Web upgrades are on the market, including the F-Web and the EWeb(15).

The F-Web adds a small shield generator that is powerful enough to block bolts from small sidearms such as blaster pistols. While providing good protection, the shield generator does require a third crew member.

The EWeb(15), released the year after Emperor Palpatine's death, offers improved fire control and targeting software. With the generator's "autoconfigure" setting, the weapon can be set up in less than five minutes. The advanced Gk7 Cryocooler offers higher power flow without the risk of overheating, allowing continuous fire for up to one hour. Many EWeb(15) units also include a shield generator.

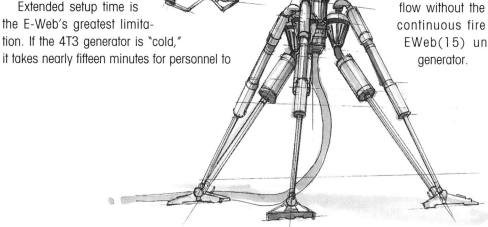

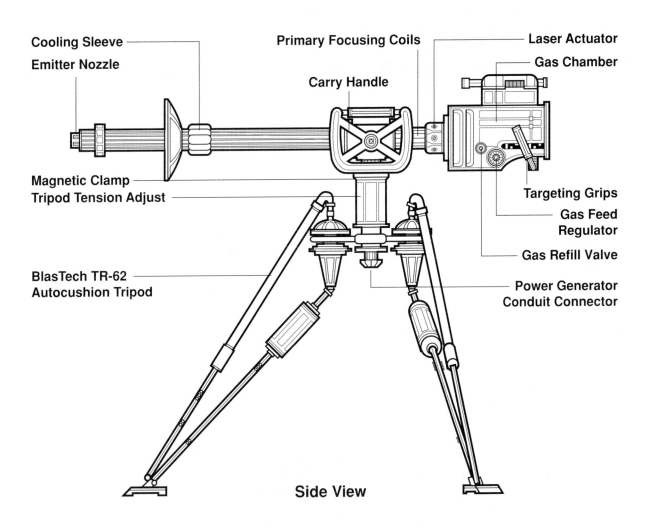

Cooling Sleeve

Emitter Nozzle

Primary Focusing Coils

Carry Handle

Laser Actuator

Gas Chamber

Magnetic Clamp

Tripod Tension Adjust

Targeting Grips

Gas Feed
Regulator

Gas Refill Valve

BlasTech TR-62
Autocushion Tripod

Power Generator
Conduit Connector

Side View

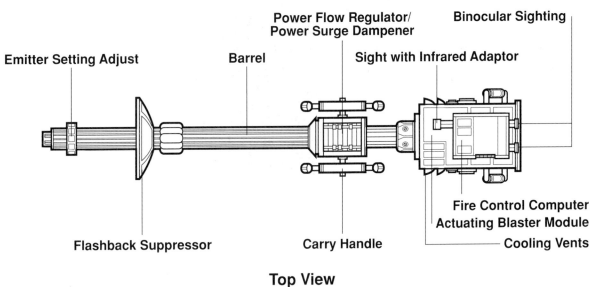

Power Flow Regulator/
Power Surge Dampener

Binocular Sighting

Emitter Setting Adjust

Barrel

Sight with Infrared Adaptor

Fire Control Computer

Actuating Blaster Module

Cooling Vents

Flashback Suppressor

Carry Handle

Top View

JAWA IONIZATION BLASTER

SCAVENGED IONIZATION BLASTER

Tatooine's Jawas are scavengers who comb the planet's desert wastes in search of discarded scrap metal, machinery, and droids. If the droid they find is active, the Jawas often use cobbled-together ionization blasters to disable the luckless target, as happened to Artoo-Detoo. They then haul the helpless machine back to their immense sandcrawler vehicle and affix a restraining bolt that compels the droid to obey their commands.

In typical Jawa fashion, this customized ionization blaster is built from an odd mixture of components haphazardly wired together and used for a purpose that completely defies the manufacturers' original specifications. Toiling away in their dank workshops, Jawa mechanics strip a blaster rifle of all internal parts except the power pack, replacing the laser components with a droid-restraining bolt and an accu-accelerator, the latter of which is pilfered from a capital ship's ion drive. (Presumably the accu-accelerators are taken from wrecked starships found and stripped by Jawa scavenger crews out in the desert.)

When a Jawa ionization blaster is fired, the power pack activates the internal restraining bolt, which releases an ion stream configured to broadcast the bolt's "halt" command. Under normal circumstances the command simply forces a droid to cease its activities; however, the ion stream is dramatically amplified when it

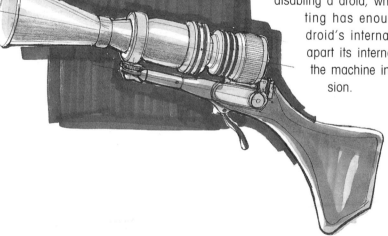

passes through the accu-accelerator. The resulting high-energy ion burst sends electrical energy racing over the droid's exterior and overwhelms its circuitry, shutting down the machine.

These custom-built blasters are about as reliable as most Jawa contraptions: when they actually do work, they are quite effective. When they don't work, they have a tendency to explode in spectacular fashion, much to the discomfort of everyone in the immediate vicinity.

The Jawa ionization blaster is a fragile weapon that is easily broken or thrown out of alignment. The blaster's optimum range is eight meters, with a maximum range of twelve meters, but hitting a target is quite easy because the ion stream is widely dispersed. The ion blast deactivates a droid for up to twenty minutes but causes no permanent damage. Should the target be organic, the ion blast causes no injury, but it inflicts a painful sting when used at close range.

Imperial soldiers have used a similar but *much* more reliable and powerful weapon, the Merr-Sonn DEMP—"Destructive ElectroMagnetic Pulse"—gun. Quite effective for missions that require soldiers to capture Rebel droids or disable security or assassin units, this gun is available in both pistol and carbine forms. The DEMP gun has adjustable settings: the low-powered stun setting is effective in temporarily disabling a droid, while the maximum setting has enough power to fry the droid's internal circuitry and blow apart its internal battery, destroying the machine in a spectacular explosion.

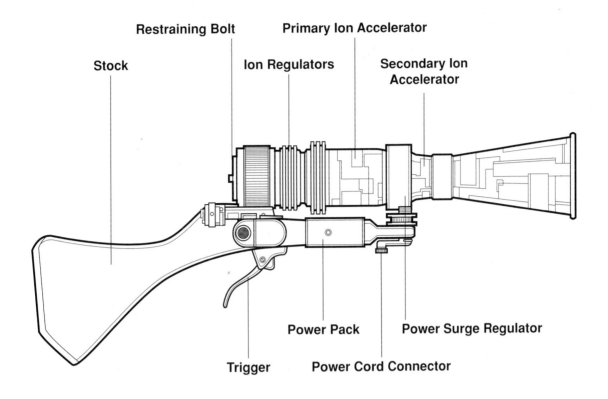

Stock

Restraining Bolt

Ion Regulators

Primary Ion Accelerator

Secondary Ion Accelerator

Power Pack

Power Surge Regulator

Trigger

Power Cord Connector

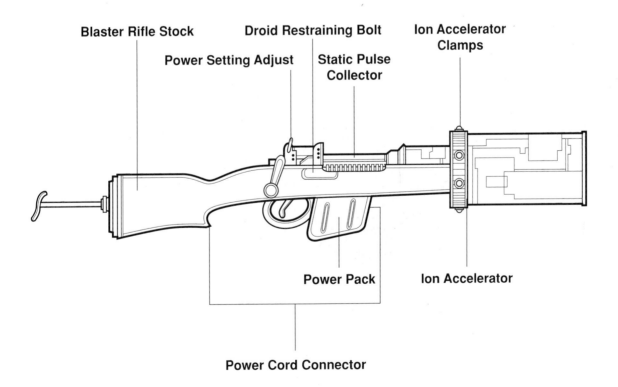

Blaster Rifle Stock

Power Setting Adjust

Droid Restraining Bolt

Static Pulse Collector

Ion Accelerator Clamps

Power Pack

Ion Accelerator

Power Cord Connector

BOWCASTER

WOOKIEE BOWCASTER

A curious combination of modern and ancient technologies, the bowcaster, or "laser crossbow," is the traditional weapon of the Wookiees of Kashyyyk. While anachronistic to those accustomed to using blasters, a bowcaster is quite deadly in the hands of a skilled Wookiee warrior such as Chewbacca, partner of the famed smuggler Han Solo.

The bowcaster is essentially a magnetic accelerator with twin polarizers that use alternating polarity pulses to accelerate a highly tensile metal bowstring and propel an explosive quarrel at extremely high speed. The fired quarrel has the appearance of an elongated blaster bolt because it is wrapped in an energy envelope that channels the quarrel's explosive force into the target. The result is a weapon that's considerably less advanced than a blaster pistol yet delivers an equivalent amount of damage.

Tremendous strength is needed to cock the weapon, which notches the bowstring and loads a quarrel from the ammo cartridge. This primitive arming system limits the bowcaster's rate of fire and places great emphasis on the Wookiee's patience and marksmanship, since it may take several seconds for the warrior to get off another shot. Some Wookiees have modified their bowcasters by adding multiple bowstrings, dual bows, or, in the case of Chewbacca's bowcaster, an automatic recocking system. During the Imperial occupation of Kashyyyk, Wookiees often bolted blaster rifles to their bowcasters for added firepower.

Bowcasters are designed for use in Kashyyyk's dense jungles, with good stopping power—for taking out the most dangerous predators—but are short-range weapons with an optimum range of thirty meters and a maximum range of only fifty meters. The weapon can be disassembled and carried in a utility pouch; it can be put back together in less than a minute. Wookiees use bandoliers to carry power packs, canisters of blaster gas, and spare ammunition cartridges that hold six quarrels each.

A bowcaster can be fired manually by moving the reserve spring into position and fashioning a bowstring from a meter-long length of kthysh vine. (Many warriors carry a treated kthysh vine in their utility pouches for emergencies.) Used in this fashion, the bowcaster's range is cut to thirty meters, but it can fire standard explosive quarrels or simple crossbow bolts carved from wood.

Hand-built by the master weapon crafters of Kashyyyk, bowcasters are bestowed to young Wookiees as they are completing adulthood rites of passage. This tradition has endured for thousands of years, and a warrior's bowcaster is considered a visible symbol of his or her courage and honor. These highly prized possessions are often engraved with clan markings and pictographs depicting a warrior's greatest accomplishments.

Imperial troops enslaved many of the great crafters during the occupation, but thanks to Kashyyyk's admittance to the New Republic, the great weapon builders are again free to continue making these magnificent weapons while diligently training new apprentices to carry on the proud tradition of bowcaster craftsmanship.

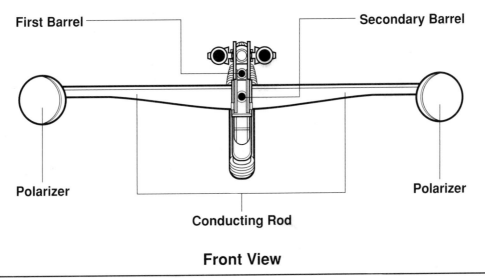

First Barrel

Secondary Barrel

Polarizer

Polarizer

Conducting Rod

Front View

Side View

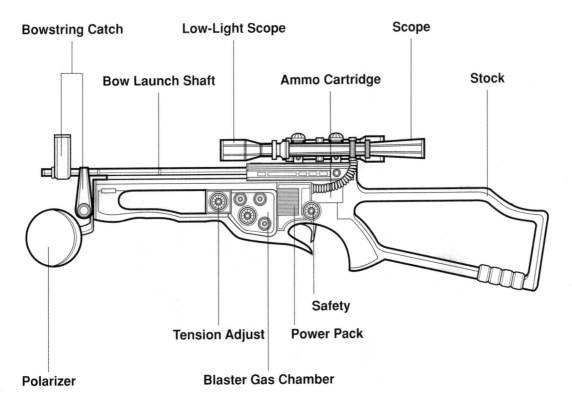

Bowstring Catch

Low-Light Scope

Scope

Bow Launch Shaft

Ammo Cartridge

Stock

Safety

Tension Adjust

Power Pack

Polarizer

Blaster Gas Chamber

BEAM TUBE

TIMMS EMPEROR-4 BEAM TUBE

Over twenty thousand years ago, during the days of barbarian warlords such as Xim the Despot and long before the rise of the Old Republic, projectile guns and magnetic accelerators ruled the battlefield. Mobile energy weapons called beam tubes were developed—prototype weapons that were the crude precursors to the blast-rifles of the Sith War, and even modern blasters.

While most citizens of the Core Worlds have seen only museum replicas, beam tubes are actually still used in some remote regions of the galaxy. For example, on the remote Tion Hegemony world of Dellalt, guardians armed with beam tubes tirelessly protect Xim's ancient treasure vaults, as they have for thousands of generations.

Despite numerous limitations, the first beam tubes changed the balance of power on those legendary battlefields. Their energy-particle beams easily defeated the armor of the day, which had been designed to protect the wearer against high-velocity projectiles, not energy beams.

The Emperor-4 beam tube is powered by a massive backpack power cell that weighs over thirty kilograms but delivers less than a hundred shots. The weapon itself severely restricts the soldier's mobility because it must be fired two-handed and weighs over fifteen kilograms.

To create and focus the high-intensity particle beam, the Emperor-4 uses four energy cyclers, twelve refinement tubes, and twelve low-grade crystals. The wasteful energy conversion process generates tremendous heat. The beam tube's sensitive electronic components are protected by twelve cooling motors, although they direct the hot air into the soldier's face, making the weapon quite uncomfortable to use. Another design limitation is manifested in the sensitive internal refinement tubes, which are easily thrown out of alignment; reconfiguring them takes nearly four hours.

The Emperor-4 requires several seconds to process enough power for a blast, with an optimum range of twenty meters and a maximum range of fifty meters. In battle, squads worked in alternating fire groups to cover each other. Because of the beam tube's limited ammunition and need for recharging, squads often carried a large power generator on a repulsorlift sled.

This beam tube's power system includes the backpack-style power cell, a recharge port, and a small refrigeration unit (to keep the cell within safe temperature levels). The entire system snaps onto a heavy blast vest that is padded with several layers of composite ceramics to absorb and disperse kinetic energy from high-impact projectiles. The vest includes a reserve power cell and a comlink with a four-kilometer range. A switch next to the comlink antenna activates an emergency homing beacon to guide rescue crews.

While these first energy weapons were quite crude, this technology proved to be superior for warfare, allowing the development of the incredibly powerful hand blasters and capital ship turbolasers that most modern soldiers take for granted.

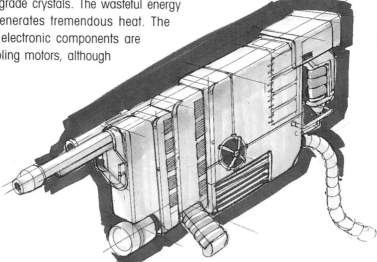

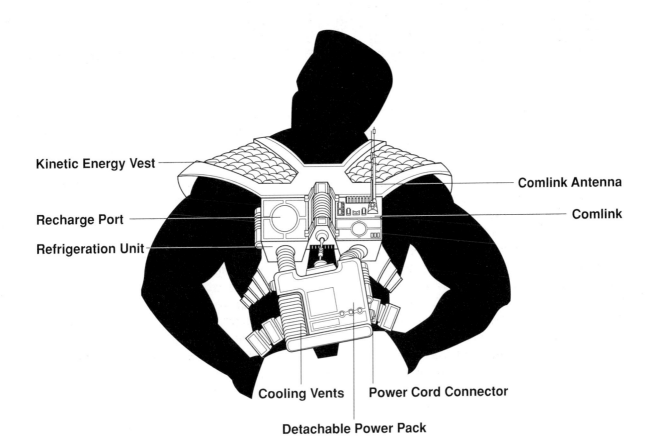

Kinetic Energy Vest

Comlink Antenna

Recharge Port

Comlink

Refrigeration Unit

Cooling Vents

Power Cord Connector

Detachable Power Pack

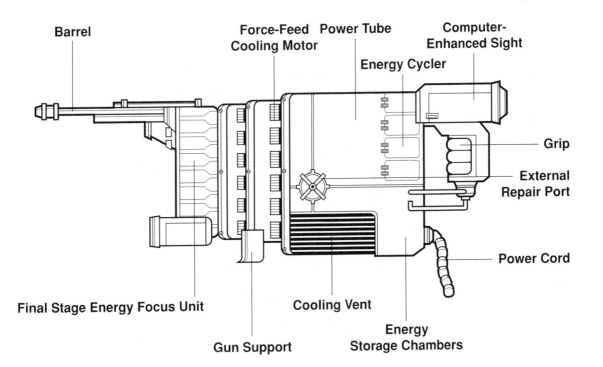

Barrel

Force-Feed Cooling Motor

Power Tube

Computer-Enhanced Sight

Energy Cycler

Grip

External Repair Port

Power Cord

Final Stage Energy Focus Unit

Cooling Vent

Gun Support

Energy Storage Chambers

SSI-RUUVI PADDLE BEAMER

SSI-RUUVI ION PADDLE BEAMER

When the mysterious aliens known as the Ssi-ruuk attacked the Imperial world of Bakura immediately after the Battle of Endor, they brought with them exotic technology and weapons that were at that time completely unknown to the Empire and the Rebel Alliance. Their primary hand weapons, called paddle beamers, are short-range energy weapons that paralyze and stun their targets.

The paddle beamer is a large disk with a simple control stock and trigger on the underside. The frame has several reinforced claw guards, so Ssi-ruuk soldiers can grasp and fire the weapon one-handed. Since the Ssi-ruuk do not wear clothing, they carry paddle beamers in shoulder bags or on tool belts or bandoliers. Dev Sibwarra, a young human brainwashed into serving the Ssi-ruuk, had a customized paddle beamer designed for human hands.

The paddle beamer creates a threadlike silver ion beam. While the ion beam can be lethal at extremely close range—Dev used a beamer to kill Ssi-ruu Elder Sh'tk'ith ("Bluescale") during his escape from the cruiser *Shriwirr*—its primary function is to paralyze its target by interfering with his or her nervous system. An ion blast can numb an extremity for several hours, and striking a primary nervous system pathway completely paralyzes the target, knocking him or her unconscious.

The Ssi-ruuk used paddle beamers to cap-

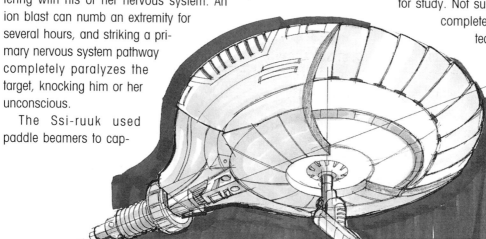

ture Luke Skywalker. They took him aboard the Ssi-ruuvi cruiser *Shriwirr*, where he learned the horrifying purpose behind this stun weapon. The Ssi-ruuk power their technology with life energies drained from living beings; this process, called "entechment," kills the subjects but provides rich reserves of energy to power Ssi-ruuvi weapons, droids, and starships. The subject *must* be alive for this process—paddle beamers allow the Ssi-ruuk to capture live subjects for entechment.

The weapon has an optimum range of eight meters and a maximum range of twelve meters, but the ion beam passes through force fields and battle armor, making both Imperial and Rebel soldiers vulnerable to these weapons. Unlike blaster bolts, the ion beam cannot be deflected by a lightsaber; the beam "bends" around a lightsaber's blade. After considerable experimentation, Luke Skywalker learned how to alter his lightsaber's frequency to deflect a Ssi-ruuvi ion beam, although this temporarily eliminated its ability to deflect blaster bolts.

After the Ssi-ruuk were driven from Imperial space, the Rebel Alliance managed to capture several paddle beamers for study. Not surprisingly, the weapons proved completely incompatible with standard technology. Soon afterward, Luke Skywalker destroyed most of the beamers, releasing the enteched spirits trapped within, and the Alliance ended its experiments with Ssi-ruuvi technology.

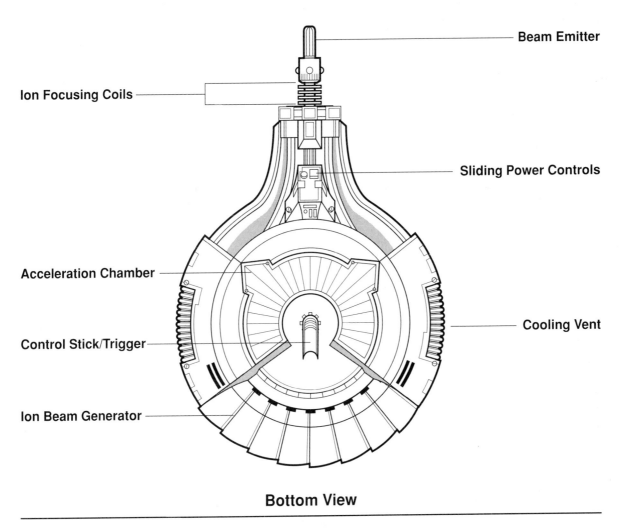

Beam Emitter

Ion Focusing Coils

Sliding Power Controls

Acceleration Chamber

Cooling Vent

Control Stick/Trigger

Ion Beam Generator

Bottom View

Side View

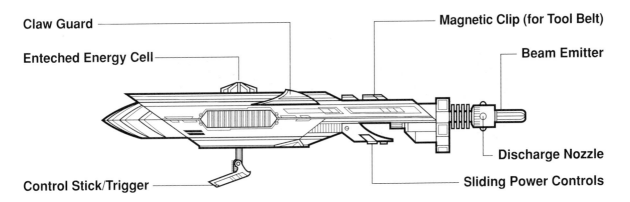

Claw Guard

Magnetic Clip (for Tool Belt)

Enteched Energy Cell

Beam Emitter

Discharge Nozzle

Control Stick/Trigger

Sliding Power Controls

DISRUPTOR

TENLOSS DX-2 DISRUPTOR PISTOL
TENLOSS DXR-6 DISRUPTOR RIFLE

Among the most controversial and reviled hand weapons in the galaxy, disruptors are energy weapons whose blasts are so powerful that they break down objects at the molecular level, leaving only a smoking pile of ash.

These small handheld pistols can disintegrate a one-meter by one-meter durasteel plate up to half a meter thick or penetrate force fields, personal battle armor, and vehicle and starship hull plating—they are virtually unstoppable. Against living targets these weapons almost always cause instantaneous death, and even a glancing blast causes horribly painful injuries that must be treated immediately in order to prevent irreparable nerve damage.

Most disruptors utilize brute force rather than technological innovations to produce their lethal blasts. The oversized XCiter and the actuating blaster module process a much greater volume of blaster gas, while the barrel's series of galven cylinders tightly focuses the beam, concentrating the blast's high-energy particles. However, because of their crude design, disruptors tend to have short ranges and limited ammunition capacity: the DX-2 pistol has an optimum range of five meters and a maximum range of seven meters and drains a standard power pack after just five shots. The DXR-6 rifle delivers even more destructive force over its optimum range of ten meters (its maximum range is twenty meters), but it, too, drains its paired power packs after only five shots. Most disruptors require an extended recycle time of five seconds or more to cool the weapon's internal components and gather an adequate charge for an additional shot.

The Merr-Sonn MSD-32 pistol, the most advanced disruptor in production, circumvents many of these limitations by using an advanced rapid-pulse energy module. The pistol creates a series of energy pulses, delivering tremendous firepower while reducing the recycle time to three seconds and extending the power pack's ammunition capacity to ten shots.

While disruptors are militarily impractical because of their limited range and ammunition, many assassins, slavers, and bounty hunters enjoy the notoriety and infamy that come with toting these weapons. The Tiss'shar assassin Uul-Rha-Shan used a miniaturized disruptor pistol against Han Solo, although its long recharge time allowed Solo to gun him down in a shoot-out at the Stars' End prison facility.

Disruptors are banned on most New Republic worlds; on some planets mere possession is grounds for the death penalty. Even under the Empire only a very small number of Imperial officials—Imperial Security Bureau interrogators and inquisitors—were allowed to carry these inhumane weapons. During the rule of the Empire some weapons manufacturers were authorized to produce these weapons in limited quantities, although most companies ceased production under New Republic law.

However, the Tenloss Syndicate and many other criminal organizations maintain back-alley labs to build disruptors and reap tremendous profits from black market sales.

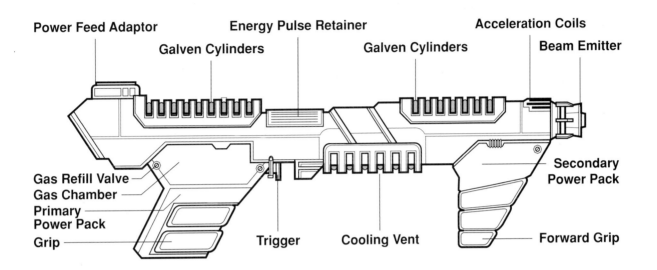

Power Feed Adaptor
Galven Cylinders
Energy Pulse Retainer
Galven Cylinders
Acceleration Coils
Beam Emitter
Gas Refill Valve
Gas Chamber
Primary Power Pack
Grip
Trigger
Cooling Vent
Secondary Power Pack
Forward Grip

Disruptor Rifle

Disruptor Pistol

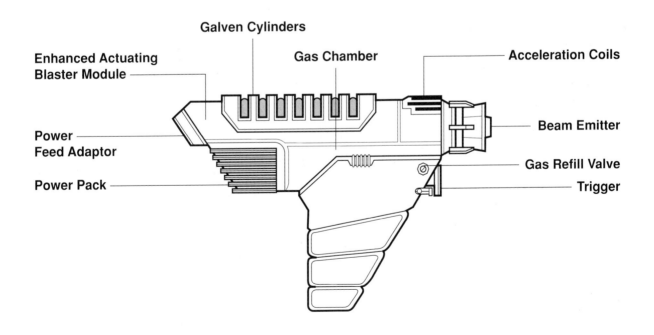

Galven Cylinders
Enhanced Actuating Blaster Module
Gas Chamber
Acceleration Coils
Power Feed Adaptor
Beam Emitter
Power Pack
Gas Refill Valve
Trigger

SONIC PISTOL

PACNORVAL DEFENSE SYSTEMS, LIMITED, SD-77 SONIC PISTOL
PACNORVAL DEFENSE SYSTEMS, LIMITED, SG-82 SONIC RIFLE

While blasters dominate the modern battlefield, sonic weapons have gained increasing acceptance because of their simple technology and utility for a number of specialized applications. SonoMax sonic pistols and rifles are used by the Corporate Sector Authority's security police, while Pacnorval's Sd-77 sonic pistol and Sg-82 sonic rifle are popular with private firms such as Santhe Security.

Sonic weapons generate a wide-dispersal cone of high-intensity sound. (They are ineffective in a vacuum since there is no atmosphere present to carry sonic vibrations.)

They offer both blast and stun settings. The first setting produces a high-intensity sonic blast comparable to a blaster bolt; at this level the sonic cone's vibrations are powerful enough to shatter solid objects and cause devastating injuries.

The stun setting releases a high-pitched wail that disrupts equilibrium, causing a loss of balance and unconsciousness in the target. The stun frequency must be recalibrated for each different species, but most sonic weapons can store several settings or be adjusted with manual controls. A new generation of advanced weapons, including the Pacnorval SIL-50 "Sleep Inducer," employ hypersonic wave energy (matching frequencies within the target's nervous system) to disorient and disable, sometimes taking effect in as little as two seconds.

Sonics have very limited ranges—the Sg-82 rifle has a maximum range of only thirty-five meters, with an optimum range of fifteen meters—but they are particularly effective for crowd control, since the stun setting incapacitates victims with-

out causing injury. The weapons are easy to operate, with simple thumb controls used to adjust the frequency, intensity, and vector of the sound cone.

Internally, these weapons are quite simple, with modular components. The only ammunition is a standard power pack. (In the Sg-82 rifle the pack also supplies energy for the stun club's electrical charge.)

The weapon's sonic projector and sound emitter precisely control the width of the sonic cone. On a tight setting the sound blast may affect only a single target, while on maximum dispersal the cone may be up to ten meters wide, still at maximum range. The sonic projector prevents the sonic blast from affecting anything outside the dispersal vector and protects the user from "sonic blastback."

Sonic weapons are quite effective underwater, an environment where blasters are useless. The sonic cone's concussive force is multiplied many times over by water's sound-conducting qualities. During the Galactic Civil War Imperial aquatic assault troopers carried sonic rifles as standard sidearms on water worlds such as Iskallon and Sedri, and greatly enhanced sonic blasters were mounted on assault skimmers.

Sonic blasts can be blocked by specialty armors that have sound-absorbing and dampening layers, but the relative rarity of sonic weapons means that these defensive measures are not widely used. Sonic stun blasts can sometimes be negated with padded sound-absorbent helmets.

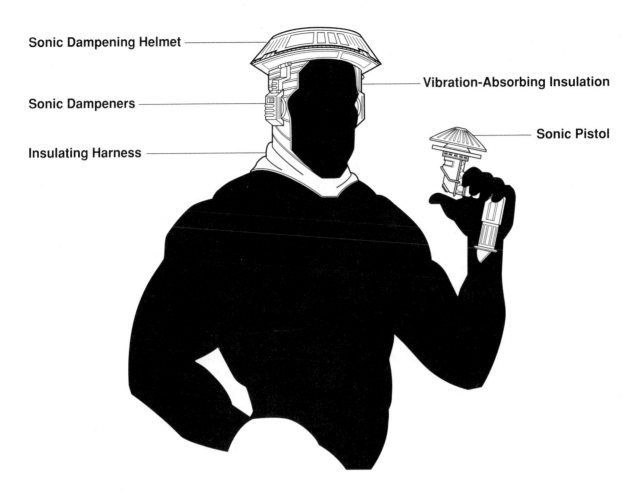

Sonic Dampening Helmet

Sonic Dampeners

Insulating Harness

Vibration-Absorbing Insulation

Sonic Pistol

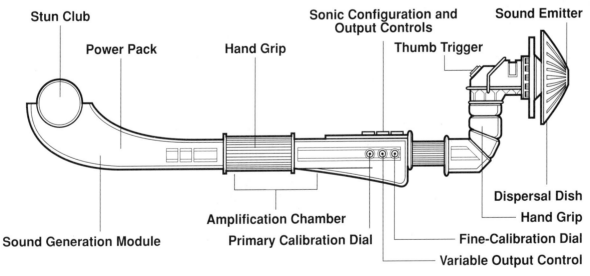

Stun Club

Power Pack

Hand Grip

Sonic Configuration and Output Controls

Thumb Trigger

Sound Emitter

Amplification Chamber

Primary Calibration Dial

Sound Generation Module

Dispersal Dish

Hand Grip

Fine-Calibration Dial

Variable Output Control

Sonic Rifle

WRIST ROCKETS

KELVAREK CONSOLIDATED ARMS MM9 ROCKET SYSTEM

A favorite of bounty hunters—who believe there's no such thing as being *too* heavily armed—wrist rockets are light yet formidable weapons. Even a basic rocket system can provide an effective last line of defense if the hunter's other weapons are disabled, while exotic warheads give the hunter a variety of options for handling unusual situations. For example, Boba Fett's Mandalorian battle armor includes a Kelvarek MM9 rocket system on the left wrist guard, adjacent to the small flame projector. Fett sometimes adds a second rocket launcher or a rocket dart launcher to his right wrist guard.

The MM9 uses both "dumb rockets" (those lacking a targeting system) and homing rockets. With homing rockets, the MM9's anti-launch cylinder (see schematic) locks the rocket in place, while the launcher's targeting computer automatically interfaces with the rocket's own system. Pressing the anti-launch release stud enables the warhead and activates the targeting laser. When the target lock activator stud is depressed, the targeting laser locks on the target—automatically tracking movement—while the targeting computer delivers constant updates to the rocket's homing system. Once the target has been selected, pressing the activation stud fires the rocket.

In addition to the targeting laser system, Fett's MM9 has a direct interface with his helmet's targeting systems, which gather data through infrared, ultrasonic, and motion sensors. Fett can use his helmet's verbal interface to launch rockets while leaving his right

hand free to reload the rocket launcher.

Fett carries several types of rocket in his belt pouches, although his preferred choices are Locris Syndicates Type-12As explosive rockets (for use on individuals) and Merr-Sonn K26 explosive rockets, which are powerful enough to destroy a speeder bike. Since many bounties include a bonus if the target is delivered alive, Fett also carries the Locris Type-12B rocket, which has a payload of FGA-583 nerve agent that can render a victim unconscious in less than six seconds.

Fett also possesses specialty rockets that deliver stun gas, ion blasts (to disable computers, droids, and other electronic devices), or luma blasts, which release a blinding flash upon detonation. Some bounty hunters "hot load" rockets with their own chemical concoctions.

Ranges vary widely, depending on how much propellant is loaded into the rocket. Many short-range rockets have an optimum range of 15 meters with a maximum range of about 25 meters, but the K26 rockets can travel up to 150 meters, with an optimum range of 75 meters.

The MM9 rocket system includes a small magnetic accelerator for launching projectiles that are similar to bowcaster quarrels. The accelerator's primary advantage is the low cost of ammunition, although the projectiles have no homing system, greatly limiting their accuracy. The accelerator's maximum range is twenty-five meters. In emergencies, the MM9 can also have a small dart clip mounted to the front of the launcher's anti-launch cylinder. The clip's five short-range rocket darts are often dipped in poison or a stun agent.

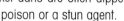

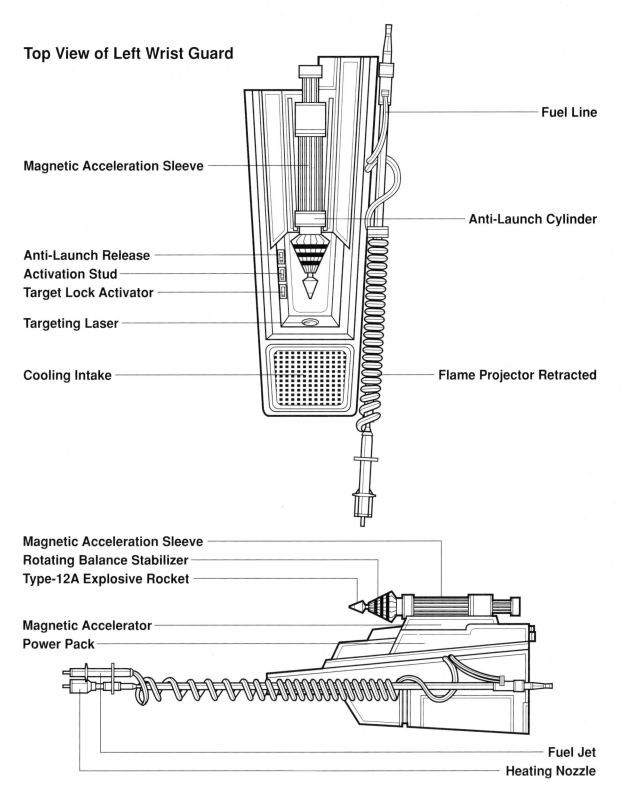

Top View of Left Wrist Guard

Fuel Line

Magnetic Acceleration Sleeve

Anti-Launch Cylinder

Anti-Launch Release
Activation Stud
Target Lock Activator

Targeting Laser

Cooling Intake

Flame Projector Retracted

Magnetic Acceleration Sleeve
Rotating Balance Stabilizer
Type-12A Explosive Rocket

Magnetic Accelerator
Power Pack

Fuel Jet
Heating Nozzle

Side View of Left Wrist Guard

STOKHLI SPRAY STICK

STOKHLI SPRAY STICK

Stokhli spray sticks are named after the Stokhli nomads of the planet Manress. The nomads developed these weapons for capturing and subduing large animals during hunting expeditions. Stokhli spray sticks offer good range, and the spraynets generate a powerful enough stun charge to take down a gundark.

The stick is a thin, meter-long metal tube that weighs only four kilograms. When fired, the weapon emits a sharp hiss and has a considerable kickback. A thin, translucent mist spirals out of the nozzle at high speed. Once exposed to cooling air, the mist quickly turns to a liquid and then into a solid cylindrical net as it spins through the air. The net has an optimum range of one hundred meters and a maximum range of two hundred meters.

The net wraps around its target, entangling the subject and delivering a powerful electrical stun charge. Tremendous strength is needed to rip free of the netting. Most spray sticks are fitted with stun pads in case the trapped animal remains conscious.

Spray sticks are elegant weapons with simple controls. Tension resistance allows the user to adjust all the weapon's functions without taking his or her eyes off the target. A spinning dial is used to determine the width of the net, and by pressing the control button, the user determines the intensity of the stun charge. Sliding the thumb trigger sets the range finder (to determine how quickly the net forms). Spraymist is released as long as the thumb trigger is held down, allowing the user to determine the length of the net precisely.

The spraymist solution, manufactured exclusively by the Stokhli people, is highly resistant to most solvents and vibroblades, although it decays naturally over the course of several hours. Even lightsabers don't do much good against the netting while it is still in flight, since the net constantly re-forms itself until it strikes its target. Each stick holds ten spraymist cartridges, with each cartridge yielding five hundred meters of netting.

Stokhli spray sticks have a hefty price tag of fourteen thousand credits and are difficult to find off Manress. While they are intended for recreational big-game hunting, Noghri death commandos working for Grand Admiral Thrawn revealed another use for the stun sticks: kidnapping.

More than two dozen Noghri confronted Luke Skywalker, Leia Organa Solo, and Han Solo while they were on a diplomatic mission to the planet Bimmisaari. But despite the skill these alien commandos displayed, they were unable to capture the New Republic heroes, who managed to escape thanks to the timely arrival of Chewbacca aboard the *Millennium Falcon*.

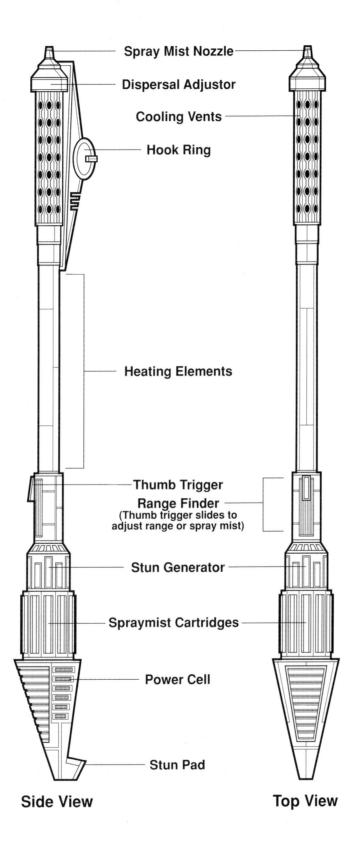

Spray Mist Nozzle

Dispersal Adjustor

Cooling Vents

Hook Ring

Heating Elements

Thumb Trigger

Range Finder
(Thumb trigger slides to
adjust range or spray mist)

Stun Generator

Spraymist Cartridges

Power Cell

Stun Pad

Side View

Top View

PROJECTILE WEAPONS

ORIOLANIS STRIKER PROJECTILE PISTOL
DRESSELIAN PROJECTILE RIFLE

Projectile weapons, commonly referred to as "slugthrowers," remain in common use, particularly on isolated worlds where blasters are not readily available. They are also commonly used by criminals on worlds with strict weapons policies: while customs authorities can be quite effective in stopping smugglers from bringing in blasters from off-world, there's very little to stop a gang from designing slugthrowers on computers and manufacturing them on cheap tooling machines.

In their most basic form slugthrowers are exceedingly simple, using an explosive chemical reaction to propel a metal slug at very high speed. While slugthrowers built on frontier worlds vary widely in capabilities and quality, modern slugthrowers built by reputable companies such as Czerka, Merr-Sonn, and Oriolanis are sophisticated weapons, ranging from pistols and hunting rifles to rapid-fire, high-caliber machine guns that can shoot thousands of rounds per minute.

Ammunition is also varied, as slugs are made of metal, ceramic, and hardened plastics. Specialty rounds can release toxic or stun gases, or acid, or carry explosive heads. During the Galactic Civil War, several Rebel SpecForce units carried explosive-tipped rounds that were quite effective in blowing through stormtrooper armor.

Projectile weapons have a number of advantages: they are cheap and easy to repair and can be built with a minimum of

high technology. Unlike a blaster, a slugthrower produces no visible beam and is easily silenced; a clever attacker can strike without giving away his or her position.

The slugthrower's main disadvantage is the need for the soldier to carry ammunition: blaster gas canisters and power packs are considerably lighter, particularly for weapons with a high rate of fire. It can be difficult to find compatible ammunition since slugthrower calibers vary so widely.

The Oriolanis Striker pistol is a standard short-range slugthrower with an optimum range of thirty meters, a maximum range of sixty meters, and a slug cartridge that holds eight slugs. As with a hold-out blaster, only a vital hit is likely to kill. This weapon is normally easy to acquire, even on worlds with strict weapons laws.

The Dresselian rifle is a far more crude weapon, normally hand-built with primitive tools. The long barrel gives the rifle a respectable maximum range of 300 meters and an optimum range of 150 meters. The rifle's magazine holds six shells. The Dresselians (nicknamed "Prune Faces" by some) managed to drive Imperial occupation forces off their world despite their limited technology. Several Bothan clans aided the Dresselians by supplying strategic information and delivering thousands of similar rifles. By limiting their aid to slugthrowers—a technology the Dresselians had already developed—the Bothans were able to conceal their involvement.

After freeing their homeworld, many Dresselians went on to serve with the Rebel Alliance, and several units participated in the Battle of Endor.

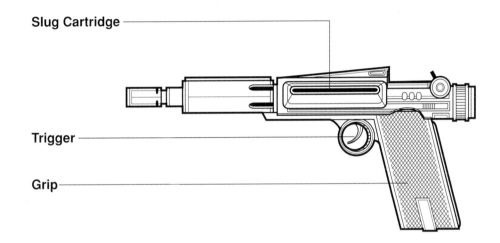

Slug Cartridge

Trigger

Grip

Pistol

Rifle

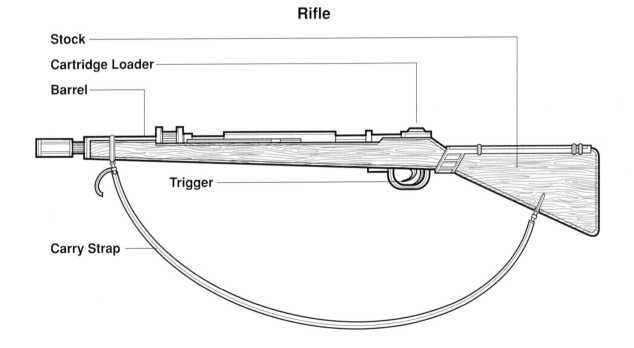

Stock

Cartridge Loader

Barrel

Trigger

Carry Strap

FLAME PROJECTOR

MERR-SONN C-22 FLAME CARBINE
MERR-SONN CR-24 FLAME RIFLE

Flame projectors combine high-energy flammable liquid fuels with air and heating elements to produce superheated cones of flame. This makes them powerful tools of intimidation as well as effective military weapons. While limited in both ammunition and range, flame projectors provide outstanding options for close-quarters combat and some specialty operations.

Military units commonly use flame projectors to quickly flush enemy soldiers out of bunkers, force back soldiers in close-range combat, and clear paths through thick vegetation. Imperial soldiers often used them to sweep through Rebel installations in efforts to force Rebel soldiers out of hiding. Flame projectors also can be rigged in makeshift trip-wire traps, with devastating results. Since most soldiers don't carry flameproof clothing or portable oxygen supplies, the danger from burns and smoke inhalation is great.

A single blast from a flame projector can cause tremendous damage to enemy equipment and vehicles, and the fuel burns for several minutes. Under the right circumstances the fire will spread uncontrollably and with horrifying speed. Imperial soldiers and Corporate Sector Authority security police ("Espos") frequently used flame projectors to break up civilian demonstrations and enforce martial law on rebellious worlds; those incidents were invariably reported to the local media as "Rebel-orches-

trated revolutionary movements" in an effort to justify the excessive casualties that were incurred.

Space pirates often use flame projectors as boarding weapons; since narrow starship corridors limit the mobility of opponents, the flamers can quickly eliminate any resistance.

Flame projectors come in a wide variety of sizes and capabilities, ranging from Boba Fett's wrist-mounted Czerka ZX unit to the deadly flame carbines and rifles favored by military forces. Fett's flame projector produces a cone of flame up to five meters long and a meter wide; the backpack fuel canister supplies him with over fifty shots. His projector can be activated via a control stud, or it can be voice-activated through Fett's computer control system located inside his helmet.

The Merr-Sonn C-22 flame carbine was issued to CSA Espos as a secondary weapon to back up the standard-issue blaster or riot gun. It has an optimum range of three meters, a maximum range of seven meters, and a small fuel canister clips to the user's belt, holding enough fuel for ten six-second discharges. The larger CR-24 flame rifle has a slightly longer maximum range—ten meters—an optimum range of five meters, and a canister holding enough fuel for twenty-five shots. The Corporate Sector Authority also mounted powerful CR-28 flamers on numerous ground vehicles for use in crowd control efforts; the CR-28 has an optimum range of ten meters, a maximum range of twenty meters, and enough fuel for fifty blasts.

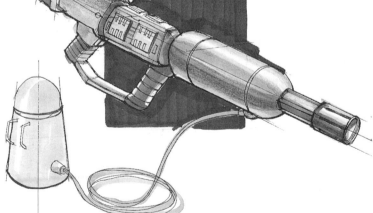

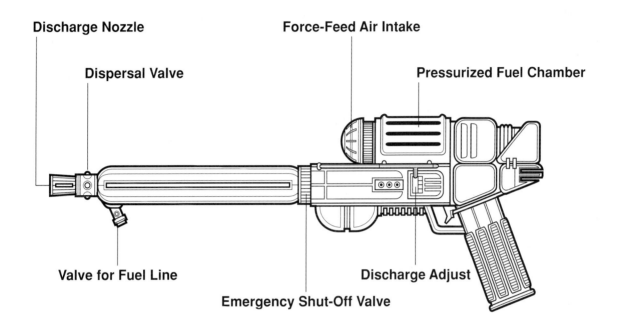

Discharge Nozzle

Dispersal Valve

Force-Feed Air Intake

Pressurized Fuel Chamber

Valve for Fuel Line

Emergency Shut-Off Valve

Discharge Adjust

Carbine

Rifle

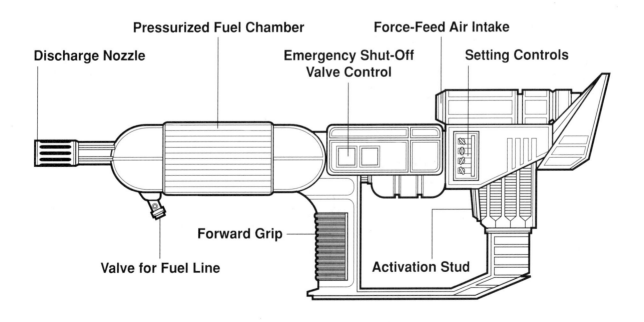

Pressurized Fuel Chamber

Discharge Nozzle

Emergency Shut-Off Valve Control

Force-Feed Air Intake

Setting Controls

Forward Grip

Valve for Fuel Line

Activation Stud

DART SHOOTER

PRAX ARMS STEALTH-2VX PALM SHOOTER
PRAX ARMS PROTECTOR PRP-502 HOLD-OUT SHOOTER

Small dart shooters are designed to fool even the most sophisticated weapons detectors, and so they are essential tools for espionage agents and assassins, who rely on secrecy and stealth to accomplish their missions. Dart shooters are also favored by private citizens who feel the need to carry a weapon but want something that's less conspicuous than a blaster or vibroblade.

Such weapons are simple in design. Each uses a high-tension spring to launch a small metal dart coated with poison, nerve toxin, or a chemical stun compound.

The Prax Arms Stealth-2VX palm shooter is among the smallest and lightest of these weapons. It can be hidden inside a pocket, slipped up a sleeve, or even concealed in the user's palm. Some agents carry them inside a false comlink or restraining bolt caller. The Stealth-2VX has a short range—only three or four meters—but makes an outstanding emergency defense weapon. Its noiseless operation provides a great advantage for secret attacks, such as close-range assassinations. In this unit three darts load directly into the weapon, and extra darts can be hidden by the user in a deceptively unremarkable wristband.

The Prax Arms Protector PRP-502 is a more typical dart pistol that uses a high-tension spring to achieve an optimum range of ten meters and a maximum range of twenty-five meters. The PRP-502

holds a clip of six darts and can be fired once every three seconds; its sliding release lever allows clips to be changed in two or three seconds. Noiseless and exceptionally light—it weighs barely a hundred grams—this dart shooter is also easy to hide. Its lack of energy emitters or power cells allows it to evade detection by most standard weapon scanners. Twisting the PRP-502's assembly release causes this weapon to snap into four separate pieces so that it can be hidden in luggage to more easily slip it past security sensors or random searches. Reassembly requires less than five seconds.

The darts normally are less than five centimeters long, may be hollow or solid, and may be made of many different metals or plastics. In and of themselves the small darts are harmless, but there are a wide variety of compounds that can be used to achieve specific results.

Malkite themfar and Fex-M3 nerve toxins are among the most potent dart coatings and can cause death in less than ten seconds once they are injected into the target's bloodstream. Concentrated symoxin, originally developed as a contact painkiller, can knock a target unconscious in less than fifteen seconds, allowing the victim to be transported for interrogation or simply "moved out of the way" without injury. More esoteric dart payloads may include homing beacons (for tracking suspect individuals) or molecular acid for sabotage and to defeat security locks and binders.

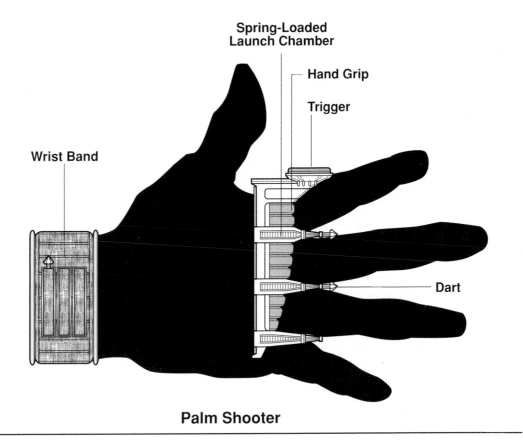

Spring-Loaded
Launch Chamber

Hand Grip

Trigger

Wrist Band

Dart

Palm Shooter

Hold-Out Shooter

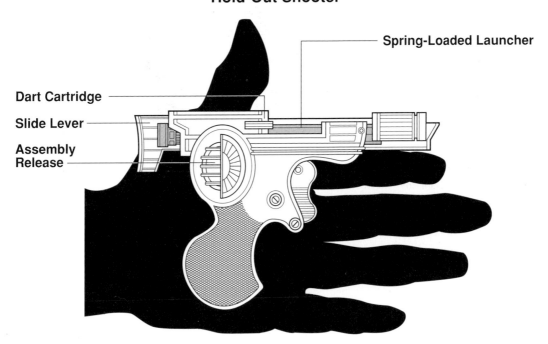

Spring-Loaded Launcher

Dart Cartridge

Slide Lever

Assembly
Release

FLECHETTE LAUNCHER

MALAXAN FIREPOWER INCORPORATED FWG-5
GOLAN ARMS FC1 FLECHETTE LAUNCHER

Flechette launchers are tube weapons that shoot canisters and small missiles designed to explode close to their targets, releasing hundreds of razor-sharp flechettes at high velocity. These weapons allow a single soldier to deliver devastating firepower against troops and small vehicles.

The Malaxan Firepower FWG-5 flechette pistol is a typical handheld flechette launcher. With an optimum range of fifty meters, a maximum range of one hundred meters, and stopping power equal to that of a heavy blaster pistol, the small pistol offers a viable alternative to a blaster. The FWG-5's miniature laser tracking system "paints" the target with an electronic homing signature, enabling the flechette cartridge to follow the target's movements while in flight. Once the cartridge is within three meters of the target, it explodes, releasing dozens of tiny flechette darts powerful enough to puncture blast vests, ceramic armor, and even the plasteel armor plate worn by stormtroopers. Since the cloud of flechettes spreads over a two-meter-diameter area, even a "near miss" can severely injure the target. The FWG-5's ammunition clip holds eight flechette cartridges.

The Golan Arms FC1 is a traditional shoulder-braced flechette weapon widely used by the Corporate Sector Authority's security police squads. During one of his many smuggling adventures, Han Solo used one of these launchers to force back attacking slavers while escaping from the hijacked luxury cruiser *Lady of Mindor*.

The FC1 has an optimum range of 100 meters, a maximum range of 250, and can fire both antipersonnel and antivehicle canisters. Through the scope's range finder, the user must manually program each canister's detonation range, targeting for a detonation point ten meters in front of the target to achieve maximum flechette dispersal. In emergencies the launcher can be fired without setting the detonation range—the canister explodes on impact—but this mode dramatically reduces the effectiveness of the flechettes.

The FC1 holds four canister tubes, each with a single canister, and has a reserve chamber for two additional canisters. Lightly tapping the firing stud selects the tube that is fired, allowing the soldier to carry several canister types and fire the specific type needed as different combat situations arise.

The standard antipersonnel canister is a small globe that releases hundreds of flechettes over a ten-meter-diameter area. A well-placed shot can eliminate an entire squad of enemy troopers. Antivehicle rounds consist of eleven-centimeter-long missiles; their razored flechettes are considerably larger than those of the antipersonnel canister, and the missile's shaped charge focuses the flechettes over a concentrated target area no more than five meters in diameter. A cloud of antivehicle flechettes can rip through ten centimeters of durasteel armor plating, destroying snowspeeders and other lightly armored repulsorcraft. Once through the armor, multiple flechette strikes can cause catastrophic damage, destroying internal electronic components and flight systems, scrapping power generators and laser cannons, and causing serious injury to any crew members.

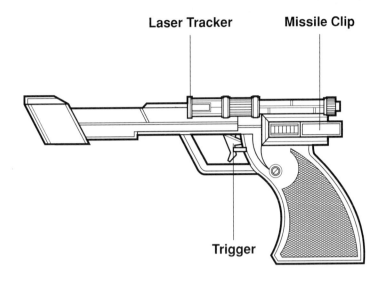

Laser Tracker   Missile Clip

Trigger

Flechette Pistol

Flechette Launcher

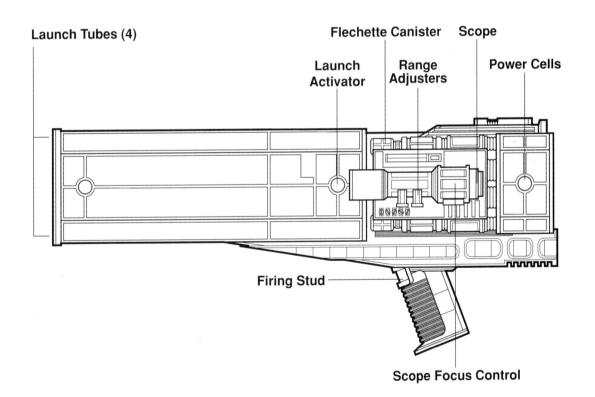

Launch Tubes (4)

Flechette Canister   Scope

Launch
Activator

Range
Adjusters

Power Cells

Firing Stud

Scope Focus Control

MISSILE TUBE

MERR-SONN MUNITIONS PLX-2M

The Merr-Sonn Munitions PLX-2M—or "Plex-Twoem"—is a portable missile system designed to destroy airspeeders, atmospheric fighters, and other medium-size vehicles. A refined version of the older Merr-Sonn PLX-2 launcher developed for the Empire, the PLX-2M is a lightweight launcher that levels the battlefield for infantry, giving troops the opportunity to destroy vastly more powerful opponents while allowing them to retain the mobility that is their greatest advantage.

Missile weapons are not widely used in modern military arsenals because most speeders and starships have outstanding countermeasures systems designed to fool missiles' homing systems. However, a skilled operator who fires at precisely the right moment can use the PLX-2M and similar systems to great effect against enemy speeders.

These light missile launchers have several advantages over conventional artillery blasters, which require large power generators and are limited to line-of-sight fire. Missile systems are lighter for easy transport, while targeting systems give the missiles greater range. As more sophisticated targeting computers are developed, missile systems are becoming more popular among military forces.

The PLX-2M consists of a shoulder-carried launcher paired with a sophisticated computer targeting system. Setup takes barely a minute, allowing soldiers under fire to assemble and use the system quickly. The weapon weighs nearly fifty kilograms,

but the built-in microrepulsorlift unit stabilizes and supports the launcher, replacing a tripod. The repulsorlift generators and the support collar absorb the recoil from each missile's ignition, allowing the user to launch multiple missiles without sacrificing accuracy.

The PLX-2M's computerized tracking system has heads-up sighting, using holograms to display range, speed, and other vital tracking data. The conventional scope (under the holographic projector) allows targeting in heavy rain, darkness, and fog. Once a target has been selected, its silhouette is fed to the missile's homing system. The weapons officer has a choice of targeting methods, using either EPR, which programs the missile to home in on intense infrared sources (such as the target's exhaust), or "smart" Gravity-Activated Mode (GAM) targeting, which allows the missile to lock onto gravity-wave anomalies generated by the target's repulsorlift drive. Once the "gravity-wave lock" is achieved, even the most skilled pilots are hard-pressed to lose the missile, which has a maximum range of fifty kilometers.

The missiles can also be "dumb fired" using unguided line-of-sight targeting. This option is selected if there are "friendly" craft nearby that might be targeted accidentally by the missile's homing computer.

The PLX-2M carries six Arakyd 3t3 missiles, each equipped with miniature proton warheads. The missiles are powerful enough to cause an instant kill against a combat airspeeder; a lucky shot can inflict significant damage against even an AT-AT walker or starfighter.

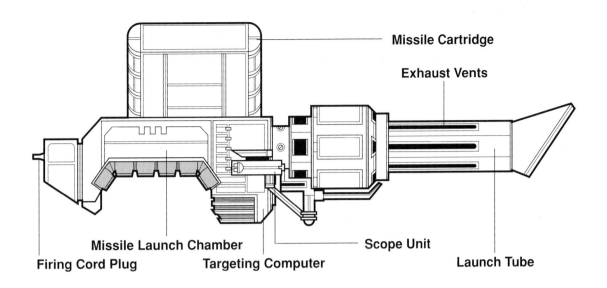

Missile Cartridge

Exhaust Vents

Missile Launch Chamber

Firing Cord Plug

Targeting Computer

Scope Unit

Launch Tube

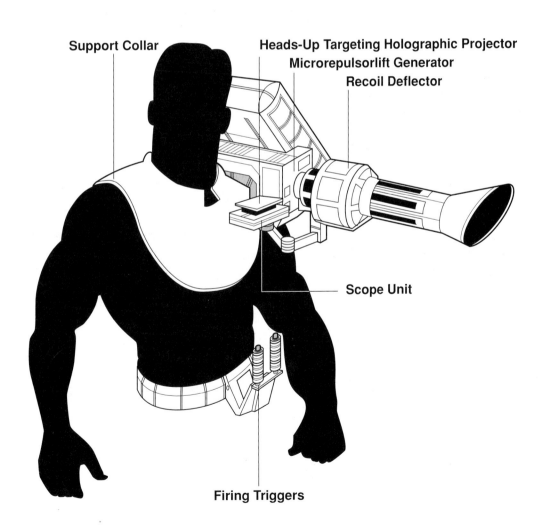

Support Collar

Heads-Up Targeting Holographic Projector

Microrepulsorlift Generator

Recoil Deflector

Scope Unit

Firing Triggers

THERMAL DETONATOR

MERR-SONN MUNITIONS CLASS-A THERMAL DETONATOR

When the bounty hunter Boushh threatened to explode a thermal detonator inside Jabba the Hutt's throne room, everyone inside had good reason to cower. No one would have survived the intense explosion. Fortunately, the masked hunter—actually Princess Leia Organa in disguise—had other objectives, namely, to rescue Han Solo from Jabba's clutches.

Thermal detonators are immensely powerful—and strictly regulated—explosive devices. The small metal ball looks like a common grenade, and the device's thermite casing contains the synthetic explosive known as baradium. When the detonator's sliding thumb trigger is pushed, warning lights and alarms are activated as the six-second timer counts down. The detonator can be deactivated at any time by returning the trigger to its original position. The timer also may be reset manually to offer a maximum countdown of five minutes, or the trigger's control pins can be programmed to act as a deadman's switch. In this setting, unless a tiny switch near the indicator light is flipped to the safety position, the detonator will explode instantly when the trigger is released.

When a detonator explodes, the baradium's fusion reaction creates a particle field that quickly expands outward, releasing enough energy and heat to virtually disintegrate anything caught in the blast sphere. Within a few seconds, the baradium core burns out and the particle field sphere collapses in on itself. Everything within the blast sphere is gone, while anything beyond the sphere's outer boundary is left unharmed.

Standard-issue Imperial detonators have a small baradium core and yield a blast radius of about five meters. The Class-A thermal detonator carried by Princess Leia would have resulted in a blast radius of twenty meters. Some criminals have custom-built detonators with enough baradium to create hundred-meter blast spheres.

Baradium is dangerously unstable, sometimes triggering a fusion reaction if the detonator is jarred or exposed to excessive heat. Detonators have been known to explode when dropped or thrown through the air or for no apparent reason. As a result, they are *strictly* military-issue and illegal for civilian possession, although their usefulness creates intense demand for them, pushing black market prices up to two thousand credits per detonator.

Since a single blast can disintegrate up to two meters of permacrete, military crews often use detonators for demolitions work and detonator booby traps sometimes are set to cover retreating soldiers.

Princess Leia used a thermal detonator to lend credibility to her impersonation of Boushh, since the infamous Ubese bounty hunter was known to be fond of explosives. Leia received the weapon from Lando Calrissian, who used two similar detonators to destroy the opulent palace of Prince Xizor, ruler of the criminal organization known as Black Sun.

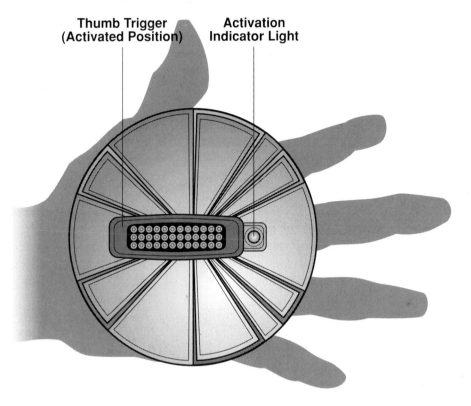

Thumb Trigger
(Activated Position)

Activation
Indicator Light

Top View with Hand (for scale)

Side View

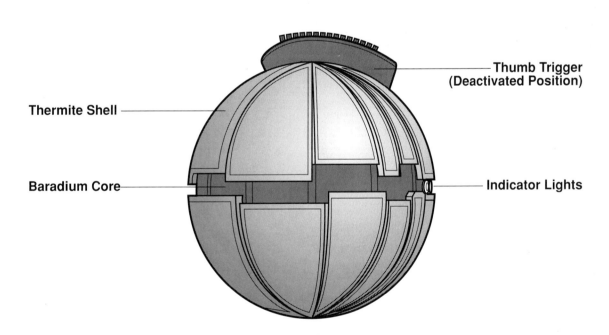

Thumb Trigger
(Deactivated Position)

Thermite Shell

Baradium Core

Indicator Lights

MERR-SONN GLOP GRENADE
MERR-SONN C-22 FRAGMENTATION GRENADE
MERR-SONN WW-41 CRYOBAN GRENADE

Standard issue as secondary weapons for New Republic and Imperial ground troops, grenades are particularly effective for use in cluttered terrain, where blasters are of limited use. Soldiers most often carry fragmentation grenades because they are equally effective in damaging physical structures and inflicting casualties on enemy forces.

The Merr-Sonn C-22 fragmentation grenade is fairly typical, consisting of a small detonite charge encased in a pre-stressed chrome shell. The grenade's explosion fills a ten-meter-diameter area with lethal shrapnel. Twisting the timer dial sets the grenade's delay for up to a maximum of two minutes, and pressing the activation panel primes the grenade's detonite charge and starts the timer. Holding the activation panel stops the timer, and entering an access code deactivates the primer, allowing the user to reset the weapon. While the C-22 grenade can be thrown, the magnetic grapple allows it to be placed precisely for demolition work.

New Republic soldiers use a similar grenade, the C-16, which has a detonator switch and a preset delay of four seconds; twisting a small dial alters the timer's delay. The C-16's low mass and small spherical design make it perfect for throwing.

Soldiers may also carry a number of specialty grenades. Merr-Sonn glop grenades use high-pressure jets to spray an extremely strong adhesive foam over a ten-meter-diameter area, trapping anyone

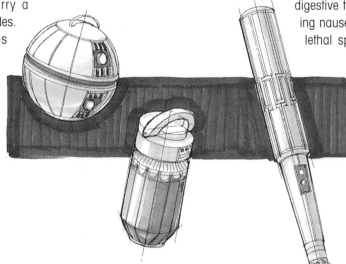

found in the blast area. The glop grenade can be set to explode on contact, or the timer may be used to select up to a fifteen-second delay. This reusable grenade is extremely useful for subduing targets without causing injuries and was used extensively throughout the Corporate Sector.

The Merr-Sonn WW-41 CryoBan grenade uses a chemical agent that absorbs heat energy, effectively creating an area of intense cold at the detonation point. An outstanding fire suppressant, CryoBan also can destroy electronic components, droids, and vehicles not adapted for cold-weather duty. Soldiers exposed to CryoBan experience numbing cold and, unless treated immediately with bacta, may lose limbs or suffer severe nerve damage.

Smoke and dye grenades are used as location markers (for incoming vessels) and can be employed to obscure the vision of enemy troops. Luma grenades release intense light, acting as flares and illuminating target areas. They are also effective for blinding opponents.

There are a number of specialty grenades with payloads designed solely to injure enemy soldiers. Microscopic Bothan stun spores cause disorientation and unconsciousness. Plank gas is a corrosive chemical that eats away at exposed skin, causing extremely painful injuries; it can also destroy space suits, electronic components, and droids. While generally not lethal, the chemical agent T-238 attacks a soldier's digestive tract, causing severe, debilitating nausea for several hours. The most lethal specialty grenades release billowing yellow clouds of Fex-M3 nerve agent, which can cause death after just ten seconds of exposure.

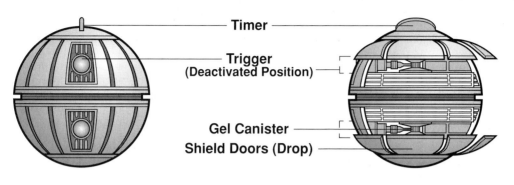

Timer

Trigger
(Deactivated Position)

Gel Canister

Shield Doors (Drop)

Glop Grenade

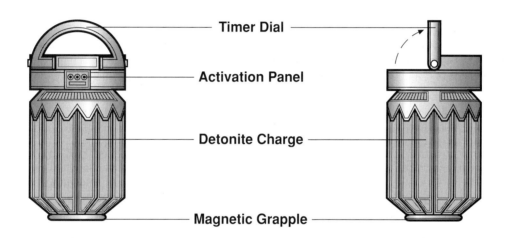

Timer Dial

Activation Panel

Detonite Charge

Magnetic Grapple

Fragmentation Grenade

CryoBan Grenade

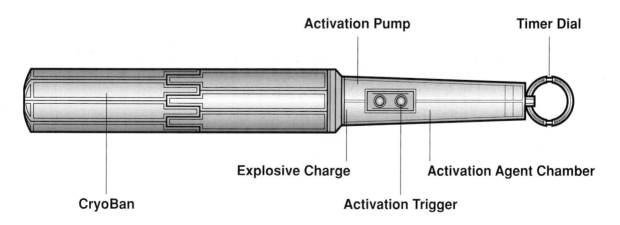

Activation Pump

Timer Dial

Explosive Charge

Activation Agent Chamber

CryoBan

Activation Trigger

GRENADE MORTAR

MERR-SONN MOBILEMORTAR-3

Grenade mortars are powerful long-range grenade launchers that normally serve as infantry support. The MobileMortar-3 combines a long-range MM-s3 grenade launcher with a WW-676 repulsorlift platform, resulting in a light combat vehicle that can quickly move to any position and lend fire support where it is needed most while demoralizing enemy infantry units with a constant barrage of grenades.

The MM-s3 grenade mortar is a portable high-volume grenade launcher. It can fire once every 1.2 seconds, while the barrel's internal rotation module stabilizes grenades in flight for an optimum range of five hundred meters and a maximum range of one kilometer. The barrel's sound dampener greatly muffles blast noise, lending added stealth on the battlefield. The targeting computer provides range and fire-vector data, but the scope's awkward position leads experienced gunners to rely on visual targeting, resorting to the scope only in limited-visibility conditions, such as darkness, smoke, and heavy fog. The MM-s3's magazine holds twelve C-22 fragmentation grenades (or any specialty grenade that can be fitted into a C-22 shell). Attaching a motorized grenade pack to the rear refill door increases the ammunition supply to one hundred grenades. The microrepulsorlift makes the weapon easy to transport and also absorbs most of the mortar's recoil, providing a stable platform for multiple firings.

The MobileMortar-3's WW-676 repulsorlift sled has a top speed of 250 kilometers per hour, with exceptional acceleration and a flight ceiling of thirty meters. Propulsion is provided by an X-7a repulsor engine, while the four thrust vectors located inside the main drive, the secondary XA7 drive unit (under the gunnery chair), and dual steering vanes work in conjunction to provide tremendous maneuverability. The sled's ability to climb rapidly and perform elaborate midair maneuvers makes it a challenging target for enemy artillery pieces and laser cannons. A pilot often hugs the ground for maximum cover, climbing just long enough to allow the gunner to pepper enemy troops with grenades before they can return fire.

The speed and maneuverability come at a steep price, however: The WW-676 has virtually no armor and provides no protection to the pilot and gunner, who are secured only by restraint belts. Since even a blaster rifle bolt can severely damage the vehicle, pilots normally withdraw as soon as they encounter enemy fire.

The large ammunition locker set underneath the pilot's station holds five hundred grenades, which can be fed directly into the mortar through the reload tube. The WW-676 also can carry an E-Web heavy repeating blaster with the power generator mounted inside the ammunition locker. MobileMortar-3 units are assigned to army platoons as support, or four of them may operate as a light mechanized infantry squad. Pilots and gunners are either army specialists or biker scouts.

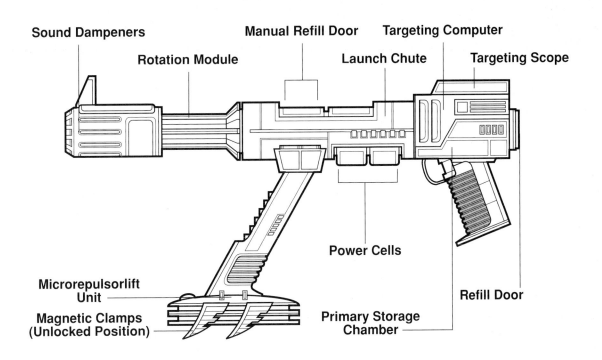

Sound Dampeners

Rotation Module

Manual Refill Door

Targeting Computer

Launch Chute

Targeting Scope

Power Cells

Microrepulsorlift Unit

Magnetic Clamps (Unlocked Position)

Primary Storage Chamber

Refill Door

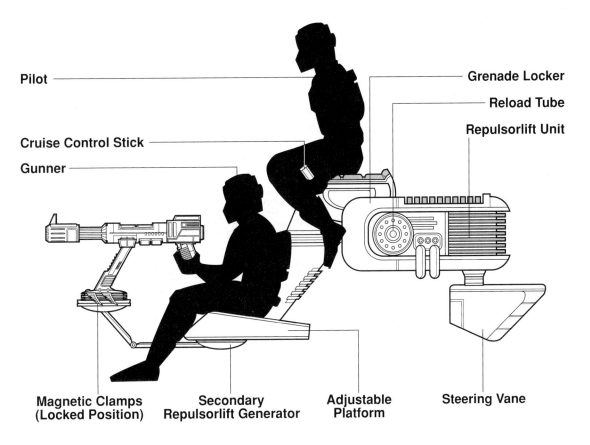

Pilot

Cruise Control Stick

Gunner

Grenade Locker

Reload Tube

Repulsorlift Unit

Magnetic Clamps (Locked Position)

Secondary Repulsorlift Generator

Adjustable Platform

Steering Vane

BLASTER ARTILLERY

Loronar MAS-2xB

A descendent of fixed-position turbolasers such as the Speizoc Arms C-136 "Grandfather Gun" and the Loronar Turbolaser System I, the Loronar MAS-2xB is among the most powerful ground-based siege weapons in the galaxy. The New Republic's MAS-2xB is a mobile system, providing a turbolaser pulsor that can be mounted inside a repulsorcraft vehicle.

During full-scale planetary invasions these artillery systems play a key role in knocking out targets such as transportation centers, troop bases, and military fortresses. In addition to siege assaults, the pulsor can be quite effective against capital ships at low altitudes. The pulsor is designed to destroy even the most sophisticated defense systems, which frequently consist of hardened armor plating, shields fed by massive fusion generators, and/or networks of long-range artillery and laser cannons.

The MAS-2xB's tremendous power requirements are met by a single massive Republic Engineering Corporation 4.2FC fusion power core. The MAS-2xB's primary turbolaser "pulsor" uses an amplification dish positioned around the turbolaser actuator to galven (or focus) the energy beam, boosting its optimum range to ten kilometers and maximum range to thirty kilometers. With an energy output that matches a Star Destroyer's turbolaser, the beam can blast through up to twenty meters of durasteel plate, although the energy demand is so great that the pulsor can fire only once per minute. Four rows of cooling chambers filled with meter-long cryogenic cylinders wrap the power core, the energy capacitors, and the pulsor itself to prevent critical meltdowns during combat.

To defend the system from counterattack, two turbolaser turrets and a quad heavy laser cannon turret deal with approaching airspeeders, repulsortanks, and AT-AT walkers. Six small shield generators and two-meter-thick armor plating ward off enemy blasts, making this weapon all but impervious. The MAS-2xB's mass is so great that even the seven repulsorlift drives provide limited performance with painfully slow acceleration, virtually no maneuverability, a maximum altitude of fifty meters, and a top speed of only forty-five kilometers per hour. At over twice the size of an AT-AT walker, this vehicle is truly terrifying to behold and its firepower produces a deafening roar that literally shakes the ground.

The MAS-2xB requires a crew of fifteen soldiers, including six technicians and engineers needed to maintain the fusion generator and repulsorlift drive systems, which are prone to power surges and burnouts. Only its sixteen energy dampers prevent catastrophic power overloads and normally at least half of them must be replaced after each battle. MAS-2xBs are incredibly maintenance-intensive, requiring special docking platforms for maintenance and repair. Because of their incredible cost—nearly one million credits per unit—the New Republic maintains only a few thousand of these units, deploying them only in the most important ground campaigns.

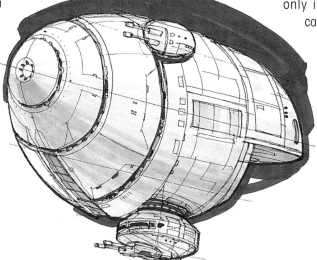

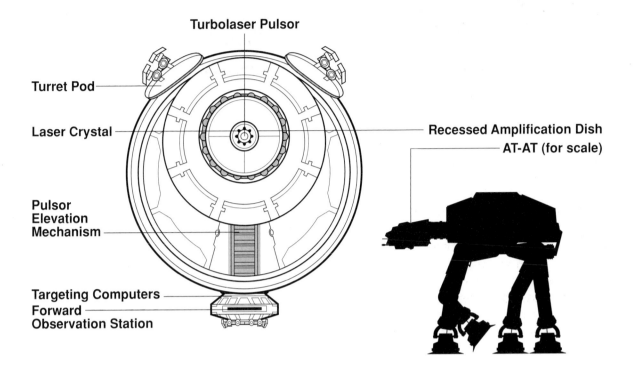

Turbolaser Pulsor

Turret Pod

Laser Crystal

Recessed Amplification Dish

AT-AT (for scale)

Pulsor
Elevation
Mechanism

Targeting Computers
Forward
Observation Station

Front View with AT-AT (for scale)

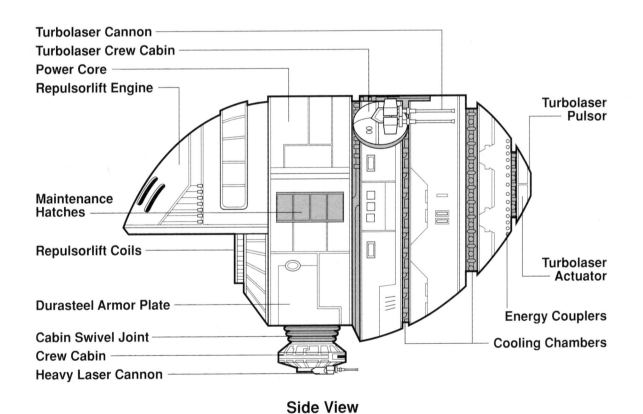

Turbolaser Cannon
Turbolaser Crew Cabin
Power Core
Repulsorlift Engine

Turbolaser
Pulsor

Maintenance
Hatches

Repulsorlift Coils

Durasteel Armor Plate

Turbolaser
Actuator

Cabin Swivel Joint
Crew Cabin
Heavy Laser Cannon

Energy Couplers

Cooling Chambers

Side View

ANTIVEHICLE ARTILLERY

ATGAR 1.4 FD P-TOWER

Antivehicle artillery pieces are permanently placed defensive laser cannons designed to destroy enemy vehicles such as landspeeders, airspeeders, and repulsortanks. They vary widely in size and energy output, ranging from massive CoMar G-003 Tri-Tracker units to small, inexpensive systems such as the Atgar 1.4 FD P-Tower, which was used by the Rebel Alliance at numerous bases, including Echo Base on Hoth.

The dish-shaped Atgar P-Tower offers a single light laser cannon with an optimal range of up to two kilometers and a maximum targetable range of ten kilometers. In this older weapon design, the P-Tower's primitive galven circuitry and focusing lens produce a low-power energy beam that is dangerous only to lightly armored repulsorcraft such as landspeeders and airspeeders. The armor on AT-AT walkers and repulsortanks can easily deflect its bolts. Though the energy beam strikes instantly, the outdated targeting computer cannot accurately predict high-speed airspeeder maneuvers, and so scoring a hit is difficult for all but the most experienced gunners. In practice, the P-Tower has often proved more effective against stormtroopers than against Imperial vehicles.

The P-Tower's platform rotates 360 degrees, providing a full field of fire, while light armor plating protects the targeting computer and the small Atgar C-6 battery, which stores enough energy for eight shots. The P-Tower uses an out-dated firing system: the battery must charge the weapon's sixteen micropower routers (placed evenly around the outer edge of the dish) and eight energy conversion cells. As a result, the weapon needs a full ten seconds to build up an adequate charge, the result being an exceptionally low fire rate. Additionally, a single burnout in any of the sixteen converters disables the weapon, making it prone to failure in combat.

The P-Tower has a crew of three support members while the main gunner handles the portable fire control computer, which has a readout screen and a small joystick for aiming. The weapon provides no protection for crew members, forcing them to stand out in the open, exposed to enemy fire.

Even though the Atgar 1.4 FD P-Tower was at one time the most common antivehicle artillery piece in the Rebellion—many P-Towers were deployed at Echo Base on Hoth and other major Rebel bases—the weapon is almost universally detested by New Republic commanders. It is underpowered, difficult to move, and too expensive to abandon on the battlefield. Experiments to upgrade the weapon—improving the range, overhauling the power system to deliver more damage, or adapting the unit to take a power feed from a larger generator—invariably ended in failure because of the system's decades-old electronics.

With improved antivehicle artillery pieces now available to the New Republic, the P-Tower is currently found only in the hands of mercenary units and pirate gangs that can't afford better.

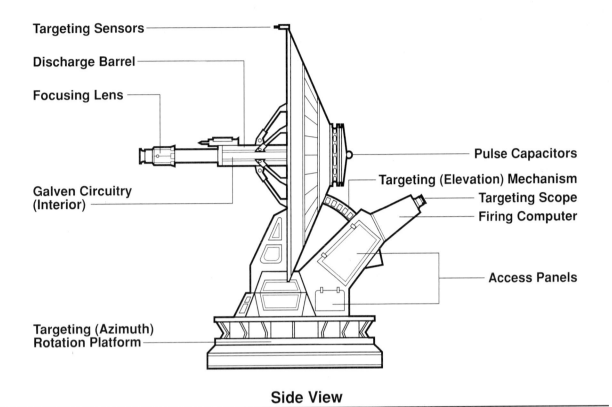

Targeting Sensors

Discharge Barrel

Focusing Lens

Galven Circuitry
(Interior)

Pulse Capacitors

Targeting (Elevation) Mechanism

Targeting Scope

Firing Computer

Access Panels

Targeting (Azimuth)
Rotation Platform

Side View

Front View with Figure (for scale)

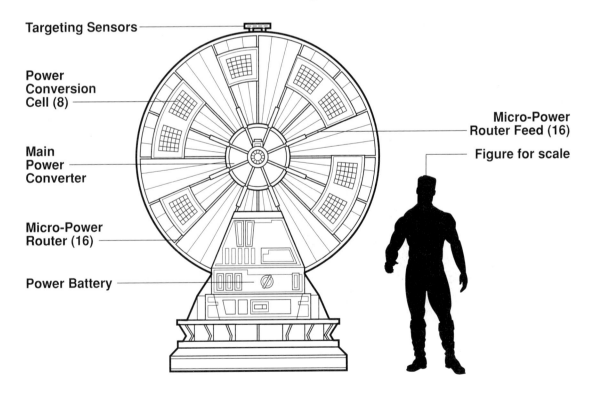

Targeting Sensors

Power
Conversion
Cell (8)

Main
Power
Converter

Micro-Power
Router (16)

Power Battery

Micro-Power
Router Feed (16)

Figure for scale

ANTI-INFANTRY BATTERY

GOLAN ARMS DF.9 ANTI-INFANTRY BATTERY

Anti-infantry batteries use precision targeting computers to direct high-energy blaster bolts into the heart of advancing enemy infantry formations, inflicting heavy casualties and destroying support equipment. The popular DF.9 anti-infantry system delivers far more firepower than do heavy repeating blasters such as the E-Web and often is used in conjunction with antivehicle batteries to protect military bases, spaceports, and other strategic facilities.

The DF.9 laser cannon has an optimal range of three kilometers and a maximum range of sixteen kilometers—much greater than that of the most powerful hand weapons—and so the DF.9 can decimate an enemy infantry unit long before the soldiers can return fire. Capable of firing once every three seconds, the DF.9 uses an energy beam to scatter explosive energy over an eight-meter-radius impact point, allowing a single blast to destroy an entire squad. The armored, proton-shielded turret rotates 180 degrees, but the fixed-position emplacement means the weapon cannot be moved easily from location to location. The crew of three consists of the gunner, a targeting computer technician, and a technician who monitors and regulates power flow from the generator.

During the Galactic Civil War, the Golan Arms DF.9 battery was among the most popular anti-infantry artillery pieces on the market and could readily be found in the arsenals of both the Alliance and the Empire. DF.9 units played a key role in

protecting the Alliance's Echo Base on Hoth and have been used extensively at other Alliance bases, including Tierfon Rebel Outpost, Arbra Base, and Oracle Base on Tel III. Rebel technicians often upgraded the laser cannon's actuator and first-stage barrel to allow it to deliver more energy and make the weapon effective against light vehicles such as AT-ST walkers and CAVw PX-10 ground assault vehicles. However, these upgraded weapons proved useless against AT-AT walkers at the Battle of Hoth.

Although the DF.9 design is more than two decades old, it has remained popular with New Republic, Imperial, and independent military groups such as planetary armies, militias, and mercenary units. Easy availability on the black market—with an average cost of around ten thousand credits for refurbished units—means that DF.9s also tend to end up in the hands of pirates, revolutionaries, and other outlaw bands.

Imperial and New Republic forces have used at least two variants of this weapon. The Twin DF.9 features twin rapid-fire laser cannons, a larger power generator, and advanced laser actuators to achieve a fire rate of one per second. The SP.9 has an improved DF.9 laser cannon mounted on a self-propelled repulsorlift sled. Like the Twin DF.9, the SP.9 cannon can fire once per second, while the sled has a maximum speed of sixty kilometers per hour.

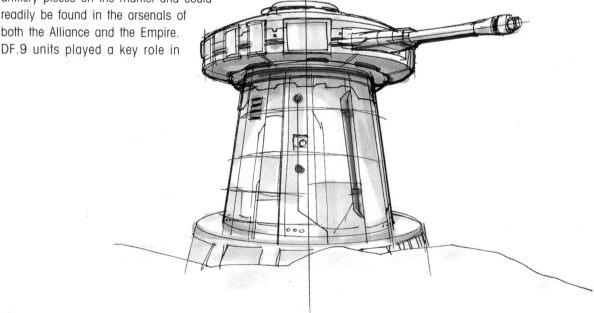

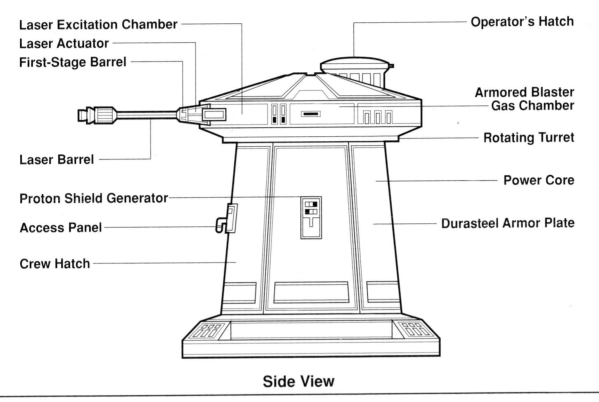

Laser Excitation Chamber

Laser Actuator

First-Stage Barrel

Laser Barrel

Proton Shield Generator

Access Panel

Crew Hatch

Operator's Hatch

Armored Blaster Gas Chamber

Rotating Turret

Power Core

Durasteel Armor Plate

Side View

Front View with Figure (for scale)

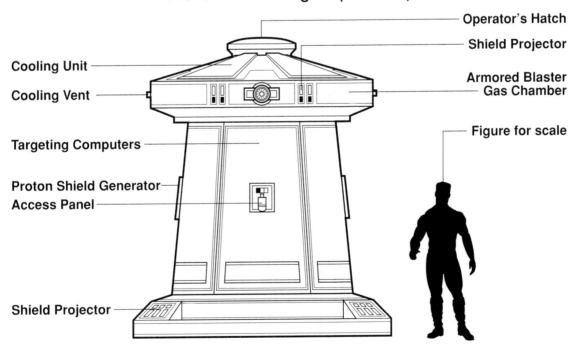

Cooling Unit

Cooling Vent

Targeting Computers

Proton Shield Generator

Access Panel

Shield Projector

Operator's Hatch

Shield Projector

Armored Blaster Gas Chamber

Figure for scale

MELEE WEAPONS

EVOLUTION OF MELEE WEAPON TECHNOLOGY

For centuries melee weapons have been designed to help warriors in hand-to-hand combat situations, extending their reach while adding force to the blows that are delivered through the use of weighted clubs, sharpened blades, and the like. The first melee weapons included knives, clubs, and axes, and they were made of wood, stone, and eventually metal. However, just as advances led to the development of high-tech ranged weapons, technology has been applied to melee weapons, resulting in stunning improvements that have made them far more deadly than their ancient counterparts.

Current melee weapons most often are made of ultra-strong metal alloys, composite ceramics, and reinforced plastics. This makes them lighter and easier to wield, and they are less likely to break in battle. Many melee weapons feature some sort of enhancement that is powered by a long-use energy cell. For example, blades are now equipped with vibration generators that cause rapid movement, allowing them to inflict substantially more damage. While an unpowered blade requires the user to apply significant force in order to injure an opponent, vibroblades need only make glancing contact. The vibrating blade automatically cuts into the victim, resulting in severe injuries. A direct hit can kill the victim immediately.

Current melee weapon design also emphasizes durability for extended operation with minimal maintenance. Most vibroblades incorporate self-sharpening diagnostic modes, while the blades and shafts are virtually indestructible. It's not uncommon for vibroweapons that have been abandoned for decades to work quite well, once the vibration generator has been recalibrated and the power cell has been replaced.

The lightsabers built by the Jedi Knights can last for thousands of years. Lightsabers discovered in ancient Jedi crypts have been known to require no adjustment whatsoever, and their power cells can still create the deadly energy blades that are capable of cutting through almost any substance.

Advanced technologies also have allowed the development of specialized weapons such as shock generators, which dispense modulated electrical charges to paralyze targets temporarily. These generators are useful for crowd control and for capturing enemy soldiers for later interrogation. Nonlethal shock generators have been incorporated into many melee weapons, from stun batons to shock nets and blast shields.

ALIEN TECHNOLOGY AND MELEE WEAPONS

While the blending of thousands of alien cultures—a natural result of interstellar travel—has led to the development of many hybrid weapons, others have remained unique to the originating culture. For instance, Wookiees are fearsome opponents when they use their ryyk blades in close-quarters battles, but few other beings have the strength to wield those heavy swords. As another example, the Noghri of the planet Honoghr customarily carry short-bladed knives into combat. These aliens are barely a meter tall, yet they are exceedingly quick, much stronger than their size would suggest, and frighteningly ferocious. In hand-to-hand combat Noghri can easily bypass their opponents' defenses, strike a lethal blow with unerring precision, and then retreat before their opponents can respond. A longer, bulkier weapon such as a vibrosword would only slow them down.

EVOLUTION OF COMBAT TECHNIQUES

The advantages of modern weaponry—lethality, lightweight design, and reliability—have led warriors to develop their own advanced combat styles and techniques. After years of study many warriors have developed masterful attacks and parries designed to overwhelm an opponent completely, and traditions of weapon mastery endure in many warrior sects.

However, some of these tactics have come about as a result of necessity, since defenses also have improved over the millennia. Modern suits of armor are light, yet their high-strength metal alloys and plastoid panels allow them to deflect blades and absorb impacts from clubs and other weighted weapons. Often it is only through carefully planned attacks that warriors can expect to outmaneuver their opponents and pierce their defenses.

Some melee weapons incorporate unusual technologies that allow their wielders to craft unique combat strategies. This may give them an advantage against opponents who are expecting to face more conventional weaponry. Again, the classic example would be that of soldiers using vibroblades. Swordsmen who are accustomed to standard dueling methods can deliver a series of attacks, parries, and feints before the final deadly strike is scored. But

lightsabers in turn can easily slice through the vibroblades' shafts, and so defenders cannot parry attacks and have little choice but to retreat from an advancing Jedi Knight.

MELEE WEAPONS IN MODERN COMBAT

Even though ranged weapons have come to dominate combat, soldiers will always carry melee weapons, since hand-to-hand engagements will ever remain part of warfare. Whereas blasters need to be aimed, melee weapons can be quickly hefted and utilized reflexively, enhancing the combatant's inherent skills.

Hand-to-hand skirmishes may be fought on the open battlefield, but they are even more common inside buildings and in other areas where there is little room to maneuver. Melee weapons become essential in such close-quarter situations. The Rebel Alliance won several battles against Imperial stormtroopers in circumstances where the Imperials' bulky armor limited their movement, while the Rebels were able to strike and retreat with virtual impunity.

Melee weapons are also used widely on worlds where the governments strictly control access to blasters. Since criminals seldom pay attention to such official prohibitions, many citizens feel the need to carry melee weapons for self-defense. Small weapons such as vibroshivs are cheap and small enough to be carried conveniently. Concealability always offers the wielder a distinct advantage; someone who is threatened by an attacker needs only a split second to pull the weapon and provide an unwelcome surprise for a thug who has moved in on an apparently unarmed victim.

And of course there are many worlds with primitive and isolated cultures that still rely predominantly on melee weapons because blasters and other high-tech goods are impractical. A classic example are the Tusken Raiders of Tatooine, who use axlike gaderffii sticks as their primary weapons. These simple blades are well suited to the Raiders' rough, nomadic lifestyle since they are durable, require no energy sources or maintenance, and have no moving parts. As long as this sort of culture exists, the melee weapon will remain a vital part of military life.

LIGHTSABER

DARTH VADER'S LIGHTSABER
LUKE SKYWALKER'S LIGHTSABER

Among the Old Republic's many legends, none endure more than the stories of the Jedi Knights and their incredible lightsabers.

A lightsaber's handgrip is approximately twenty-four to thirty centimeters long and features a mirrorlike concave metal disk called a blade emitter on one end. Controls include an activation lever, a recharge socket, diagnostic readouts, and in some cases blade length and intensity controls. Opening the small access panel reveals a tiny but very sophisticated power cell as well as at least one—and sometimes several—multifaceted crystals or jewels.

The lightsaber's jewels focus the power cell's energy charge into a tight parallel beam that emerges from the blade emitter as a vibrant blade of pure energy. The blade is a closed energy loop. Its amplitude determines when the energy beam arcs back to the negatively charged high-energy flux aperture that rings the outer edge of the lightsaber's concave disk. The power cell can last for years because it is fed by the energy that enters the flux aperture; the weapon loses energy only when the blade makes contact with another object.

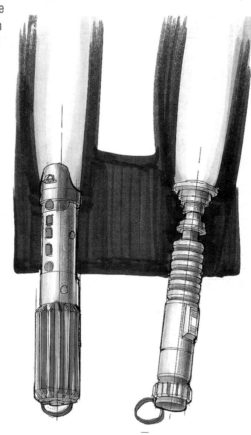

The lightsaber's deadly energy blade can cut through almost any substance. Because the blade itself has no weight and emits no heat, a novice may easily miscalculate its path. A Jedi Knight undertakes years of study to master the weapon, developing the skill that allows him or her to block incoming blaster bolts or fend off as many as a dozen attackers.

Each lightsaber is custom-built, normally by the Jedi student as one of the tests of an apprentice's skills. After his disastrous defeat at Cloud City, Luke Skywalker retired to Obi-Wan Kenobi's hut on Tatooine to build his new lightsaber, perhaps hoping that that familiar and comfortable place would provide solace as he grappled with the knowledge that Darth Vader might be his father.

Most lightsabers have customized features such as pressure-sensitive activation levers (so that the blade disappears as soon as the saber is released) and multiple crystals that enable the user to alter the amplitude and length of the blade. The lightsaber's handgrip is as much a work of art as a practical weapon, often featuring a design native to the Jedi's homeworld or built by the student in a style reminiscent of his master's lightsaber.

The Jedi drew their lightsabers only as a last resort—when negotiation failed to resolve a dispute peacefully—but their skills were unquestioned once these magnificent energy blades flashed. The Empire nearly succeeded in exterminating the Jedi, but Luke Skywalker has been training a new generation of Jedi Knights, who proudly wield their lightsabers in defense of the New Republic, reaffirming traditions of courage and honor that have endured for a thousand generations.

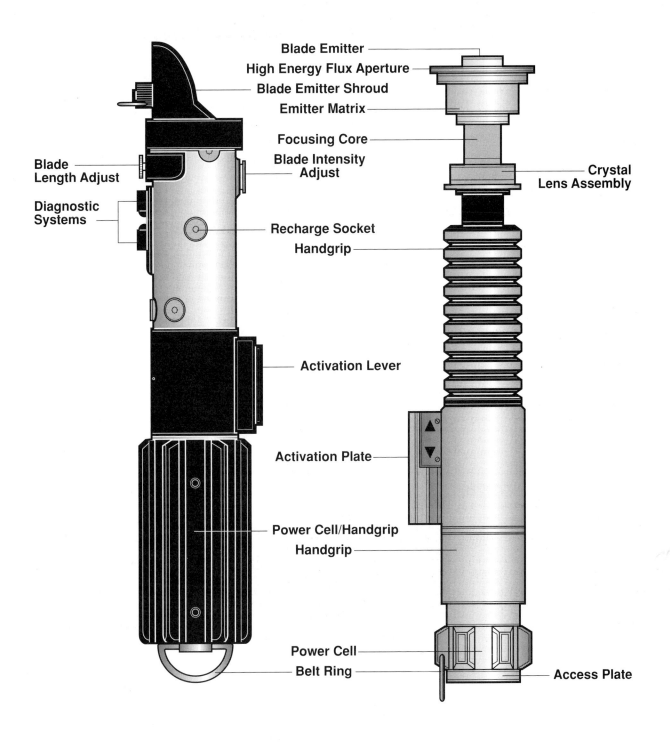

Blade Emitter

High Energy Flux Aperture

Blade Emitter Shroud

Emitter Matrix

Focusing Core

Blade Intensity
Adjust

Crystal
Lens Assembly

Blade
Length Adjust

Diagnostic
Systems

Recharge Socket

Handgrip

Activation Lever

Activation Plate

Power Cell/Handgrip

Handgrip

Power Cell

Belt Ring

Access Plate

Darth Vader's Lightsaber

Luke Skywalker's Lightsaber

EXAR KUN'S LIGHTSABER

DOUBLE-BLADED LIGHTSABER

Some unique objects are invariably associated with their remarkable owners. The unusual double-bladed lightsaber of the fallen Jedi Exar Kun is one such artifact. This weapon was as distinctive and dangerous as its builder, the Dark Lord of the Sith, who initiated the great Sith War and nearly toppled the Old Republic.

Once a young and ambitious Jedi studying under Master Vodo-Siosk Baas, Exar Kun was lured to the dark side of the Force. After turning away from the teachings of his master, Kun gathered armies of followers and initiated a campaign to exterminate the Jedi Knights, with the ultimate intention of conquering the Republic.

As the battles against the Jedi escalated, Kun altered his normal lightsaber into a more deadly and dangerous weapon. Kun added a second emitter matrix on the opposite end of the handgrip, allowing him to release two blue-white blades simultaneously. The dark Jedi wielded the saber much as he would a quarterstaff, using one blade to block incoming attacks, then quickly spinning the handgrip to use the second blade to strike a killing blow against his opponent.

Customized controls allowed him to adjust each blade's length from half a meter to one and a half meters. Panels controlled each blade's intensity: at its highest setting, a blade was like any other lightsaber, with the ability to cut through dense materials such as armor plating and durasteel with virtually no resistance. At the lowest power setting a blade became a simple shaft of light, delivering no damage and providing no resistance against incoming lightsaber attacks. By abruptly shortening a blade or dropping it to the lowest power setting, Kun tricked his opponents into overextending themselves during attacks, giving him an opportunity for a deadly counterstrike. By coupling these tactics with his Force abilities to predict the actions of his opponents, Kun became virtually unstoppable in combat.

Truly corrupted by the dark side of the Force, Kun showed no mercy and his plan to exterminate the Jedi nearly succeeded. He even dared to challenge Master Baas on the Republic Senate's floor, striking him down in front of the horrified senators and Jedi Knights.

However, Kun's reach was too great and his thirst for power too unquenchable for even him to control. One of his former disciples, the fallen Jedi Ulic Qel-Droma, turned on the Dark Lord of the Sith, leading the Republic to Kun's main fortress on Yavin Four. The jungle moon was devastated in the battle, and Exar Kun's twin-bladed lightsaber and numerous other artifacts were destroyed. Kun was thought dead, although his spirit later manifested itself after Luke Skywalker established his Jedi academy, or *praxeum*, in the Massassi ruins on the moon's surface.

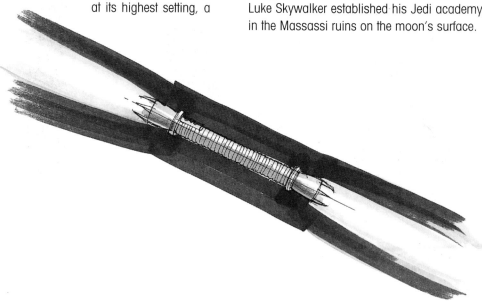

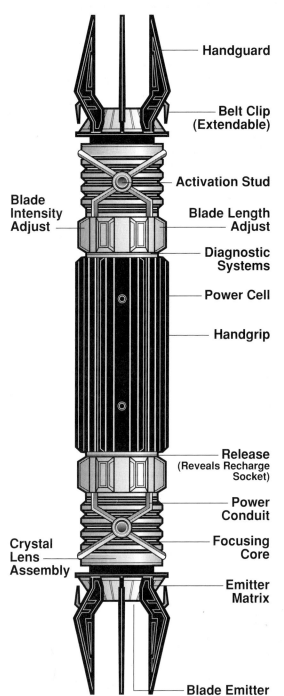

Handguard

Belt Clip
(Extendable)

Activation Stud

Blade
Intensity
Adjust

Blade Length
Adjust

Diagnostic
Systems

Power Cell

Handgrip

Release
(Reveals Recharge
Socket)

Power
Conduit

Crystal
Lens
Assembly

Focusing
Core

Emitter
Matrix

Blade Emitter

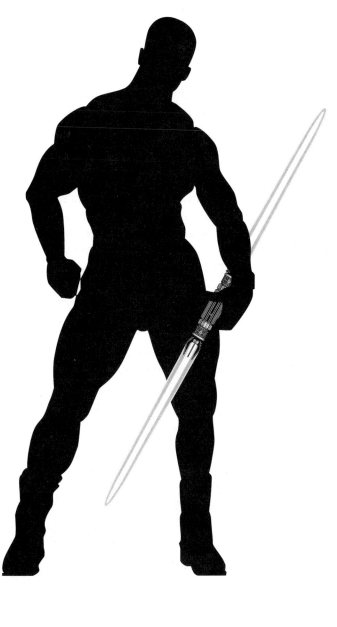

GADERFFII

GADERFFII

Gaderffii, also known as gaffi sticks, are the dangerous bladed weapons wielded by Tatooine's fearsome Sand People, also known as Tusken Raiders. Fashioned with metal scavenged from wrecked starships, these handcrafted weapons are crude, dangerous, and sturdy enough to last for years.

The simple design consists of a hollow durasteel tube with a cutting blade affixed on one end and a weighted club or a second blade attached to the other end. The double-edged ax blades are sharpened to a razor's edge, able to cleave blasters—or living beings—in two with a single blow. The primary blade often has a spike used for spearing attacks. Gaffi sticks equipped with a second blade allow a Raider to deliver multiple cutting swings or strikes in quick succession, while sticks armed with a weighted club head can be used to knock victims unconscious or batter and break apart objects such as droids, speeders, and vaporators.

Conflict and intimidation play significant roles in Tusken Raider culture, with individuals often brandishing their gaffi sticks during loud quarrels that determine social standing within the clan. The weapons double as eminently practical tools that can be used as walking sticks during arduous trips through the mountains, and the ax blades can be used to carve marks that indicate clan territories or leave warnings on rock faces. A gaffi stick is in many ways far more practical than a blaster, which may run out of power or break if not handled carefully, although the Raiders do maintain a small number of hunting blasters that have been stolen during raids on moisture farms.

Extremely territorial and violent, the Sand People have perfected the art of hiding in Tatooine's desert wastes and attacking with surprise acting heavily in their favor. They often attack at night, and ride their banthas single-file to hide their numbers. Superstitious by nature, these tall, powerful humanoids largely avoid high technology. Indeed, many Sand People seem afraid of mundane objects such as landspeeders, which they approach with great caution, as if expecting them to rear up and attack like some kind of metal beast.

Luke Skywalker learned about the perils of encountering the Sand People when he was attacked while trying to retrieve his runaway droid, Artoo-Detoo. Luke's hunting rifle was destroyed by a single swing from a Raider's gaffi stick, and the inexperienced young man promptly fainted…an act that probably saved his life, as it led the attacker to immediately join his fellows in the more important duty of looting Luke's landspeeder.

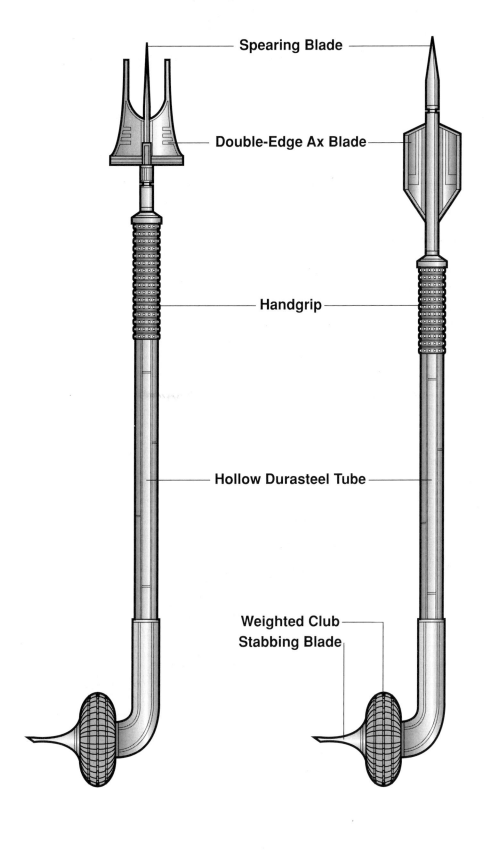

Spearing Blade

Double-Edge Ax Blade

Handgrip

Hollow Durasteel Tube

Weighted Club
Stabbing Blade

FORCE PIKE

SoroSuub Controller FP

Cloaked in flowing red robes and full body armor, their faces completely hidden by masks, the Imperial Royal Guards were Emperor Palpatine's personal bodyguards, charged with protecting him and defending the most important treasures of the Empire, including the Imperial throne room in the Imperial Palace on Coruscant. Afforded the best military training and mental conditioning in the Empire, the Royal Guards never hesitated to demonstrate their formidable skills at wielding their imposing force pikes, making quick work of any transgressors.

The force pike is a two-meter-long pole-arm weapon topped with a charged power tip. Weighing barely seven kilograms, it is light for its size, allowing someone with sufficient training to manipulate the weapon with stunning swiftness. As is typical of other vibroweapons, the force pike's power cell energizes an ultrasonic vibration generator and so produces a distinctive low hum when activated. Conductive circuits that line the pole's interior carry the ultrasonic charge to the power tip, which emits thousands of microscopic vibrations per second. This rapid motion allows the blade to slice effortlessly through stone, metal, and of course flesh and bone. The blade's vibrating action means

that even a grazing attack can cause serious lacerations, dismemberment, and other grievous injuries. Even with the generator deactivated, the metal blade is extremely sharp.

A force pike also can be set to release a stun charge, which is delivered as soon as the power tip comes within four centimeters of the target. The painful shock charge is powerful enough to knock a full-grown Wookiee unconscious. The force pike's long pole is perfect for thrusting attacks, giving the weapon a considerably longer reach than standard vibroblades while allowing for precisely controlled strikes. This design also allows the wielder to apply his or her full physical strength to an attack. The pole's spun graphite composition strengthens the shaft while allowing it to flex and temporarily bend rather than break under extreme pressure.

Besides their noted use by the Emperor's Royal Guards, force pikes are often carried by honor guards and diplomatic corps troops as "ceremonial" (but nonetheless deadly) weapons. Force pikes are also quite effective for crowd control measures, allowing police officers and military troops to disperse bystanders quickly and round up demonstrators for detention and questioning.

Force pikes are useful weapons for boarding actions, since they allow attackers to slice through bulkheads and air locks in a few seconds without having to resort to dangerously unpredictable explosive charges.

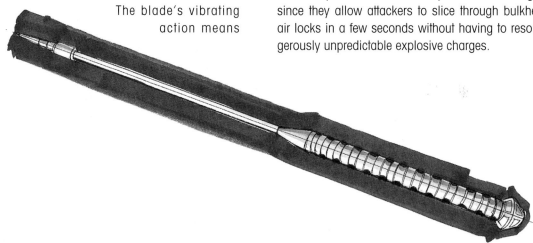

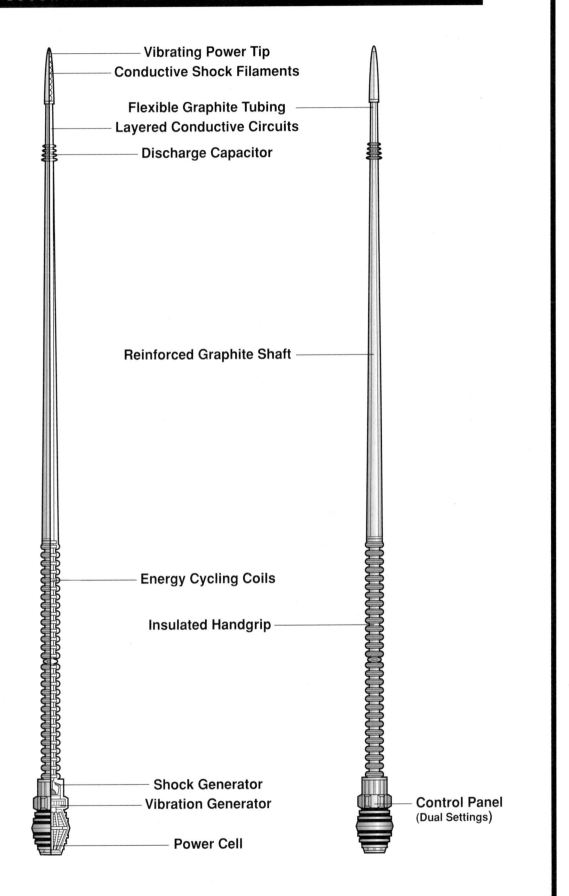

Vibrating Power Tip
Conductive Shock Filaments
Flexible Graphite Tubing
Layered Conductive Circuits
Discharge Capacitor

Reinforced Graphite Shaft

Energy Cycling Coils

Insulated Handgrip

Shock Generator
Vibration Generator

Power Cell

Control Panel
(Dual Settings)

VIBRO-AX

CLAN GROOGRUN VIBRO-AX
SOROSUUB BD-1 CUTTER VIBRO-AX

Jabba's palace on Tatooine was home to some of the mangiest, vilest criminals in all the Outer Rim Territories. Knowing the likelihood of frequent outbursts of mayhem, Jabba equipped his guards with an assortment of deadly weapons.

Vibro-axes, a particular favorite among the Gamorreans, were essential to Jabba's amusement, since their blades proved most effective in herding unsuspecting visitors over the rancor pit's trapdoor. In the hands of his ill-tempered skiff guards, these rather nasty weapons also ensured speedy yet entertaining feedings of the Sarlacc at the Great Pit of Carkoon.

Vibro-axes vary widely in quality and power output, although all of them have the same basic function: A power cell supplies energy to an ultrasonic vibration generator, which propels the cutting blade through thousands of microscopic vibrations per second. The result is a hand weapon that is significantly more dangerous than its unpowered counterparts.

Despite the availability of better weapons, Jabba's nine Gamorrean guards stubbornly insisted on carrying crude vibro-axes built by Snogrutt, a master weapon maker from their home clan of Groogrun. Led by a brutish fellow by the name of Ortugg, the Gamorreans patrolled the palace's dungeons, searching for spies who were plotting against Jabba's best interests and keeping a close eye

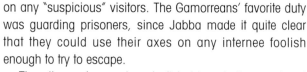

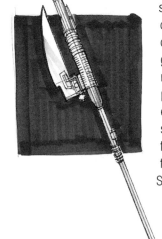

on any "suspicious" visitors. The Gamorreans' favorite duty was guarding prisoners, since Jabba made it quite clear that they could use their axes on any internee foolish enough to try to escape.

The vibro-ax's wooden shaft holds a hollow ax head that contains both the ultrasonic generator and the power cell. A tremendous amount of vibration is transferred down the wooden handle, and Gamorreans are among the few creatures with enough strength to handle these difficult devices. The Gamorreans often chose to use their weapons in *unpowered* mode to demonstrate their great strength...although most of Jabba's guests believed the simple creatures tended to forget to power up their weapons, caught up in the excitement of battle.

Jabba's other guards, including a number of Weequay and Nikto warriors, were considerably more practical, favoring modern weapons such as the SoroSuub BD-1 Cutter vibro-ax. This weapon has a hollow durasteel shaft with internal dampeners that absorb vibrations from the ax blade. The high-powered ax head can slice through armor plating as if it were rotting cloth, while the quick-release switch allows the user to replace a damaged ax blade in seconds. Six power cells permit up to eight hours of continuous use, while the intensity switch gives the wielder the ability to determine precisely how much damage the blade will cause. (Jabba's guards, not known for finesse, normally left the dial set at maximum power.) These weapons are sturdy enough to take rough handling, with superior weight distribution to make them easy to handle in combat. Still, they proved no match for Luke Skywalker's lightsaber blade, which sliced right through them.

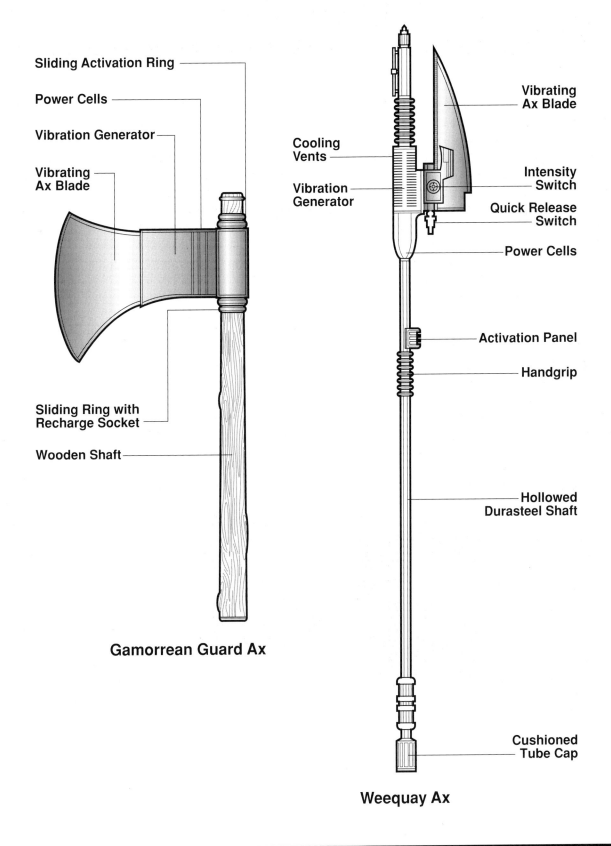

Sliding Activation Ring

Power Cells

Vibration Generator

Vibrating
Ax Blade

Sliding Ring with
Recharge Socket

Wooden Shaft

Gamorrean Guard Ax

Cooling
Vents

Vibration
Generator

Vibrating
Ax Blade

Intensity
Switch

Quick Release
Switch

Power Cells

Activation Panel

Handgrip

Hollowed
Durasteel Shaft

Cushioned
Tube Cap

Weequay Ax

VIBROBLADE

MERR-SONN TREPPUS-2 VIBROBLADE
CZERKA VIBROKNUCKLER

"Vibroblade" is the generic term applied to any powered cutting blade, ranging from tiny vibroshivs to sword blades that can be up to a meter long. As with the vibro-ax, these weapons use small ultrasonic generators to produce thousands of microscopic vibrations per second along the blade's edge, greatly improving the ability to slice through dense materials. Originally developed for industrial uses, vibroblades are used in factories and are carried in the field by scouts, mechanics, and other laborers. Medical applications are numerous, since vibroscalpels allow for very precise, effortless incisions.

Almost inevitably, this technology was applied to warfare, leading to the development of exceptionally dangerous hand weapons. Whereas an unpowered blade may simply cause lacerations, even a glancing blow with a vibroblade can cut off a limb or cause other very serious injuries. Vibroblades are so powerful and inexpensive that they have all but replaced unpowered blades on many worlds.

The Merr-Sonn Treppus-2 is a standard knife-sized vibroweapon with a blade nearly fifteen centimeters long. The power cell (located in the handgrip) supplies energy for up to ten hours, while the sheath can include an optional automatic recharging unit.

Pressing the activation stud powers up the weapon, although the blade can be preset to activate as soon as it is pulled from its sheath. When powered, the blade vibrates so quickly that it seems to blur,

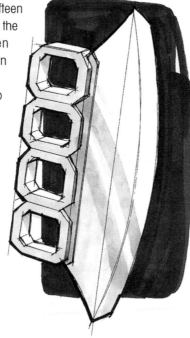

while the low hum of the vibration generator can be heard from several meters away. The blade effortlessly cuts through duraplast, ceramic armor, and metal alloys. The handgrip's padding absorbs excess vibration, resulting in a weapon that is extremely easy to wield. Its excellent weight distribution allows it to be thrown with great accuracy.

The Czerka vibroknuckler is a small self-defense weapon designed for someone who's accustomed to brawling with bare fists. Once it is slipped over the fingers, the knuckler's cutting blade activates as soon as the wielder clenches his or her hand into a fist. While the knuckler has a very short blade, it is almost impossible for unarmed opponents to block its blows.

Vibroblades and vibrobayonets are commonly carried by New Republic commandos and other soldiers as backup weapons. In lawless locales such as the Mos Eisley spaceport, vibroblades are openly carried both to intimidate and to ward off potential attackers. On worlds with strict prohibitions against weapons, many street thugs carry small, easily concealed vibroshivs, which generally have blades less than six centimeters long but are still quite deadly in close-quarters combat.

During his early days as a smuggler Han Solo had a close call with a thug wielding a vibroblade. With no means of retreat or escape, Solo had to rely on his most potent weapon: his wits. The Corellian smuggler momentarily distracted the attacker, allowing Solo's associate, Fiolla of Lorrd, to run over the thug with a swoop.

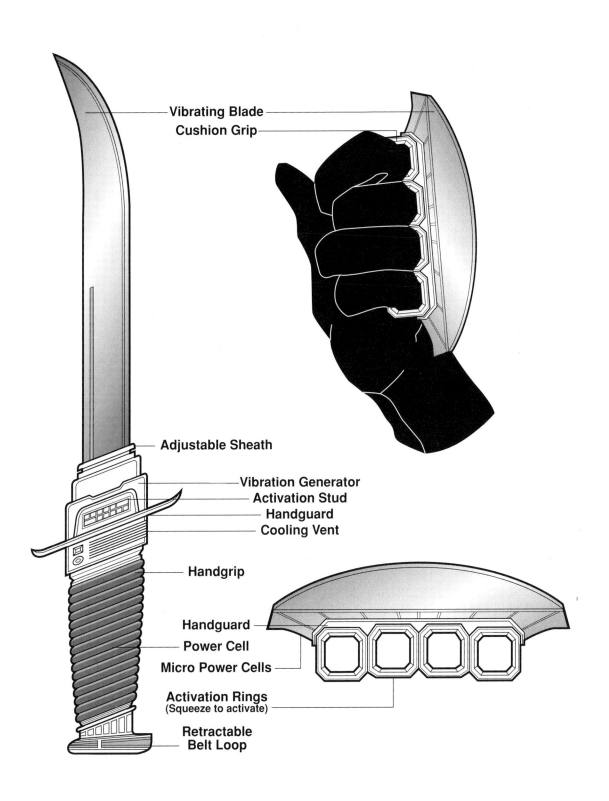

Vibrating Blade
Cushion Grip

Adjustable Sheath

Vibration Generator
Activation Stud
Handguard
Cooling Vent

Handgrip

Handguard
Power Cell
Micro Power Cells

Activation Rings
(Squeeze to activate)

Retractable
Belt Loop

RYYK BLADES

RYYK BLADES

Ryyk blades are the traditional hand weapons carried by the Wookiees of Kashyyyk. Essentially long machetes, they consist of sharpened blades with hide-wrapped grips. Specific blade and handgrip designs vary from clan to clan, and each warrior often etches personal markings into his or her blade.

A warrior's ryyk blade is a prized personal possession and, like a bowcaster, is believed to be something akin to an extension of his or her being, representing the warrior's courage, strength, and honor. Any Wookiee who manages a successful hunt using only a ryyk blade is regarded with great respect by his or her clan mates.

Although ryyk blades weigh at least fifteen kilograms, Wookiees can use them to make slashing attacks at blinding speed. Wookiee combat styles traditionally emphasize brute strength over finesse, but warriors wield these weapons with great precision, wasting no strength or motion: They are deadly opponents in combat.

Ryyk blades were first developed when the Wookiees were still technologically primitive. The Wookiee clans lived in the uppermost branches of Kashyyyk's trees, but hunting parties often ventured to the dangerous lower levels of the jungles, using their ryyk blades to carve paths and create intricate networks of vines for swinging from tree to tree. Before the development of

bowcasters, hunting parties relied solely on spears and ryyk blades to feed their clans and protect their villages.

Wookiees still carry these weapons even when within the confines of their own treetop communities, since some particularly aggressive creatures are known to sneak into the outskirts of their cities when prowling for food. These animals are so dangerous that Wookiee nurseries are placed in the uppermost branches, where they are vigilantly guarded.

Predators such as katarns and webweavers can seemingly materialize from the trees and attack without warning. In these situations a warrior doesn't have time to draw and fire a bowcaster—when a creature pounces, a ryyk blade kept within easy reach often means the difference between life and death.

During the Imperial occupation of Kashyyyk, Wookiees resisting the Empire often used their ryyk blades to carve new paths through the jungles, which they used to set up ambushes of Imperial troops, which were completely unprepared to deal with the planet's terrain...or the ferocity of their opponents.

Years later, after the Wookiees gained their freedom and joined the New Republic, Princess Leia Organa Solo was brought to Kashyyyk by Chewbacca. Leia was guarded by Ralrracheen and Salporin. Those two warriors displayed great skill with these simple weapons when they defended Leia from attacks by Noghri death commandos who were serving the legendary Grand Admiral Thrawn.

Ryyk Kerarthorr Blade

Ryyk Blade

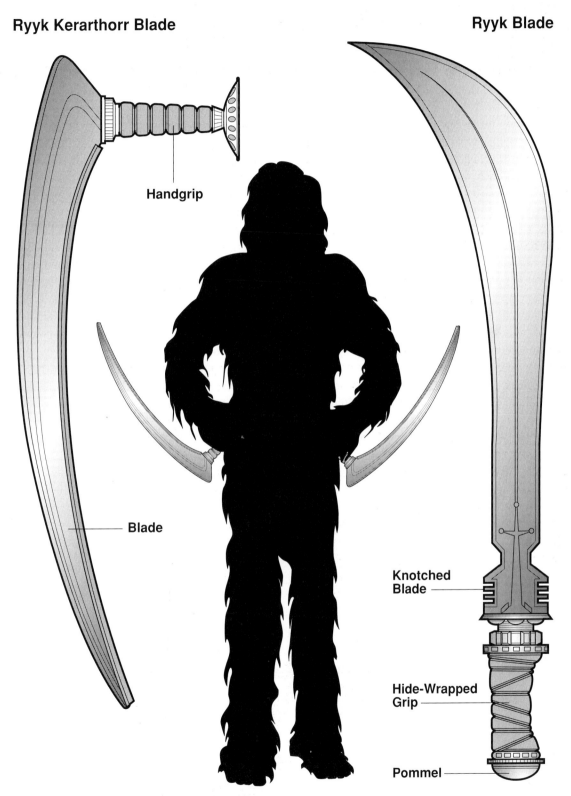

Handgrip

Blade

Knotched Blade

Hide-Wrapped Grip

Pommel

Wookiee brandishing Ryyk Kerarthorr Blade

STUN BATON

MERR-SONN STUN BATON
MERR-SONN KZZ RIOT ARMOR

When discontent turns to public protest, some governments seek ways of dispersing angry mobs with a minimum of public bloodshed. As a result, many nonlethal stun weapons have been designed to break up demonstrations. One of the most recognizable of these weapons is the Merr-Sonn stun baton, which was used widely by both the Empire and the Corporate Sector Authority.

The Merr-Sonn stun baton is a weighted club that has been coupled with a shock charge generator. While of an exceptionally simple design, it is *quite* effective, particularly against unarmed protesters. The club's ridges have scores of miniature shock projectors that deliver a stunning and painful charge that can paralyze a person for as much as several minutes; most victims slump into unconsciousness after just one blow.

The baton has a variable charge setting—adjusted by spinning a small dial above the recharge socket—that allows the soldier to set the exact severity of the electrical shock. (Though marketed as a humane crowd-control weapon, a stun baton at full charge can kill.) A weight inside the club can be slid toward one end or the other to alter the amount of physical damage delivered with each swing. The rechargeable power cell lasts for three hours of continuous use.

The stun baton is but one tool available to security forces, which often carry blastshields and wear full riot armor. Merr-Sonn's KZZ riot armor has hardened ceramic plating to deflect rocks, bullets, and other projectiles, although it does nothing to stop blaster bolts. Armored helmets have retractable blast visors to negate the effects of luma and flash grenades, while insulated bodysuits worn under the armor block stun blasts. In particularly dangerous situations, troops may be issued oxygen processors and sealed environment suits to block stun gases, nerve agents, and other toxins. Blast shields made from a ceramic/transparisteel composite can deflect energy bolts from pistols and other small hand weapons and can be fitted with shock projectors that will stun and force back protesters.

After the collapse of the Empire, the Corporate Sector Authority experienced widespread civil unrest, and Authority "Espos" (security police) dressed in riot armor were often dispatched to quell protests. These soldiers, never known for their tolerance or compassion, grimly waded into the crowds and attacked anyone within reach. After these demonstrations had been brutally suppressed, "troublemakers" who had been brought down by Espo stun batons were frequently detained for questioning—and most were never seen again.

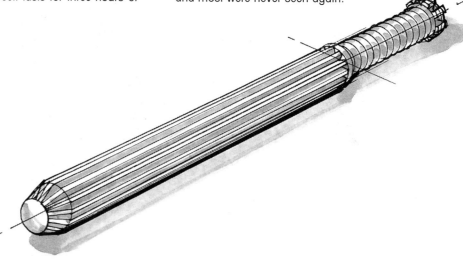

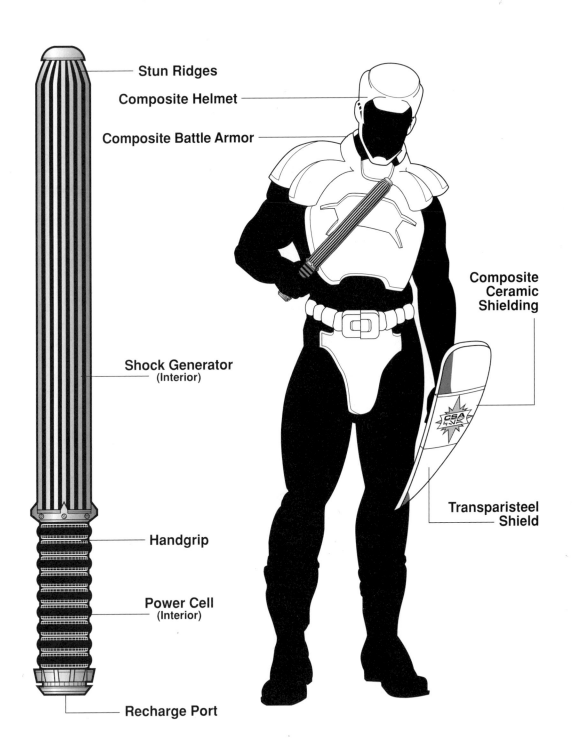

Stun Ridges

Composite Helmet

Composite Battle Armor

Shock Generator
(Interior)

Handgrip

Power Cell
(Interior)

Recharge Port

Composite
Ceramic
Shielding

Transparisteel
Shield

INDIVIDUAL FIELD DISRUPTOR

Aeramaxis Evasive-13 Individual Field Disruptor

Individual field disruptors are high-power portable energy projection systems that are used to defeat energy screens and fences. However, a disruptor also can serve as an impromptu personal weapon, delivering a potent energy blast to anyone who touches the person wearing the disruption field equipment.

Energy fences project walls of visible, deadly energy. Anything touching one of these fences is repulsed by the equivalent of a heavy repeating blaster bolt. While these are formidable defensive systems, a sufficiently powerful individual field disruptor allows the wearer to slip through unharmed, although the disruptor does nothing to counteract sensors, trip lasers, and other common security systems.

Individual field disruptors have one notable drawback—if they cannot compensate for the fence's power rating, a person wearing a disruptor will suffer the full brunt of the fence's blast.

First released during the reign of the Empire, the Evasive-13 is one of many individual field disruptors on the market. Its fifteen-centimeter-long case holds the power cell, a control computer, and twin projection shells. Each of these holds a disruption bubble unit. Sliding the twin shells away from the power cell will activate the unit, at which time the twin disruption bubble integrators generate a small energy field, completely enveloping the user.

At the minimum setting the Evasive-13 can pass through low-power fences, and the power cell lasts for over an hour of continuous use. However, maximum output, which is is necessary to counteract many military-grade fences, drains the cell in less than four minutes. The Evasive-13 also can be used as a close-quarters weapon, since anyone who touches a full-power disruption field receives a very nasty and sometimes fatal energy blast.

When it was released over a decade ago, the Evasive-13 used cutting-edge (for the time) disruption bubble technology and had a price of over twenty-five thousand credits. More advanced disruption bubble generators have become available—in turn leading to the development of more powerful energy fences—so that the Evasive-13 is now considered a midlevel system, and its price has dropped to around eight thousand credits. The Evasive-13 can defeat most civilian energy fence systems, but many military units have high enough energy ratings to counteract this disruptor.

Evasive-13 disruptors were used by paramilitary operatives who planned to kill the infamous Doctor Evazan by infiltrating his secured fortress on the planet Ando. These agents, hired by families that had been victimized by the insane doctor's failed experiments, used disruption bubble generators to slip through several layers of power screens, but their attack was foiled and they were killed by Evazan and his companion, the Aqualish thug Ponda Baba.

Military operations specialists have access to much more sophisticated disruption bubble generators. Elite Imperial Storm Commandos and the New Republic's top operatives, Page's Commandos, often use advanced field disruptors such as the Aeramaxis Evasive-226-R.

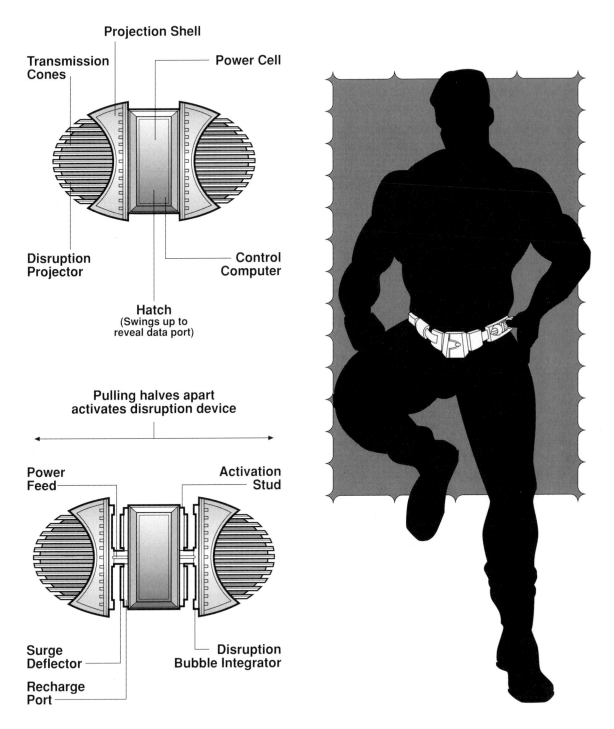

Projection Shell

Transmission
Cones

Power Cell

Disruption
Projector

Control
Computer

Hatch
(Swings up to
reveal data port)

Pulling halves apart
activates disruption device

Power
Feed

Activation
Stud

Surge
Deflector

Disruption
Bubble Integrator

Recharge
Port

Figure Activating Field Disruptor (on utility belt)

Starship and Planetary Weapons and Defenses

Evolution of Space Combat

The history of space travel has been marked by great triumphs as species have expanded across the stars, but it also has been plagued by numerous conflicts. Galactic anthropologists believe that long-range weaponry has been used since the first days of chemical rockets, and the earliest starship weapons included guided missiles, projectile launchers, and low-energy microwave lasers. Defenses were limited to thin armor plating, primitive shield banks, and reflective hull coatings designed to deflect energy beams. Projectiles and homing rockets were used to detonate attacking missiles, while clouds of charged particles diffused incoming energy beams.

Over thousands of years starship technology advanced continuously, often rapidly, leading to the development of sublight ion drives and advanced sensors. New technologies brought improved weapons and defenses, and struggles for the control of territory and resources erupted.

In the days before the founding of the Old Republic, Xim the Despot and other warlords commanded vast fleets and built the first stellar empires. More than twenty thousand years ago the Old Republic brought peace to the stars. Vast space fleets and the powerful Jedi Knights protected the Republic through many horrible conflicts. By the time of the Sith War, four thousand years before the rise of the Empire, starship energy weapons had evolved into pulse-wave cannons, laser cannons, and turbolasers. High-acceleration slugthrowers and mass drivers became smaller and lighter than their predecessors, yet they hurled their increasingly dangerous payloads over far greater ranges. Starship defenses improved in parallel, with thicker armor plating and more powerful shield banks developed to absorb and deflect deadly blasts.

The need for starship weapons remains strong as the New Republic tries to bring peace to the galaxy. Starships must defend themselves from any of a number of threats, including space pirates and Imperial remnant ships, which capture thousands of civilian vessels each year. Hostile aliens lurking on the edges of New Republic space often raid colony worlds, while internal conflicts between New Republic members still arise, leading to battles between competing species, disputes involving colonies seeking to win their freedom, and corporate wars fought over valuable resources.

WEAPON TERMINOLOGY

A number of standardized terms are used in the discussion of starship weapons. Energy weapons include lasers, turbolasers, and ion cannons. Their beams carry high-energy particles that interact with the target to cause explosive damage.

Particle (or physical) weapons are those that deliver a physical warhead. These include concussion missiles, proton torpedoes, and old-fashioned slugthrowers and magnetic accelerators. Many modern physical weapons—such as concussion missiles and proton torpedoes—wrap their warheads in sheaths of energy to prevent accidental detonations.

Starfighter weapons can be used to destroy other starfighters but have little chance of damaging a larger capital ship. Their primary advantages include the incorporation of tracking systems that can target highly maneuverable ships and the opportunity for top pilots to utilize their individual skills. Capital weapons, by contrast, release phenomenally powerful blasts that are capable of penetrating meters of armor plating and inflicting devastating damage, but they cannot be used accurately to target starfighters and small freighters.

Various factors are considered in determining a starship weapon's overall effectiveness. The first step is to measure the weapon's destructive capability. The second element is the measure of the weapon's range. For instance, most capital-scale weapons have much longer ranges than do starfighter weapons. As with other ranged weapons, starship weapons have an optimal range—at which a modestly skilled gunner can expect to hit a target—and a maximum range, at which point a hit is possible only for the best gunners.

Another critical factor is a weapon's rate of fire—how often the weapon can be fired—since a delay of a few seconds between shots can prove to be a critical factor in deciding the outcome of a battle.

The final major consideration is the quality of the weapon's targeting computers. An outstanding targeting computer often can predict a target's flight path, thus allowing even mediocre pilots to make long-range hits. Poor targeting systems can force pilots to rely purely on their own reflexes if they are to score a hit.

STARSHIP DEFENSES

Starship defensive systems also tend to follow standardized configurations. The most common defensive resource is armor plating, which absorbs the destructive energy from all types of attacks. Starships also use shield generators to absorb and divert enemy attacks. Starship systems normally include countermeasures, such as jammers and stealth devices, to confuse the homing systems found aboard proton torpedoes and concussion missiles. Finally, most small fighters rely on their often-incredible maneuverability to evade attacks.

PLANETARY WEAPONS

Planets are especially strategic resources in space combat since they offer great quantities of raw materials, high-tech weapons-manufacturing facilities, and staging points for use by entire fleets. As a result, possession and control of worlds, particularly those in key locations, may be essential for victory in space warfare.

Many fleets use orbital bombardments to destroy cities and their defending armies before landing armies that will occupy such worlds. Aside from the usual array of turbolasers and fighter raids, fleets have been known to employ nuclear missiles, mass drivers, and asteroids to destroy a planet's entire infrastructure.

To prevent this kind of wholesale destruction, many worlds have employed sophisticated defensive networks complete with surface turbolasers and ion cannons used to attack orbiting ships. Planetary shields can block projectiles and energy beams and can even incinerate vessels that collide with the shields. Sensor stations, mines, defensive fleets, and space stations with dozens of turbolaser emplacements also can be used to protect a planet.

Thus, planetary weapons and defensive systems reflect the vastness of modern warfare and represent the cutting edge of military technology as it is employed by all spacefaring civilizations.

PROTON TORPEDOES

KRUPX MG7-A PROTON TORPEDO
KRUPX MG7 PROTON TORPEDO LAUNCHER

Proton torpedoes are high-speed concussion projectiles that carry high-yield proton-scattering warheads. They deliver tremendous explosive energy and are among the most powerful weapons that can be carried by starfighters. While these weapons are best known for their role in destroying the first Death Star at the Battle of Yavin, they have had many military applications including assaults on capital ships and precision ground bombing.

Proton torpedoes normally are used as secondary weapons, complementing a starfighter's primary laser cannons. While their utility is limited (since fighters can carry only a limited number of torpedoes), each pair of torpedoes has nearly twice the explosive power of an X-wing's four laser cannons combined. Because they are physical weapons, proton torpedoes are unaffected by energy shields, allowing them to blast directly into the target's hull and particle shields. Proton warheads can destroy starfighters and even inflict serious damage on large capital ships.

Proton torpedoes use sophisticated guidance computers to home in on their targets. Each torpedo is wrapped in a protective energy envelope to prevent accidental detonation caused by collisions with debris or near misses by laser cannon blasts. The torpedo's guidance system normally has a margin of error of less than three meters, although fast-moving craft can outrun or outmaneuver a torpedo. One limitation of the guidance system is that torpedoes that lose their initial targets sometimes lock onto the nearest passing ship. To prevent this, some pilots launch their torpedoes with the homing computers deactivated, using only visual targeting. While this tactic is much more difficult, it also greatly reduces the chances of a torpedo accidentally target-locking on a friendly vessel.

The New Republic X-wing carries a pair of Krupx MG7 torpedo launchers, each with a magazine containing three torpedoes. The Y-wing carries a pair of Arakyd Flex Tube launchers (for a total of eight torpedoes), while the B-wing's two Krupx MG9 launchers each carry six torpedoes. Imperial assault ships such as the TIE bomber, the Delta Class DX-9 Stormtrooper Transport, and the KonGar Ship Works ATR Assault Transport each carry a pair of proton torpedo launchers. Many capital ships and orbital defense stations also maintain these weapons systems, though with a much greater ammunition capacity.

The first Death Star was destroyed when Luke Skywalker launched a pair of proton torpedoes into an unshielded thermal exhaust port, destroying the station just seconds before its superlaser would have blasted the main Rebel base on Yavin Four into oblivion. Perhaps most amazing is the fact that Luke made the shot with his X-wing's targeting computer deactivated, using only his natural abilities to hit the target area, which was only two meters across.

Some infantry units carry shoulder- or backpack-mounted proton torpedo launchers. While heavy and relatively expensive, they are quite effective in protecting infantry from starfighter attacks. Some military units have even begun retrofitting their vehicles to carry similar proton torpedo racks.

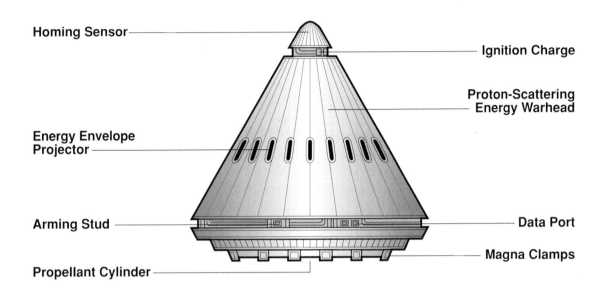

Homing Sensor

Ignition Charge

Proton-Scattering
Energy Warhead

Energy Envelope
Projector

Arming Stud

Data Port

Magna Clamps

Propellant Cylinder

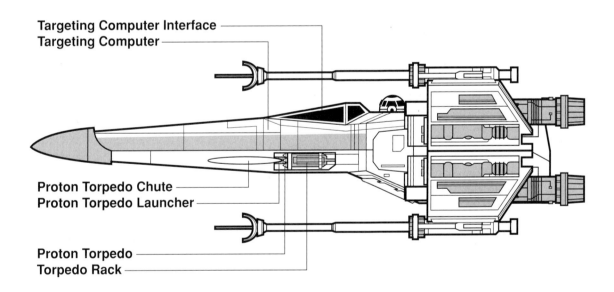

Targeting Computer Interface
Targeting Computer

Proton Torpedo Chute
Proton Torpedo Launcher

Proton Torpedo
Torpedo Rack

X-Wing Fighter Cutaway with Proton Torpedo (for scale)

CONCUSSION MISSILES

ARAKYD ST2 CONCUSSION MISSILE
ARAKYD ST2 CONCUSSION MISSILE RACK

Concussion missiles are self-contained projectile weapons armed with explosive warheads. While designed for bombing attacks in an atmosphere—where the concussion blast can cause tremendous devastation—concussion missiles are also effective for outer space combat.

The concussion missile's armored tube carries the warhead, a guidance computer, and a propellant system. Exterior shield projectors wrap the missile in a protective energy shroud, giving it the appearance of an elongated laser cannon. Concussion missiles share many of the advantages of proton torpedoes—they are unaffected by energy shields, and their warheads are very powerful—but also have the same primary disadvantage: they are short-range weapons with an optimum range of three hunded meters and a maximum range of seven hundred meters. The missiles' homing sensors are outstandingly effective against stationary and slow-moving targets, making them ideal for planetary bombing runs and attacks on capital ships.

Concussion missiles normally are fired in staggered pairs, with the second missile launching a fraction of a second after the first. The first missile slips through the target's energy shields undisturbed, and its blast eliminates defensive shields and armor plating. A fraction of a second later the second missile impacts the same area, inflicting maximum damage on the now-vulnerable target. In atmospheres, the concussion warhead's explosion generates sonic booms and ground tremors at close range, lev-

eling walls, destroying equipment, and inflicting heavy casualties. In space combat concussion missiles normally are used to eliminate a capital ship's shield generators so that turbolasers can finish off the target vessel.

The *Millennium Falcon* carries a pair of Arakyd ST2 missile launchers, each with a magazine of four missiles. More than a meter long, the ST2 missile is as powerful as a standard proton torpedo. During the Battle of Endor the ST2's warheads easily pierced the armor plating around the Second Death Star's main reactor, triggering the chain-reaction explosion that destroyed the station.

The powerful ST2 concussion missile system is a favorite of independent ship owners, since it can be purchased for about 1,500 credits, compared to the over 2,000 credits needed to purchase a proton torpedo launcher. Concussion missile systems are easier to maintain than proton torpedo launchers, although they end up being fairly expensive in the long run, since each missile costs 750 credits.

For smaller ships, where mass significantly affects flight performance, miniaturized launchers such as the Krupx MG5 may be used. This launcher has a magazine of four missiles and often is mounted on Z-95 Headhunters and other light craft. The New Republic has added a pair of small Dymek HM-6 launchers (each with a magazine of six torpedoes) to many of its A-wing fighters, giving the light interceptors some badly needed offensive punch.

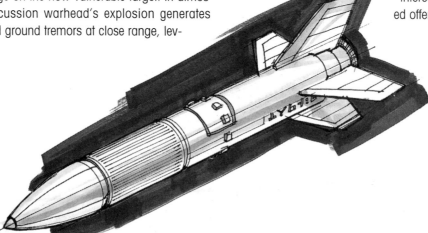

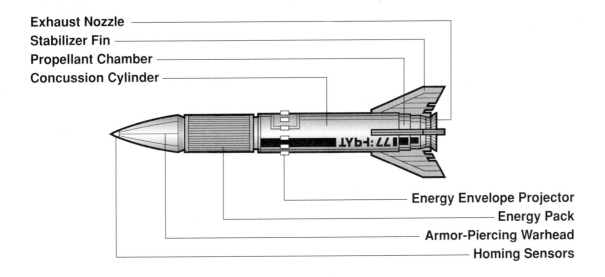

Exhaust Nozzle
Stabilizer Fin
Propellant Chamber
Concussion Cylinder

Energy Envelope Projector
Energy Pack
Armor-Piercing Warhead
Homing Sensors

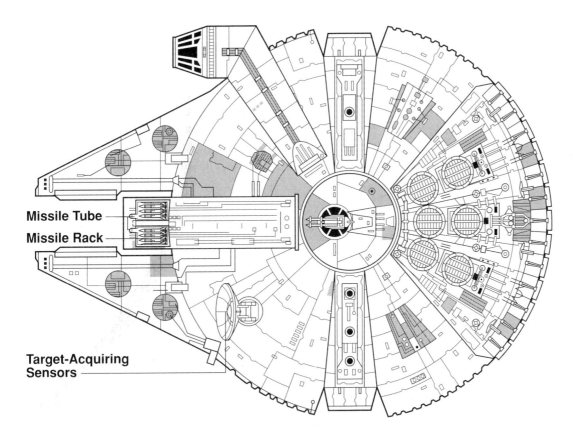

Missile Tube
Missile Rack

Target-Acquiring
Sensors

Millennium Falcon Cutaway with Concussion Missiles (for scale)

LASER CANNONS

Taim & Bak KX9 Laser Cannon
Corellian Engineering Corporation
AG-2G Quad Laser Cannon

Laser cannons are the most common starship weapons in the galaxy, ranging from the low-power units found on independent freighters to the high-output military models used by fighters and smuggling ships such as the *Millennium Falcon*. Some capital ships also utilize laser cannons to deal with starfighters.

Laser cannons are similar to blasters, only much more powerful. The cannon's laser actuator combines high-energy blaster gas with a large power charge. (The actuator's prismatic crystal produces the high-energy beam of charged particles coupled with light.) A laser cannon is supplied by a power generator or fed from the ship's main reactor, while volatile blaster gas must be stored and carried in supercooled, puncture-proof chambers. Laser cannons use long barrels—with interior galven coils and circuits—to maintain the beam's cohesion over incredible distances.

Laser cannons are comparatively light and have a high rate of fire, with good stopping power when used against fighters and other light craft, though they cannot puncture the high-power shielding and thick armor plating of capital ships. Although laser cannons are exposed to the icy vacuum of space, the energy conversion process generates tremendous waste heat, and sophisticated cooling systems are needed to protect the internal components.

While most pilots prefer visual sighting—which is why most energy beams are configured to the visible light spectrum—integrated combat computers and turret servos automatically make minute adjustments to improve fire accuracy. In space combat there's nothing more deadly than a highly skilled gunner paired with a good targeting computer.

The New Republic's X-wing fighter uses four KX9 laser cannons. These fixed-position lasers can be programmed to fire simultaneously or in alternating pairs. The KX9's barrel keeps the beam focused over long distances, while the cannon produces one of the most powerful energy beams found among starfighter weapons. The KX9's standard pilot interface is a Fabritech ANq 3.6 tracking computer paired with an IN-344-B "Sightline" holographic imaging system. Upgraded X-wings have improved interface systems to keep this older ship competitive against newer fighters.

The *Millennium Falcon* has two turrets with AG-2G quad laser batteries. Installed by Lando Calrissian and modified by Han Solo, the AG-2G cannons draw directly from the *Falcon*'s Quadex power core. Enhanced power cyclers, high-volume gas feeds, and custom-modified laser actuators (with larger energization crystals) greatly increase the AG-2G's energy output, and the weapon can destroy a TIE fighter with a single shot. The *Falcon*'s cannons have enhanced cooling packs and compressors for prolonged use without the risk of overheating. The unusual splitter coupling slightly disperses the energy beam, forcing the target's shields to deflect energy simultaneously from two hits and increasing the likelihood of overloading the shields and inflicting greater damage.

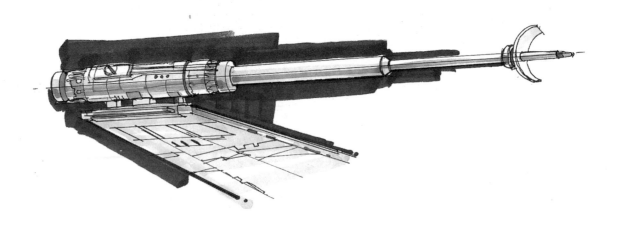

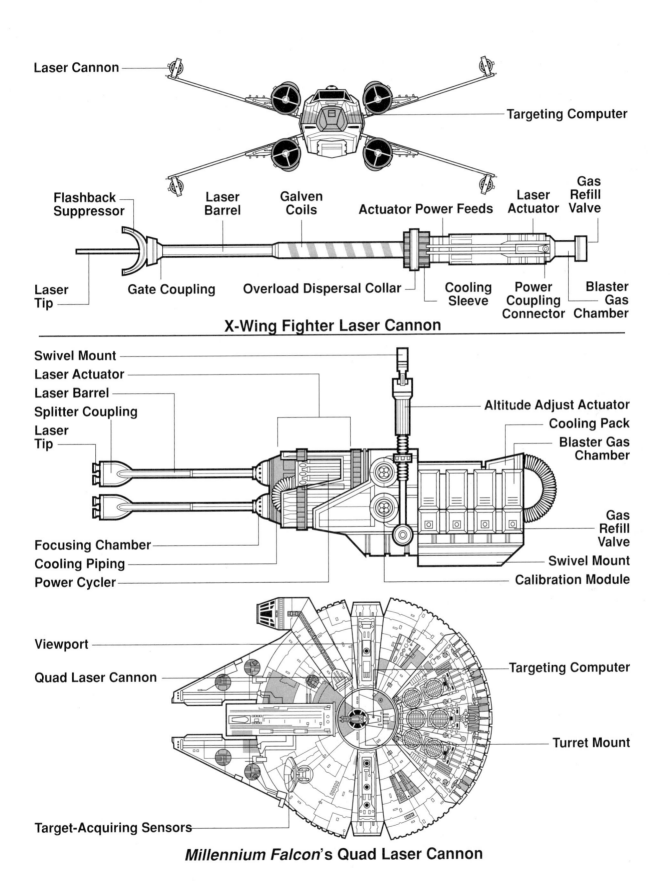

Laser Cannon

Targeting Computer

Flashback Suppressor

Laser Barrel

Galven Coils

Actuator Power Feeds

Laser Actuator

Gas Refill Valve

Laser Tip

Gate Coupling

Overload Dispersal Collar

Cooling Sleeve

Power Coupling Connector

Blaster Gas Chamber

X-Wing Fighter Laser Cannon

Swivel Mount

Laser Actuator

Laser Barrel

Splitter Coupling

Laser Tip

Altitude Adjust Actuator

Cooling Pack

Blaster Gas Chamber

Focusing Chamber

Cooling Piping

Power Cycler

Gas Refill Valve

Swivel Mount

Calibration Module

Viewport

Quad Laser Cannon

Targeting Computer

Turret Mount

Target-Acquiring Sensors

***Millennium Falcon*'s Quad Laser Cannon**

DEFLECTOR SHIELD GENERATOR

KDY ISD-72x DEFLECTOR SHIELD GENERATOR DOMES
CHEMPAT SHIELD GENERATOR

Deflector shields provide a starship's first line of defense. These electronic energy dampeners wrap the vessel in a protective screen that blocks incoming attacks. While they are expensive and require plenty of power, shield generators are much lighter and take up far less volume than armor plating. The two most common shield types are particle shields and ray, or energy, shields.

Particle shields are standard equipment on all starships. They absorb kinetic energy from physical impacts, protecting a ship during collisions with debris and other ships, and blunt the effects of proton torpedoes and concussion missiles. Particle shields provide no protection against energy attacks such as laser or turbolaser fire.

These shields greatly enhance a ship's hull integrity by using energy charges to strengthen the molecular bonds of the hull plating. They are kept powered at all times to deflect micrometeors and other small particles. Ships must lower their particle shields when launching carried craft or firing their own physical weapons. Computers are used to drop and raise the shields with microsecond precision in order to leave the ship vulnerable for only a minimal time.

Ray shields will absorb blasts from laser cannons, turbolasers, and other energy weapons. Since these shields consume a tremendous amount of energy, they are raised only when battle is immi-

nent. Shield energy permeates the ship's hull and wraps the vessel in layers of energy that may extend anywhere from a few millimeters to several centimeters away from the hull. (An energy shield carries so much power that touching one can be fatal.) Energy shields often absorb enough of the impact that any blast merely rocks the ship, scoring its armor plating but leaving it otherwise undamaged.

As with most starfighters, the Y-wing's single Chempat generator uses several projectors to wrap the entire ship in shield energy. Larger ships may call upon multiple generators: Imperial Star Destroyers carry a pair of ISD-72x generators on top of their conning towers. Shield operators allocate energy as needed to deflect incoming attacks and protect particularly vulnerable portions of a ship.

When overloaded by incoming energy charges, a shield projector's matrix boards will burn out rather than flooding the generator with energy and destroying the entire shield system. Tech crews can repair burned-out projectors in just a few minutes to get the shields back up to full power.

A ship without shields can be quite vulnerable. When the Super Star Destroyer *Executor*'s shields went down at the Battle of Endor, its bridge was destroyed by a single Rebel A-wing fighter. This triggered a series of chain reactions that eventually detonated the *Executor*'s main reactor. Mon Calamari Star Cruisers maintain three sets of backup shield generators in order to prevent this type of catastrophic failure.

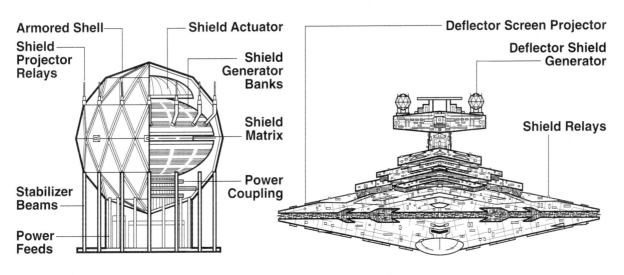

Armored Shell
Shield Projector Relays
Shield Actuator
Shield Generator Banks
Shield Matrix
Stabilizer Beams
Power Coupling
Power Feeds

Deflector Screen Projector
Deflector Shield Generator
Shield Relays

Deflector Shield Generator Cutaway

Star Destroyer (for scale)

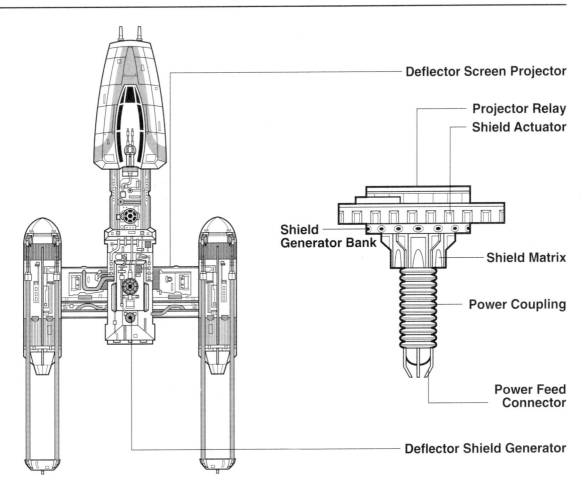

Deflector Screen Projector
Projector Relay
Shield Actuator
Shield Generator Bank
Shield Matrix
Power Coupling
Power Feed Connector
Deflector Shield Generator

Y-Wing Starfighter (for scale)

Deflector Shield Generator

ION CANNONS

BORSTEL NK-7 ION CANNON

Ion cannons are similar to laser cannons, but their energy beams, which appear to be standard laser blasts, actually disable the targeted ship's electronic and computer systems instead of causing physical damage. Ion energy blasts overload and fuse circuitry, blowing out computers, flight control systems, sensors, shields, and weapons—even life-support and communications systems are damaged.

While low-powered bolts may cause only minor system failures, a powerful blast can cripple a ship for several minutes. As internal electronic systems short out, streams of blue lightning play across control panels and electronic interfaces. (Laser cannons sometimes cause an ionization effect, as happened to Luke Skywalker's snowspeeder during the Battle of Hoth.)

Since ion blasts are unimpaired by energy shields, ships have no defense against them short of reconfiguring their shields—and this would make the shields useless for absorbing standard laser blasts.

Aboard capital ships, ion cannons may be as numerous as turbolasers. Imperial Star Destroyers have sixty Borstel NK-7 ion cannon emplacements, while Mon Calamari Star Cruisers carry nearly two dozen ArMek SW-7 ion batteries.

The original Death Star's defenses included 2,500 ion cannons, while Death Star II had double that number.

Star Destroyers use gunnery control stations to concentrate fire from several ion emplacements against a single target, and so they often disable a target vessel with the opening volley. The ionization effect lasts long enough to allow assault crews to board and capture the stricken vessel, although some Star Destroyer commanders use the ship's tractor beams to hold the ionized vessel immobile so that it can be destroyed by turbolaser blasts before it sends out a distress signal.

Ion cannons also can be potent starfighter weapons. During the early days of the Galactic Civil War, Rebel Y-wings and B-wings often used them to disable Imperial freighters and capture them with their cargoes intact. As a result, Alliance soldiers received the best equipment the Empire could buy, while the captured ships supplemented the Alliance's meager cargo fleet. Fighter attacks utilizing ion cannons also helped the Alliance capture combat starships, including many of the Nebulon-B escort frigates and Corellian corvettes that formed the backbone of the Rebel fleet before the arrival of the Mon Calamari Star Cruisers.

Ion cannons are popular among privateer and pirate fleets for the same reason: they give raiders the highest odds of capturing ships—and their valuable cargoes—undamaged. These weapons are also favored by the alien species known as the Ssi-ruuk, who attacked the Imperial world of Bakura shortly after the Battle of Endor, using their ion cannons to capture Imperial and Rebel vessels alike.

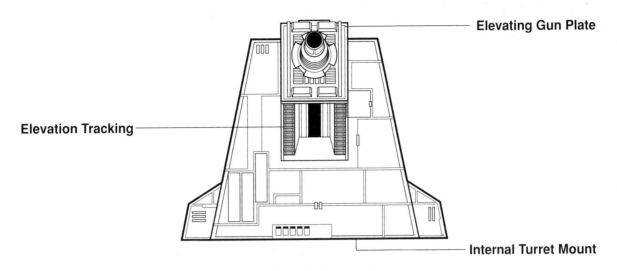

Elevating Gun Plate

Elevation Tracking

Internal Turret Mount

Front View

Side View with TIE Fighter (for scale)

Ion Tube

Barrel

Energy Coupler

Cooling Grid

Ion Accu-Accelerator

Capacitor Banks

TIE fighter (for scale)

Maintenance Hatches

Gunnery Crew Station

Tracking and Targeting Computers

Turbine Generator

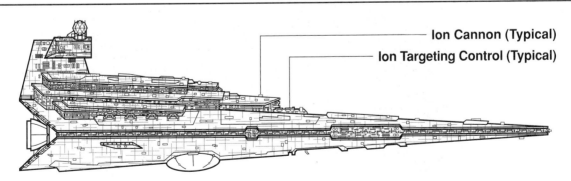

Ion Cannon (Typical)

Ion Targeting Control (Typical)

Imperial Star Destroyer with Ion Cannon Placement

TRACTOR BEAM PROJECTOR

PHYLON Q7 TRACTOR BEAM PROJECTOR

A tractor beam is a powerful and invisible force field that can capture and move objects with great precision. The more powerful the tractor beam, the greater its range and the mass it can move. The force field is produced by a tractor beam generator, then released by a tractor beam projector—also called an emitter tower—which normally is mounted on a rotating turret.

Commercial tractor beams found aboard freighters and container ships are used primarily to move cargo modules and vary widely in strength. Tractor beams located in hangar bays and spaceports can guide crippled ships for safe landings during emergencies. While these systems often have great strength, they are not suited for military purposes because of their short-range and simple targeting systems.

Military tractor beams play an important role in space combat. For example, the tractor beams on an Imperial Star Destroyer can capture a small freighter in midflight. Once captured, the ship has virtually no hope of breaking free and is likely to blow out its own sublight drives if it resists. A tractor beam's greatest limitation is that it has difficulty targeting fast and maneuverable craft, as the *Millennium Falcon* proved during its daring escape from the ice world of Hoth when it outmaneuvered Darth Vader's fleet of Star Destroyers.

Tractor beam emplacements are large and maintenance-intensive, requiring crews of up to

ten operators and technicians. An Imperial Star Destroyer has ten Phylon Q7 tractor beam projectors, and many other capital ships, including Mon Calamari Star Cruisers, Nebulon-B frigates, and Victory Star Destroyers, also maintain tractor beams. Tractor beam equipment is too massive for starfighters.

Tractor beams offer tremendous tactical and strategic advantages against capital combat starships. When tractor beams capture and slow an enemy ship, it's much easier to target and disable its vital systems. Standard Imperial procedure was to hold a ship in place and destroy its weapons, although the attacked ship could avoid this fate by signaling its surrender and powering down its main reactor, as Princess Leia's Rebel Blockade Runner did when it was captured over Tatooine. Ships that refuse to surrender are often destroyed.

The most powerful tractor beam systems ever built were those aboard the Death Star space stations. More than seven hundred tractor beam projectors ringed the first Death Star, and nearly two dozen of them could apply their force at any given point, making the tractor's grip almost unbreakable even at vast distances. The *Millennium Falcon* was captured at such a great range before its sensors could reveal that the Death Star wasn't actually a small moon! The *Falcon*'s crew couldn't hope to escape until the Jedi Knight Obi-Wan Kenobi had disabled the entire tractor beam system by severing one of seven primary couplings that led to the main reactor.

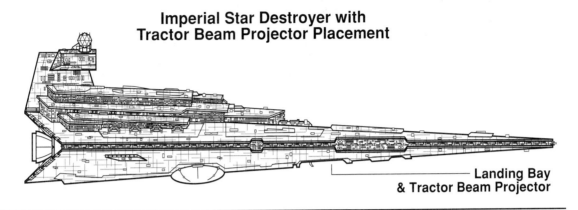

Imperial Star Destroyer with Tractor Beam Projector Placement

Landing Bay & Tractor Beam Projector

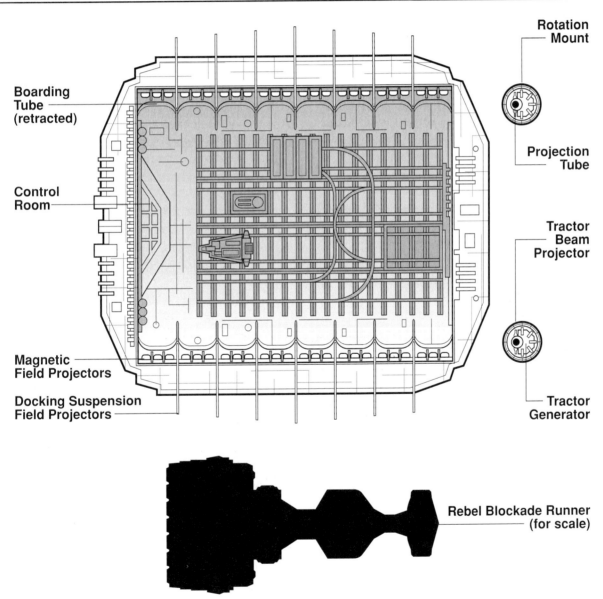

Boarding Tube (retracted)

Control Room

Magnetic Field Projectors

Docking Suspension Field Projectors

Rotation Mount

Projection Tube

Tractor Beam Projector

Tractor Generator

Rebel Blockade Runner (for scale)

Imperial Star Destroyer Landing Bay and Rebel Blockade Runner (for scale)

TURBOLASERS

TAIM & BAK XX-9 TURBOLASERS

The most common capital ship weapons in the galaxy, turbolasers are large-scale energy weapons carrying enough punch to cut through the shields and thick armor plating of modern warships. Banks of turbolasers, coordinated through computerized fire-control systems, deliver sustained volleys of energy. Imperial Star Destroyers claim *sixty* Taim & Bak XX-9 heavy turbolasers, while even small capital combat starships carry a few of these weapons.

Turbolasers are two-stage supercharged laser cannons. The small primary laser produces an energy beam that enters the turbolaser's main actuator, where it interacts with a stream of energized blaster gas to produce an intense blast. The energy bolt's destructive power is incredible, and the barrel's galven coils focus the beam, providing a range that is double or *triple* that of conventional laser cannons. Turbolasers also can target planetary surfaces for devastating ground bombardments.

Turbolasers draw so much power that each one has its own dedicated turbine, and multiple capacitor banks supplement the turbine's power feed. The power core regulates energy flow, bleeding off excess and blocking power surges that could cause the turbolaser to explode. Turbolasers use a delay of at least two seconds between shots to allow the capacitors to build up an adequate charge.

Just as with other energy weapons, turbolasers generate a tremendous amount of waste heat. The Taim & Bak XX-9 turbolasers kept

aboard Star Destroyers have three separate cryosystems. Each laser barrel has a cooling sleeve, while a large cooling unit is placed behind the laser actuator.

Turbolasers utilize computerized fire control systems to target capital ships across vast distances in deep space, though starfighters are fast enough to evade the fire from these bulky weapons. Star Destroyers rely on TIE fighters or laser cannons to handle enemy fighters.

Taim & Bak XX-9 turbolaser emplacements use servo-actuated turrets mounted outside the ship and are protected by a meter of quadanium steel hull plating. Crew stations and the main turbine are located inside the ship. The earlier XX-8 design features a taller tower that can hold both the turbine and the crew stations.

Turbolasers require intensive maintenance along with frequent replacement of cooling sleeve components, galven tube circuits, and energization crystals. A burnout of any of these components can knock the weapon off-line, while a critical failure can lead to an explosive overload, destroying the weapon and killing the crew.

Possession of turbolasers was strictly controlled under Imperial law. The New Republic maintains similar restrictions, granting waivers only to allied governments. However, through theft and black-marketeering, these deadly weapons often fall into the hands of pirates, mercenaries, and other outlaw groups.

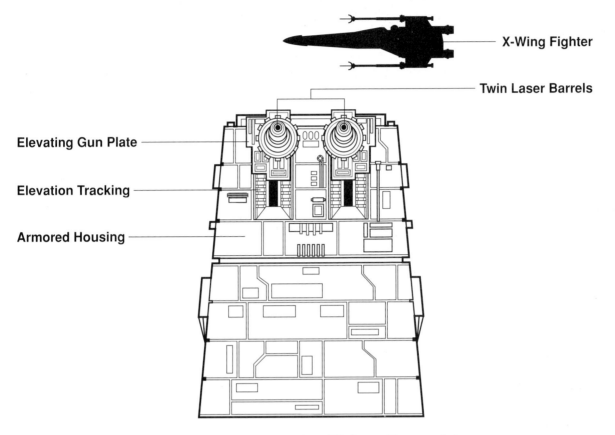

X-Wing Fighter

Twin Laser Barrels

Elevating Gun Plate

Elevation Tracking

Armored Housing

Front View with X-Wing Fighter (for scale)

Side View

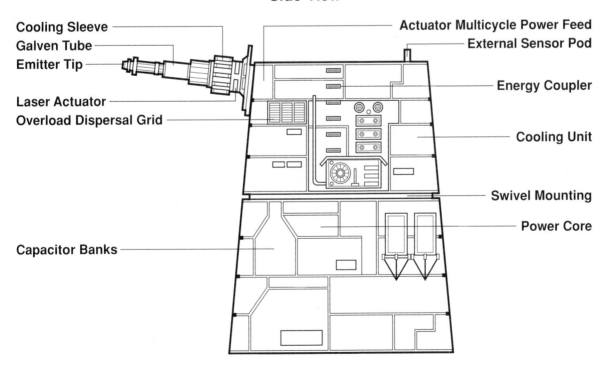

Cooling Sleeve

Galven Tube

Emitter Tip

Laser Actuator

Overload Dispersal Grid

Capacitor Banks

Actuator Multicycle Power Feed

External Sensor Pod

Energy Coupler

Cooling Unit

Swivel Mounting

Power Core

PROTON GRENADE

MERR-SONN MUNITIONS 7-PRG

Proton grenades are high-powered handheld explosives that contain a proton core, a greatly reduced version of the warheads used in proton torpedoes. Originally developed for breaching ships' hulls during boarding actions, proton grenades such as Merr-Sonn's 7-PrG also are used for large demolitions projects, such as when a Rebel commando team led by General Han Solo blew up the second Death Star's shield generator on the planet Endor.

Twisting the grenade's arming mechanism primes the battery to deliver a small electrical charge to the proton core; pressing the activation plunger starts the timer. This two-step process offers a fail-safe to prevent accidental detonations; this is very helpful, since the proton core is almost as powerful as a thermal detonator. The timer can be set for up to twenty minutes, and the weapon can be disarmed at any time by pressing the twist plunger release.

A proton grenade is much more effective than a standard detonite charge. The prestressed metal casing and shaped proton charge channel the explosion's force toward the magnetic plate that holds it to its target, and the blast can punch through a meter and a half of permacite. Electromagnetic pulses disrupt any computers, droids, blasters, and other electronic devices within twenty meters.

When the grenade is used in boarding actions, the explosion instantly blasts away armor plating; this is much quicker than carving through the hull with fusion cutters. The explosion exposes the ship's outer corridors to vacuum, eliminating any opposition in the explosive decompression, while attacking troops are free to board with minimal resistance. Unless the defenders don space suits, their only choice is to fall back as the attackers advance, cutting through bulkheads and exposing more and more of the ship's interior to space. Teams of troops boarding from multiple locations often can secure a vessel within minutes. Attackers also can use proton grenades to damage a ship's sublight drives, shield generators, and weapons.

Proton grenades are favored by Imperial spacetroopers (also known as zero-g troopers), who are often called upon to board pirate and New Republic ships. Each armored space suit holds a multitude of weapons, including laser cannons and a mini-proton-torpedo launcher.

Some starships use proton grenade launchers to *counteract* boarding actions. From close range, launchers pepper the enemy vessel with proton grenades, setting off a series of explosions that sow confusion aboard the attacking ship, granting the victimized vessel the precious seconds needed to escape. These launchers also hamper the boarding parties themselves, since the shrapnel from a proton-grenade explosion easily punctures most space suits. More than a few smugglers use these launchers to ward off Imperial and New Republic boarding teams.

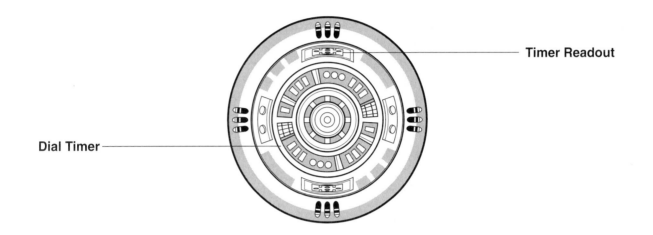

Timer Readout

Dial Timer

Top View

Profile with Hand (for scale)

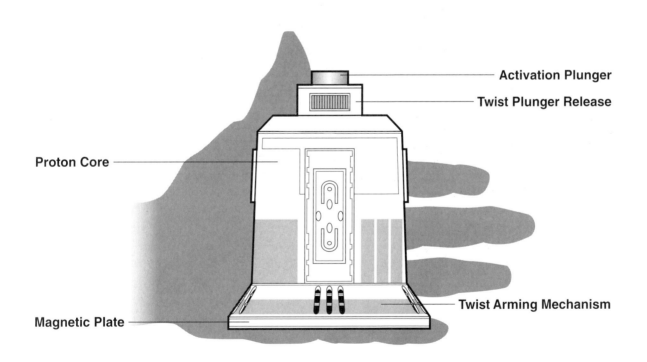

Activation Plunger

Twist Plunger Release

Proton Core

Magnetic Plate

Twist Arming Mechanism

DIAMOND BORON MISSILE

SIENAR FLEET SYSTEMS MS-15
DIAMOND BORON MISSILE

An element of the antistarfighter missile system developed at the height of the Civil War between the Rebel Alliance and the Empire, the diamond boron missile was designed to destroy multiple ships in a single blast that will consume everything within fifty meters of the detonation point. It can be particularly effective against fighters flying in formation, in which case the explosion can destroy half a dozen vessels.

The unlaunched diamond boron missile is a sleek, one-meter-long tube that can be fired from any standard large concussion-missile launcher, such as the Arakyd ST2 system. Extendable dorsal and ventral flanges at the rear of the missile provide an additional layer of armor and improve atmospheric maneuverability. As the missile streaks toward its targets, diamond boron armored blast plates expand outward, making the missile almost impervious to starfighter laser cannons. Though turbolasers are powerful enough to destroy the missile, their targeting systems normally cannot hit such a small target.

The missile's high-powered rockets outpace even proton torpedoes and concussion missiles and offer a flight time of up to ten minutes. Thrust-vector plates inside the exhaust nozzles give the missile outstanding maneuverability.

Diamond boron missiles can be programmed with detonation coordinates or can be set to explode when the internal sensor suite detects a specified number of enemy vessels—typically three—within the warhead's blast radius. Gunners also can guide the missile remotely, although this approach renders the missile vulnerable to enemy jamming systems, and it may just harmlessly race off into open space without detonating. The large blast radius effectively neutralizes starfighter countermeasures systems since the missile need only get close to the target. Of course, the weapon also can be a liability, since "friendly" craft may be destroyed by the explosion.

Diamond boron missiles nearly foiled the Bothans' attempts to steal the technical readouts for the Second Death Star. Under the leadership of Luke Skywalker and the mercenary Dash Rendar, six Bothan Y-wings descended on the cargo freighter *Suprosa*, which was secretly carrying the Death Star plans. A diamond boron missile fired by the *Suprosa* withstood repeated laser cannon blasts from Dash Rendar's *Outrider* and detonated in the middle of the fighter formation, destroying four Y-wings and killing eight Bothans.

Despite the advantages presented by this weapon, diamond boron missiles have never gained wide acceptance. At nearly twenty thousand credits each, they are prohibitively expensive compared to laser cannons and turbolasers, which can be used indefinitely. The missile's reputation has been further tarnished by incidents in which faulty warheads have exploded while in storage. Still, Sienar Fleet Systems continues to manufacture these missiles in limited numbers while trying to develop new, more cost-effective diamond boron missile designs.

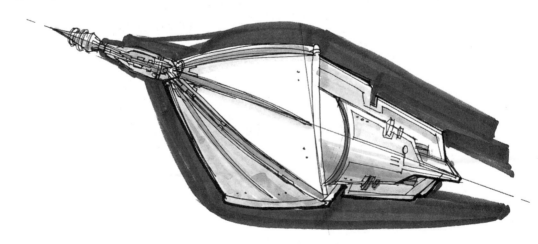

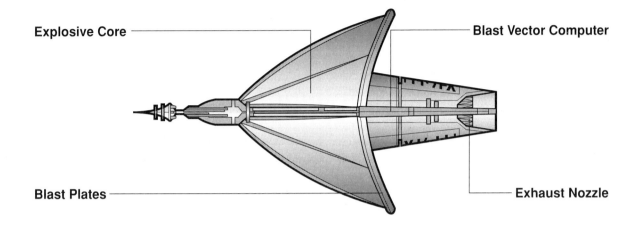

Explosive Core

Blast Vector Computer

Blast Plates

Exhaust Nozzle

Top View

Side View

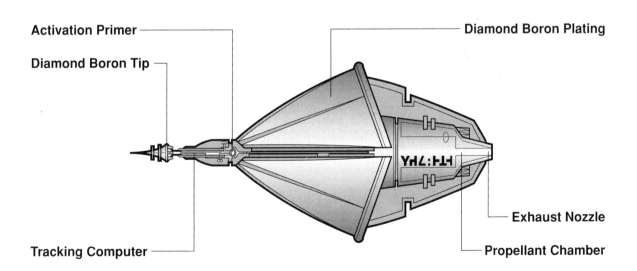

Activation Primer

Diamond Boron Plating

Diamond Boron Tip

Tracking Computer

Exhaust Nozzle

Propellant Chamber

CLUSTER BOMB

FREI-TEK CL-3 ANTISTARFIGHTER CLUSTER BOMB

Mounted on the outer hulls of Mon Calamari Star Cruisers, Nebulon-B escort frigates, and other New Republic craft, cluster bombs are effective close-range anti-starfighter weapons. Unlike turbolasers and laser cannons, each of which can target only one Imperial TIE fighter at a time, a cluster bomb can destroy multiple vessels. Like diamond boron missiles, they are most effective against closely arrayed enemy ships.

A cluster bomb (also known as a cluster trap) consists of a simple metal blister that blends imperceptibly into the host ship's hull. Cluster bombs on Mon Calamari Star Cruisers appear identical to the dozens of ovoid weapons emplacements and sensor array blisters that dot their hulls. In the case of more angular ships such as Nebulon-B frigates and Corellian corvettes, a cluster bomb may be squared off and disguised to look like an ordinary cargo air lock or sensor cluster. Some cluster bombs are built to include false signal generators that give off emissions identical to those produced by active sensor arrays. These signals lure Imperial TIE fighters to attack what seem to be tempting and helpless targets.

When activated by the ship's gunnery crew, the cluster bomb's short-range sensor suite conducts continuous scans of the immediate vicinity, searching for enemy vessels' transponder codes. Depending on its programming, the cluster bomb may activate after detecting anywhere from one to six ships in its blast radius. (Gunnery crews normally monitor their

cluster bombs and can initiate an emergency override to prevent a bomb's detonation if New Republic fighters are close enough to be damaged by the blast.)

When the bomb detonates, explosive charges and the bomb thruster propel shrapnel and dozens of magnetized proton and concussion grenades out into space. This creates a cloud of debris and explosives that measures over a hundred meters in diameter. The grenades have magnetized plates that home in on any ships in the vicinity, often creating chain-reaction explosions that can make the area a navigational hazard for several minutes.

New Republic ships broadcast warnings to friendly fighters, and most pilots memorize the locations of these blisters so they are not caught in the deadly blasts.

Explosive dampeners protect the host ship during the initial detonation, and the grenade explosions are not powerful enough to damage a capital ship's armor plating. The dampeners feature breakaway panels that allow maintenance crews to mount fresh cluster bombs on ship hulls in less than ten minutes.

Since the concussion grenades have no guidance or computer systems, they simply home in on the nearest vessel. Thus, cluster bombs have proved most effective in battles where enemy fighters vastly outnumber the New Republic's ships, greatly reducing the odds that the grenades will damage friendly fighters.

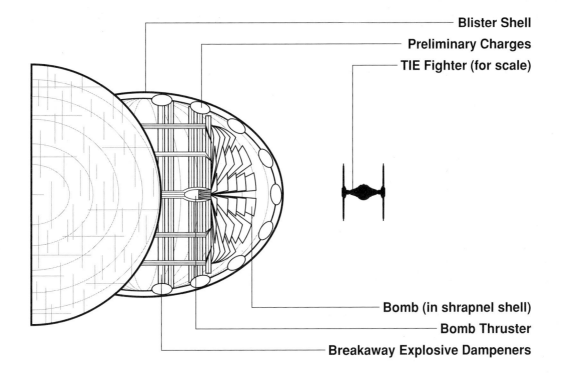

Blister Shell
Preliminary Charges
TIE Fighter (for scale)
Bomb (in shrapnel shell)
Bomb Thruster
Breakaway Explosive Dampeners

Cutaway of Cluster Bomb

Mon Calamari Star Cruiser with Cluster Bomb Placement

Cluster Bomb (disguised as blister)

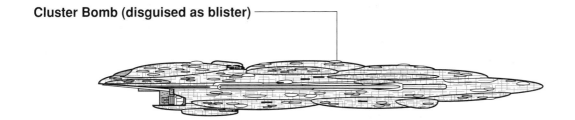

MINE

MERR-SONN DEFENDER ION MINE
CONNER SHIP SYSTEMS 3HX3 TIMER MINE

A staple of space warfare for millennia, mines are used to block travel routes and destroy enemy vessels. They prove most effective in situations where natural hazards such as pulsars, gas clouds, and ion storms limit travel to a few well-established routes. Mines also are used for planetary sieges, blocking all starship traffic onto or off a world. This tactic was favored by the Imperial Navy, which often used mines to cut off a planet, demoralizing its inhabitants and forcing them to exhaust food, fuel, and other nonrenewable resources.

There is a wide variety of space mines, ranging from crude asteroids to sophisticated devices such as the Defender ion mine. Asteroids are easily detected by sensors, making them more of a nuisance than a hazard, although they can be used to block trade routes and "herd" ships onto alternative courses where they can be ambushed. Space pirates often use asteroids to block hyperspace routes and force ships into realspace, where they can be boarded and captured.

Automated space mines pose a much greater threat to starships, since they often can home in on a vessel undetected. Mines generally operate automatically, although some military forces use remote control systems to allow friendly vessels to pass through minefields unharmed. Proximity mines—the most common type of space mine—are simple devices that explode as soon as any ship passes within their blast range.

The Merr-Sonn Defender ion mine is a multiuse deep space mine used by the New Republic, planetary governments, and even Imperial remnant forces. It features cloaking revvers and particle-beam scatter projectors that hide the mine from sensor readings, rendering it all but invisible. Once a vessel comes within ten kilometers, the Defender's ion cannon neutralizes the ship, while a narrow-band, high-frequency transmitter relays data to the mine's control station, which often is aboard a nearby ship. Thus, a capital combat starship or a customs cruiser soon arrives on the scene to search the disabled vessel.

The primary advantages of minefields are that they are relatively easy to set up, require almost no maintenance, and are *exceptionally* difficult for enemy forces to clear. To do so, unmanned drone ships must enter the field and tediously eliminate each mine.

Mines also are used widely in planetary combat, ranging from variable-altitude repulsorlift mines to simple land mines such as the Conner Ship Systems 3HX3. Each time the repulsor-field or life-form sensors detect passing troops or vehicles, the 3HX3 launches one of its explosive charges three meters into the air. Each explosive charge can severely damage light craft, such as a landspeeder or AT-ST walker, or eliminate an entire squad of enemy troopers.

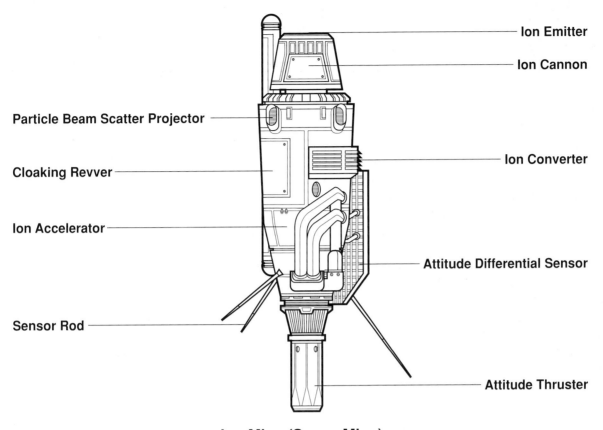

Ion Emitter

Ion Cannon

Particle Beam Scatter Projector

Ion Converter

Cloaking Revver

Ion Accelerator

Attitude Differential Sensor

Sensor Rod

Attitude Thruster

Ion Mine (Space Mine)

Timer Mine (land based)

Locking Clamp
Explosive Charge Rack
Blast Bowl
Explosive Launcher
Explosive Charge Rack

Fusion Disk
Repulsor Field Sensor
Explosive Charge
Magnetic Projector
Sliding Charge Plate

Top View

Side View

PLANETARY ION CANNONS

KUAT DRIVE YARDS V-150 PLANET DEFENDER

Planetary ion cannons are powerful ground weapons that produce intense energy beams that can reach low orbit and disable even the largest capital ships. As with smaller ion weaponry, a planetary ion cannon causes no physical damage, instead fusing and blowing out circuitry aboard the target ship and knocking out its drives, weapons, shields, computer systems, and other electronic systems.

At a cost of five hundred thousand credits per emplacement, ion cannons are prohibitively expensive, even for many planetary governments. The Kuat Drive Yards v-150 Planet Defender, which was used at the Rebel Alliance's base on Hoth, is a typical planetary ion cannon.

The v-150 consists of a spherical permacite shell, and its power is supplied by a massive reactor that normally is buried nearly forty meters below ground level. When it is activated, it takes several minutes to maneuver the ion cannon into position on its rotating base, while the blast shield retracts, exposing the cannon. A crew of twenty-seven soldiers is needed to operate the weapon and handle its targeting computers. At Hoth, targeting data also were supplied by Echo Base's electrotelescopes and long-range sensors.

Echo Base's v-150 fired the opening shots at the Battle of Hoth. A volley of ion blasts disabled the Imperial Star Destroyer *Avenger*, allowing the first Rebel transport, the *Quantum Storm*, to escape into hyperspace. While Imperial walkers relentlessly pounded Echo Base's ground forces, the v-150's crew—all natives of Alderaan—tirelessly defended fleeing Rebel ships and stayed at their posts until the very end of the battle. When they heeded the final evacuation order, they set the v-150's generator to explode to cover the liftoff of the last Rebel transports.

Ion cannons often are used to supplement planetary shields, which take several minutes to activate and are impractical to maintain at all times because of their tremendous energy demands. Since enemy ships often appear without warning, planets rely on ion cannons and similar weapons, such as planetary turbolasers, to provide covering fire until the shields can be raised.

As on Hoth, an ion cannon can be synchronized with the shields for strategic defensive fire. The shields are lowered for a split second, allowing the ion cannon to fire several volleys and inflict serious damage on orbiting enemy vessels. Then the shields are raised before the enemy can return fire.

Each ion cannon emplacement has a limited fire vector, meaning that it can protect an area no more than a few hundred kilometers square. For this reason, ion cannons are placed close to vital facilities such as military bases, planetary shield generators, starports, and major cities. Ion cannons are also limited by a low fire rate of one volley per six seconds, and so multiple weapon emplacements or shields must be provided to ensure complete protection from orbital attacks and planetary landings.

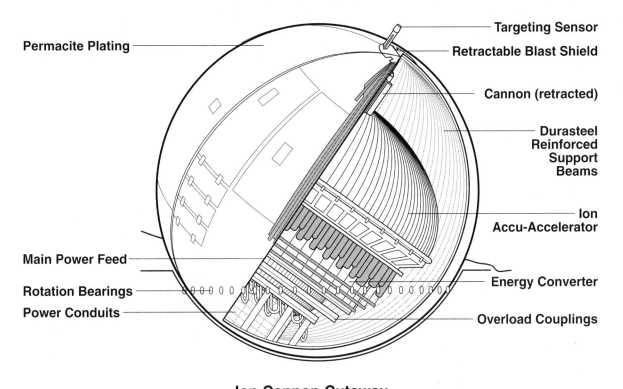

Permacite Plating

Targeting Sensor

Retractable Blast Shield

Cannon (retracted)

Durasteel
Reinforced
Support
Beams

Ion
Accu-Accelerator

Main Power Feed

Energy Converter

Rotation Bearings

Power Conduits

Overload Couplings

Ion Cannon Cutaway

Ion Cannon (land based)

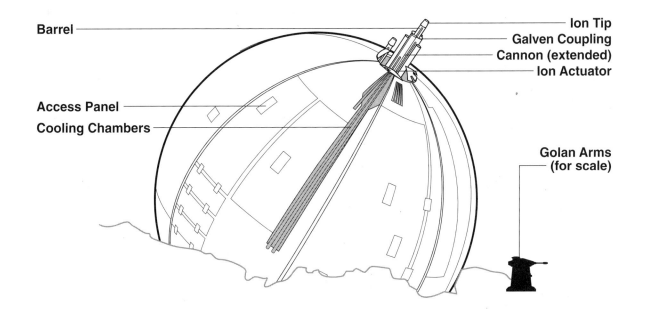

Barrel

Ion Tip

Galven Coupling

Cannon (extended)

Ion Actuator

Access Panel

Cooling Chambers

Golan Arms
(for scale)

PLANETARY TURBOLASER

KUAT DRIVE YARDS W-165 PLANETARY TURBOLASER

Planetary turbolasers are common surface-based weapons that fire supercharged bolts of destructive energy into low orbit. When deployed in sufficient numbers, they prove a deadly deterrent to planetary sieges and are capable of reducing enemy fleets to drifting hulks and debris in a matter of hours.

With a power output nearly four times that of the v-150 Planet Defender ion cannon, the w-165 is one of the most powerful turbolasers ever built. lis sustained volleys can destroy even an Imperial Star Destroyer, ripping through armor plating to pierce the ship's vulnerable main reactor and cause a titanic explosion that can literally rip apart one of those massive battle cruisers.

The w-165 requires a crew of nearly fifty, including soldiers, technicians, computer operators, engineers, and gunners. A permanent platform houses the turbolaser, crew stations, and power core. The platform's defenses include four meters of permacite armor plating and dozens of deflector screen projectors designed to block turbolaser blasts, proton bombs, and other ordnance.

Sensor arrays—located on the platform and at sensor stations or on orbiting satellites—feed data to the targeting computers. Rotation gears slowly move the turbolaser into position, making continuous adjustments for pinpoint accuracy. The w-165's reactor core is over fifty meters in diameter and allows the weapon to fire once every ten seconds. With each shot, the energy processed through the turbolaser actuator would power a large city for an entire day.

The turbolaser's barrel is nearly twenty-five meters in diameter and uses three kilometers of layered galven circuits to focus the energy bolt. Over four dozen overload dispersal tubes are needed to absorb excess energy and prevent the explosions that may occur during critical malfunctions. A cooling sleeve rings the entire turbolaser actuator to keep the weapon at a safe operating temperature, while armor plating around the actuator protects the weapon from enemy fire and reduces the blast damage in the event of an accidental explosive overload.

Because of the turbolaser's limited fire vectors, planets may use hundreds of them, and they are normally part of a larger defensive network that typically includes ion cannons and planetary shields. The w-165 has been installed on over three hundred key New Republic worlds for defense against attacks from lingering Imperial remnants and other hostile groups. Despite the weapon's incredible cost of over ten million credits per emplacement, the New Republic's government rightly considers this a wiser expenditure than having to tally up millions of casualties as a result of an enemy attack.

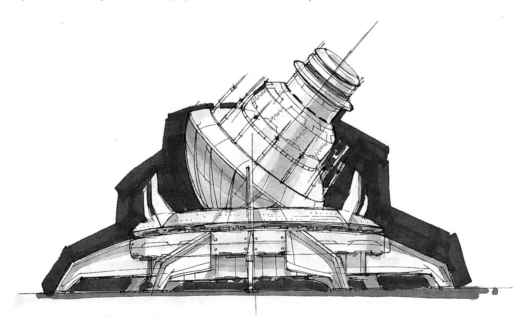

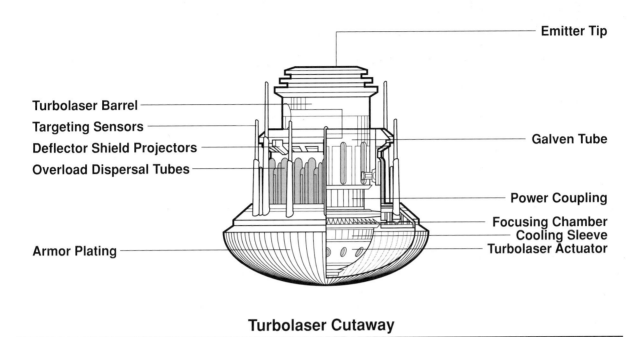

Emitter Tip

Turbolaser Barrel

Targeting Sensors

Deflector Shield Projectors

Overload Dispersal Tubes

Galven Tube

Power Coupling

Focusing Chamber

Cooling Sleeve

Turbolaser Actuator

Armor Plating

Turbolaser Cutaway

Turbolaser (land based)

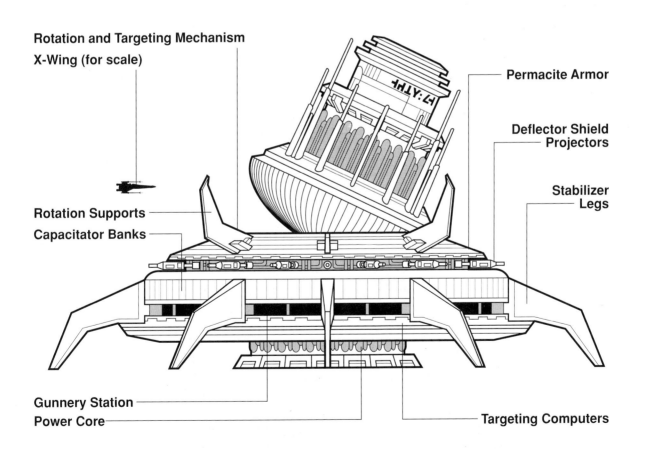

Rotation and Targeting Mechanism

X-Wing (for scale)

Permacite Armor

Deflector Shield Projectors

Stabilizer Legs

Rotation Supports

Capacitator Banks

Gunnery Station

Power Core

Targeting Computers

CLOAKING DEVICE

IMPERIAL CLOAKING DEVICE

The development of a practical cloaking shield to prevent a vessel from being detected by sensors and visual scans was one of the Empire's top military research priorities. While never put into widespread use—indeed, never even publicly acknowledged—the Empire's cloaking device represented a stunning advance in starship technology.

Imperial cloaking fields completely absorb all incoming sensor scans and block all the host ship's emissions and reflected energy. In short, the cloaked ship is rendered invisible to both sensors *and* the unaided eye. The only sensor that can detect a cloaked vessel is the relatively rare and expensive crystal gravitational trap (CGT), which searches for gravitational fluctuations created by a large mass. Since the cloaked ship is still physically present, it cannot hide from this sensor.

Despite their advantages, Imperial cloaking shields possess a number of major limitations. They consume a tremendous amount of energy—outdrawing most ships' weapons, shields, and drive systems combined—and they cost over a billion credits each.

Perhaps the greatest disadvantage is inherent in the "double-blind" nature of the shield. Because all incoming energy is absorbed and all of the host ship's emissions are blocked, the cloaked ship's scanners and communications are equally impaired; crew members cannot peer beyond the cloak's shroud, and so visual navigation is impossible. The cloaked ship is completely cut off from the rest of the galaxy. Navigation is accomplished by preprogramming astrogation routes; combat, communications, and sensor sweeps occur only if the cloaking field is lowered.

Imperial research teams conducted numerous field experiments to refine this system. Imperial Admiral Sarn directed the development of an experimental large-scale cloaking shield to be deployed aboard Super Star Destroyers, although this research project was foiled by Rebel agents. A miniaturized cloaking shield was installed aboard the Emperor's personal shuttle, which was destroyed in the explosion of the Second Death Star. No one has uncovered the plans for this advanced unit.

After the death of the Emperor, cloaking fields were considered "lost." However, Grand Admiral Thrawn learned the location of one of Emperor Palpatine's hidden storehouses—on the distant planet of Wayland—and inside it he discovered complete technical specifications for cloaking shields. Thrawn used cloaking shield technology to hide combat starships during surgical strikes against the New Republic and to claim victories at both Sluis Van and Ukio. Perhaps his most brilliant move was the siege of Coruscant, where cloaked asteroids were placed in orbit, blockading the New Republic's capital world while Thrawn's fleets systematically conquered other New Republic member worlds.

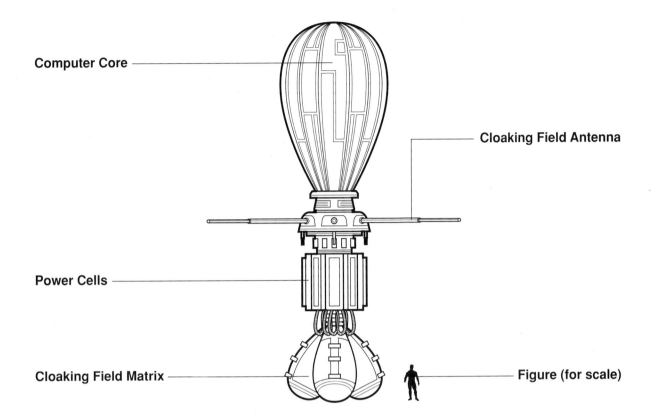

Computer Core

Cloaking Field Antenna

Power Cells

Cloaking Field Matrix

Figure (for scale)

Cloaking Device

Carrack Cruiser Cutaway

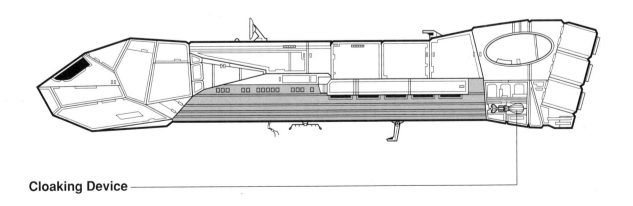

Cloaking Device

ORBITAL NIGHTCLOAK

IMPERIAL DEPARTMENT OF MILITARY RESEARCH
ORBITAL NIGHTCLOAK

Designed by the Imperial Department of Military Research, the orbital nightcloak is a siege weapon that disrupts an entire planet's climate, causing incredible destruction and upheaval while demoralizing the world's inhabitants.

The nightcloak consists of a network of hundreds of orbiting satellites, each of which distorts and absorbs light waves, completely preventing visible, infrared, and ultraviolet light energy from reaching the planet's surface. As the nightcloak is deployed, people on the ground perceive blotches of impenetrable darkness spreading through the sky, replacing their sun's warming rays. It's a terrifying sight to primitive beings who don't understand the technology that is being used—and is frighteningly unsettling even for people who know exactly what's happening.

The nightcloak wraps a planet in a state of perpetual night. Surface temperatures drop at a frightening pace. Within a day snow is falling in formerly temperate regions. Plant life withers and dies shortly thereafter as a result of the complete absence of sunlight, and the world is plunged into a perpetual deep freeze within three weeks. The nightcloak also blocks sensors and communications, effectively cutting off the world from the rest of the galaxy. People on the surface have no way of knowing how many warships are orbiting above the cloak, and the only way to get messages off-planet is to fly through the cloak's eerie darkness, then run the gauntlet of the enemy blockade.

The nightcloak's satellites are powered by the captured solar energy, making the network self-sustaining. However, this weapon has a number of limitations, the primary one being its sheer scope. Hundreds of satellites must be deployed over the course of several days. Control systems are interdependent, so that destroying only a handful of satellites can disable the entire nightcloak system. Thus, a fleet must remain in orbit to drive off attackers.

The Imperial Warlord Zsinj deployed an orbital nightcloak over the planet Dathomir during his quest to capture the New Republic's General Han Solo. Zsinj believed that Solo was being held by Dathomir's Nightsisters, a group of Force-sensitive women who manipulated the Force through "spells." Zsinj threatened to destroy the planet unless they delivered Solo. However, Zsinj's forces fell under attack from the Hapan fleet, and Luke Skywalker destroyed scores of satellites with the *Millennium Falcon*'s quad laser cannons. The siege weapon was disabled.

Refinements made to the original nightcloak system have greatly improved its utility. Improved routing systems allow up to ten percent of the satellites to be disabled before the net is affected. Mark II satellites also incorporate short-range laser cannons and targeting computers to destroy attacking ships.

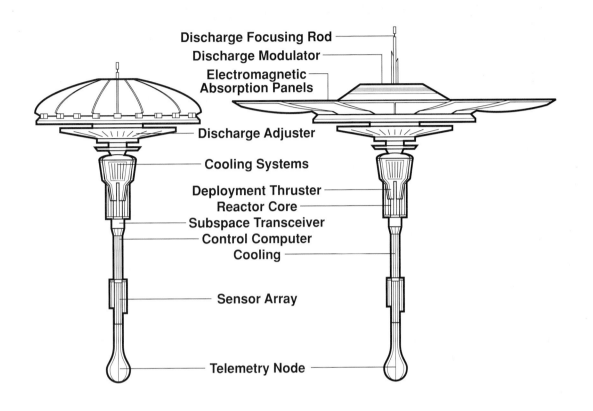

Discharge Focusing Rod
Discharge Modulator
Electromagnetic Absorption Panels
Discharge Adjuster
Cooling Systems
Deployment Thruster
Reactor Core
Subspace Transceiver
Control Computer
Cooling
Sensor Array
Telemetry Node

Satellite Off-line　　　　**Satellite On-line**

Nightcloak Deployment Graphic

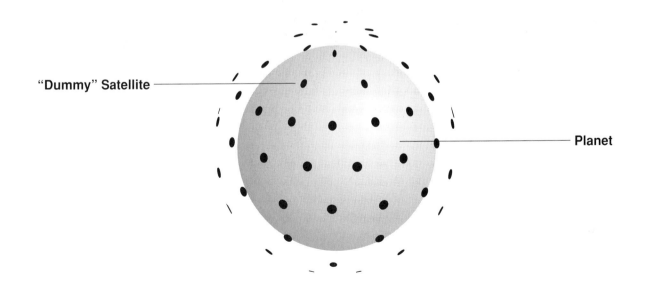

"Dummy" Satellite

Planet

PLANETARY SHIELDS

CoMar SLD-26 Planetary Shield Generator

Planetary shields use layers of charged energy to dissipate turbolaser blasts and destroy space debris on contact, protecting planets from the devastating effects of attacks as well as asteroid and comet strikes. Starships unlucky enough to career into these energy screens often are instantly vaporized, and even a glancing impact can severely damage a vessel. Since these shields are invisible, pilots rely on sensor readings to avoid contact, although enemy jamming can block the sensors, causing vessels to fly right into the shields. This nearly happened to the Rebel fleet when it attacked the Second Death Star at Endor.

Planetary shields consume so much energy that it is impractical to keep them powered at all times. Since some shields take nearly half an hour to activate, planets use networks of turbolasers and ion cannons to force back attackers until the shields can be raised.

Planetary shields vary widely in size and power output. A small unit such as the Kuat Drive Yards DSS-02, used by the Rebel Alliance at Hoth, protects an area approximately fifty kilometers in diameter. While these units are excellent at deflecting bombardments from orbit, they do nothing to prevent troopships and bombers from landing beyond a shield's perimeter. As a result, bases using these shields normally need to maintain antivehicle laser cannons and other defenses; attackers are often forced into grueling ground engagements similar to the Battle of Hoth.

On Endor, the Imperials used a CoMar SLD-26 shield generator to project a defensive energy field around the Second Death Star while it was under construction. This shield fell victim to a team of Rebel commandos who, with the assistance of the native Ewoks, infiltrated the Imperial base and used proton grenades to detonate the reactor core and destroy the shield projector array.

Grand Admiral Thrawn devised several methods of counteracting planetary shield networks. At Ukio he slipped several cloaked vessels into the planet's atmosphere while the shields were down. When Thrawn's fleet arrived later, he commanded the Jedi Joruus C'baoth to use his Force skills to coordinate his attack. The Star Destroyers' turbolaser fire splashed harmlessly against the shields, but the cloaked ships beneath the shields fired simultaneously, making it seem as though the shots were passing through the shields. The Ukians panicked and surrendered, and word of Thrawn's new "superweapons" quickly spread across the galaxy.

Later, during the siege of the New Republic's capital of Coruscant, Thrawn again crippled the enemy with a ruse. He launched twenty-two cloaked asteroids into orbit, simultaneously staging nearly three hundred *false* launches. Since a single asteroid strike on the surface could kill millions of people, Coruscant's shields were kept up at all times, effectively blockading the planet until the New Republic learned how many asteroids had actually been launched and was able to account for all of them.

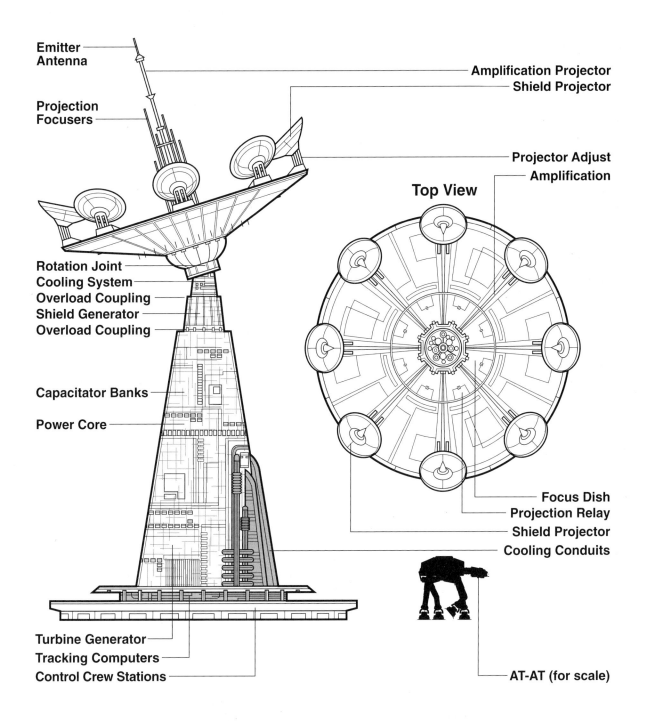

Emitter Antenna

Projection Focusers

Amplification Projector

Shield Projector

Projector Adjust

Amplification

Top View

Rotation Joint
Cooling System
Overload Coupling
Shield Generator
Overload Coupling

Capacitor Banks

Power Core

Focus Dish
Projection Relay
Shield Projector
Cooling Conduits

Turbine Generator
Tracking Computers
Control Crew Stations

AT-AT (for scale)

Side View

SUPERLASER

CUSTOM IMPERIAL SUPERWEAPON

The first of the Empire's many terror weapons, the superlaser was conceived by Grand Moff Tarkin and developed by Bevel Lemelisk. It was designed to destroy a world with a single shot. Mounted aboard the Death Star, the superlaser was the keystone of Emperor Palpatine's "Doctrine of Fear," which proposed that the peoples of the Empire could be controlled by being frightened into submission.

The superlaser was the most powerful energy weapon ever built. Fed by a fusion reactor that dwarfed even those found aboard Imperial Star Destroyers, the superlaser's eight amplification crystals produced turbolaser pulses that were fused over the weapon's central focus lens. The resulting energy beam had more firepower than half the Imperial starfleet and could instantly reduce a world to asteroid fragments and space dust.

Each amplification crystal required a separate gunnery station, where a crew of fourteen soldiers had to precisely adjust and modulate the turbolaser pulses to allow the focus lens to create a stable energy beam. Four reserve amplification crystals could be brought on line.

The Death Star's power core needed an entire day to build up enough charge for a full-power blast, although even a low-power shot had enough destructive force to crack a planet's crust and cause incredible seismic upheaval. The superlaser aboard the Second Death Star featured improved targeting computers for firing on capital ships.

Security was a primary concern: Those who controlled the Death Star's superlaser could challenge the authority of the Emperor himself. Elaborate computer safeguards, squads of stormtroopers, and the most sophisticated security checkpoints in the Empire controlled access to the superlaser's gunnery stations. The weapon could be disabled by an override command from the Death Star's overbridge. Emperor Palpatine also assigned a trusted adviser—Darth Vader in the case of the first Death Star—to remain aboard these weapons platforms to ensure that the crew remained loyal and fearful of his wrath.

The superlaser's strategic value was obvious. The weapon could have been deployed anywhere and used against a planet—a target that can neither maneuver nor hide from an attack. While the Rebel Alliance destroyed the first Death Star, the lure of wielding an ultimate terror weapon remained strong with the Emperor and with those who followed him.

Tremendous resources were funneled into developing new superlaser platforms such as the *Tarkin*, the Second Death Star, and the *Eclipse*-class Star Destroyers. After the Emperor's final defeat, the covetous Hutts turned their attention to conquering other worlds and tried to build the Darksaber, a battle station based on the Death Star's design. As with the Empire's prior attempts, the Darksaber plot was foiled by the forces of the New Republic.

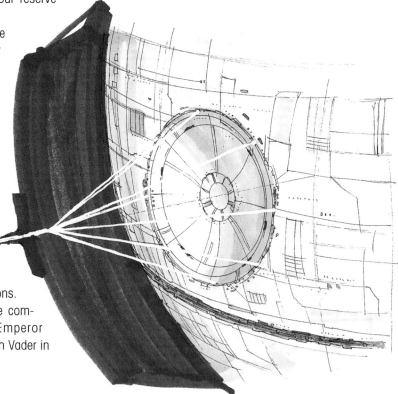

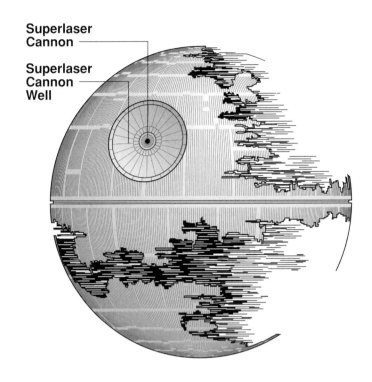

Superlaser
Cannon

Superlaser
Cannon
Well

Death Star with Superlaser Placement

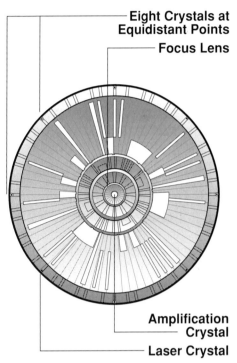

Eight Crystals at
Equidistant Points

Focus Lens

Amplification
Crystal

Laser Crystal

Top View of Superlaser

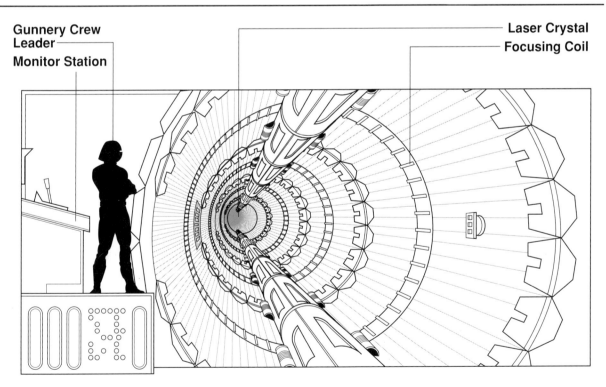

Gunnery Crew
Leader

Monitor Station

Laser Crystal

Focusing Coil

Laser Crystal Interior

SUN CRUSHER

CUSTOM IMPERIAL SUPERWEAPON

The Sun Crusher was a prototype superweapon that was developed at the Empire's Maw Installation. Using funds surreptitiously diverted from the first Death Star project, this outpost was secretly built by Grand Moff Tarkin for the development of experimental weapons technologies. Unknown even to the Emperor, the Maw Installation was forgotten after Tarkin's death at the Battle of Yavin.

However, Imperial scientists led by the researcher Qwi Xux—who devised many of the superlaser's technological innovations—continued their work despite complete isolation from the rest of the galaxy. By the time Han Solo stumbled onto the Maw Installation more than a decade after Tarkin's death, the Empire was a shattered husk of its former self, but its legacy of terror lived on in the Sun Crusher.

A starship no larger than a starfighter, the Sun Crusher had layers of quantum crystalline armor, making it impervious to turbolaser blasts. Equipped with a long-range hyperdrive, the Sun Crusher was designed to slip unnoticed into a system, fire its weaponry, and then escape before a patrol ship detected its presence.

The Sun Crusher's primary weapon was a payload of eleven energy resonance torpedoes. Each torpedo was activated when it passed through the ship's resonance energizer, emerging from the Sun Crusher's resonance projector as an oval-shaped plasma discharge.

The energized torpedo hurtled toward the system's star at near-lightspeed velocity. Upon impact, the torpedo burrowed into the star's core. Dense packets of energy released from within the torpedo made the star's core unstable, initiating a chain-reaction explosion that forced even low-mass stars to go supernova. The star was ripped apart in the blast, sending waves of energy and radiation out across the system and destroying every world in its path. The Sun Crusher's horrifying weaponry could obliterate an entire system, erasing trillions of lives in a matter of hours.

After being captured by the Maw Installation's forces, Han Solo stole the Sun Crusher in a daring escape and delivered it to the New Republic, which placed the weapon inside the gas giant of Yavin, where it was thought that the incredible atmospheric pressures would crush the craft. However, Kyp Durron, a Jedi adept consumed by the dark side of the Force, retrieved the Sun Crusher and used it in a vindictive rampage against the Empire. Durron blasted the Cauldron Nebula in an attempt to destroy Imperial Admiral Daala's fleet, then fired a resonance torpedo into the planet Carida's sun, utterly wiping out this Imperial-allied system.

The Sun Crusher was finally destroyed at the Battle of the Maw when it was captured by the gravitational forces of one of the Maw's black holes. Durron survived only by escaping in a message pod, although he suffered grievous injuries in the process.

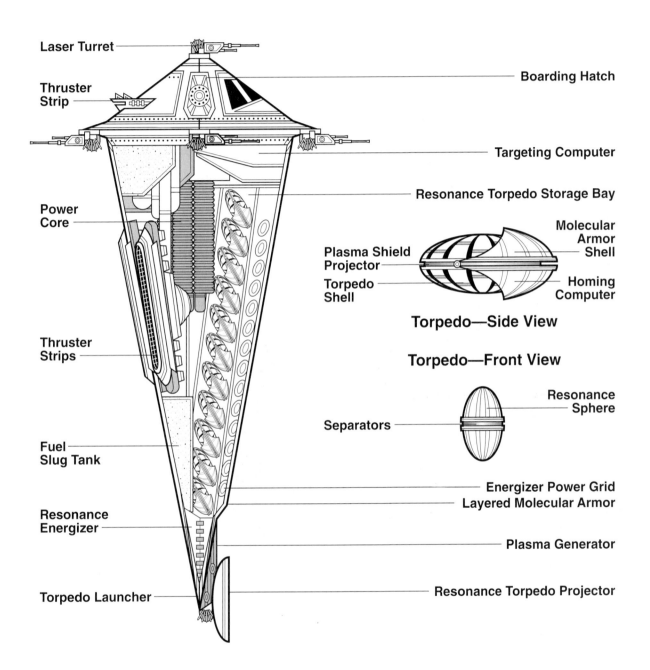

Laser Turret

Thruster
Strip

Power
Core

Thruster
Strips

Fuel
Slug Tank

Resonance
Energizer

Torpedo Launcher

Boarding Hatch

Targeting Computer

Resonance Torpedo Storage Bay

Plasma Shield
Projector

Torpedo
Shell

Molecular
Armor
Shell

Homing
Computer

Torpedo—Side View

Torpedo—Front View

Separators

Resonance
Sphere

Energizer Power Grid
Layered Molecular Armor

Plasma Generator

Resonance Torpedo Projector

Sun Crusher Cutaway

GALAXY GUN

CUSTOM IMPERIAL SUPERWEAPON

Built six years after the Battle of Endor and developed at the insistence of the reincarnated Emperor Palpatine, the Galaxy Gun was a weapon of indiscriminate terror that he planned to use to dominate the galaxy and cause the downfall of the New Republic. An immense space station built in orbit above the Emperor's new capital world of Byss, the Galaxy Gun fired missiles equipped with particle disintegrator warheads. Each missile possessed a terrifically fast hyperdrive and could travel from the Galactic Core to the outermost frontier worlds in a matter of hours.

Upon emerging from hyperspace and homing in on the target world, the missile's formidable defenses would activate. Automated laser cannon turrets blasted fighter interceptors, while armor plating and advanced energy shields easily withstood blasts from the most powerful ion cannons and turbolasers. Once within range, the particle disintegrator warhead, energized by the missile's power core, triggered massive nucleonic chain reactions that spread like wildfire across the targeted planet's surface, explosively converting matter to energy.

At the missile's full-power setting, the nucleonic reactions were sustained until all matter was converted, destroying the entire world. Reduced power settings could be used to control precisely the size of the target area in order to consume a city or military base while leaving the rest of the world undamaged.

The primary advantage the Galaxy Gun maintained over other superweapons was that it was permanently stationed above Byss and therefore was easily defended by the massed Imperial fleet. The only way to destroy the station seemed to be to mount a full-scale attack against the Empire's most heavily fortified world, an obviously suicidal undertaking even for the New Republic.

The Galaxy Gun was used as a tool of blatant terrorism in an effort to force former New Republic allies to side with the Empire. Palpatine also unleashed this weapon against the New Republic's military, destroying Pinnacle Base, which for a time served as the New Republic's main headquarters. A Galaxy Gun missile also destroyed the New Republic troopship *Pelagria*, killing a hundred thousand troops.

This Imperial superweapon was destroyed when the droid R2-D2 seized control of the Super Star Destroyer *Eclipse II*'s computer banks and programmed the ship to ram the Galaxy Gun space station. The station exploded, and a misfired missile consumed the planet Byss. This cataclysm eliminated much of the rebuilt Empire's war arsenal. In the ensuing chaos, the New Republic quickly regained much of its lost territory, while the Imperial remnants never recovered from this crippling defeat.

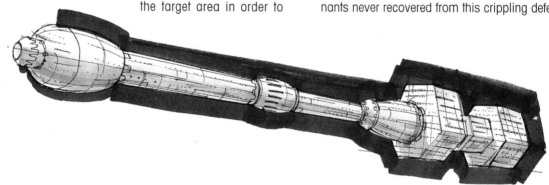

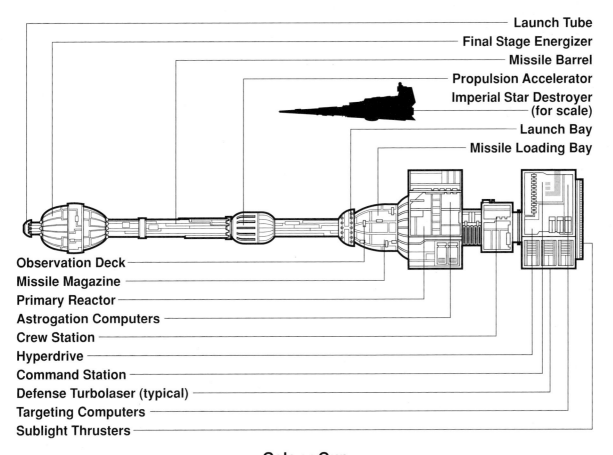

Launch Tube
Final Stage Energizer
Missile Barrel
Propulsion Accelerator
Imperial Star Destroyer (for scale)
Launch Bay
Missile Loading Bay

Observation Deck
Missile Magazine
Primary Reactor
Astrogation Computers
Crew Station
Hyperdrive
Command Station
Defense Turbolaser (typical)
Targeting Computers
Sublight Thrusters

Galaxy Gun

Galaxy Gun Missile

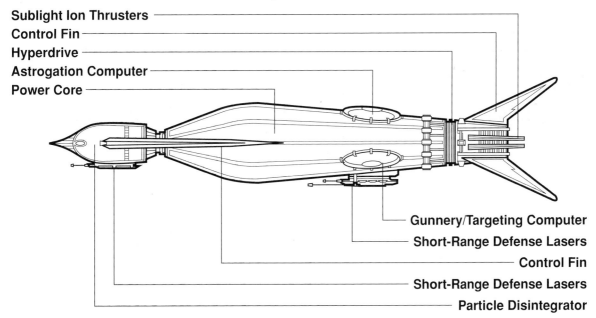

Sublight Ion Thrusters
Control Fin
Hyperdrive
Astrogation Computer
Power Core

Gunnery/Targeting Computer
Short-Range Defense Lasers
Control Fin
Short-Range Defense Lasers
Particle Disintegrator

Sensors
and
Communications

Early Starship Sensors

The early days of starship travel were quite dangerous and suited only for the bravest, most pioneering beings. There were no established travel routes, and the risks from enemy attacks and natural hazards threatened virtually every journey. Visual scanners were so limited that it was common for vehicles and vessels to collide with space debris, while marauders bent on crippling or hijacking a ship had little trouble hiding from their targets until escape became impossible. Ship navigators relied on limited electronic telescopes in order to take star readings and to determine whether they were following the correct course; ships that got lost might drift in space indefinitely.

Modern Starship Sensors

While the development of reliable faster-than-light hyperdrive proved essential for the exploration and settlement of the galaxy, it was the invention of sophisticated sensors that finally allowed safe, reliable interstellar travel. Over thousands of years of technological advancement, sensors have been constantly improved upon, and most modern vessels carry several different sensor units that allow crews to gather the data needed for accurate stellar navigation.

Ships often move at tremendous sublight velocities, and these sensitive sensor arrays allow them to avoid asteroids, radiation belts, and ion storms. Sensors also are used to detect and identify ships that are traveling together in merchant fleets and cargo convoys and to assess approaching

craft. Of course, sensor systems are essential for waging war, as they allow large military fleets to maintain cohesive formations. In battle they are used to detect and identify enemy vessels and determine the status of weapons and shield systems.

Sensor Types

A number of standardized sensors are used by ships across the galaxy. Electro-photo receptors, also known as EPRs, are short-range visual scanners that gather data provided by normal light, infrared, and ultraviolet telescopes; they are also the primary sensors used in targeting computers.

Full-spectrum transceivers (FSTs), nicknamed "universal sensors," employ clusters of scanners to detect a wide range of objects, energies, and fields, although these transceivers are not very sensitive. Dedicated-energy receptors (DERs) are used to gather more detailed data by allowing crews to detect electromagnetic emissions such as comm transmissions, navigational beacons, heat, and laser light. These sensors must be run by a skilled operator; poor operators have been known to misinterpret stray cosmic rays as comlink transmissions or to dismiss energy surges as solar flare activity when in truth they were facing a starship armed with an energy baffler unit.

There are many other specialized sensor types, such as life-form indicators and crystal gravfield traps. While these tend to be more expensive than the general sensors outlined above, the images they produce are much more detailed.

Sensor Countermeasures

Some ships utilize a variety of devices and methods, collectively known as sensor countermeasures, to hide their presence from nearby ships.

Sensor stealth systems electronically muffle or hide a ship's engine, weapon, and power generator energy signatures. To further enhance sensor stealth measures, a ship may "run silent," prohibiting communications transmissions. In extreme situations a ship may power down completely, shutting down its engines, sensors, weapons, and power generators and drift in space until the need for stealth has passed.

Sensor jamming and dampening involve flooding the

immediate area around a ship with static and random signals in order to confuse and blind enemy sensors. However, jamming creates so much interference that it is exceptionally easy to detect: Though it is hard for other ships to determine exactly what is within the jammed area, everyone knows that *something* is causing the jamming.

Some vessels carry sensor decoys—small pods or shuttles—that electronically duplicate the parent ship's sensor signatures. When these decoys are activated, enemy sensor operators suddenly seem to be faced with two *identical* vessels and must decide which one to pursue.

PLANETARY SENSORS

Many planets maintain networks of sensor satellites in order to detect approaching ships as soon as they emerge from hyperspace. While established to control commercial traffic, such networks often serve as early-warning systems in the event of military incursions. Other planets maintain minimal sensor networks, using only starport sensor arrays to detect ships as they come in for landings. When not in the vicinity of a starport, ships must rely on their own sensor capabilities.

PERSONAL SENSORS

Short-range portable sensor packs are issued as standard equipment for scouts, soldiers, and many other professionals. They allow their users to gather very detailed information within a given unit's scanning range. There are an astonishing number of specialized sensor types, ranging from atmospheric and metal scanners to communications units that monitor all comlink activity, and life-form detectors that detect and identify creatures or beings within the unit's range.

COMMUNICATIONS

Three primary communications applications are used throughout the galaxy: comlinks, subspace transceivers, and HoloNet technology.

First, comlinks were developed to generate lightspeed waves for short-range transmissions, and these devices range from personal comlinks to starship comm systems. Many worlds maintain planetary comm networks—using either hardwired systems or open-air broadcast relays—built around comlink technology.

The development of subspace transceivers allowed for real-time broadcasts over vast distances. The technology proved to be a major step in unifying the galaxy. Before the creation of subspace technology, worlds often existed in a state of relative isolation, separated from their neighbors by the amount of time it took a hyperdrive starship to cross the distances between the stars. With the coming of subspace transceivers, worlds in different systems could establish links and exchange messages instantly.

And finally, the development and deployment of the HoloNet proved to be one of the Old Republic's crowning achievements. This communications system used new technology to link all of the Republic's member worlds through an instantaneous three-dimensional holographic network. Messages could be transmitted instantly from the capital of Coruscant to all the far-flung worlds of the Republic. While the HoloNet was tremendously expensive, it also created a sense of belonging among all the Republic's citizens. After the fall of the Republic, the Empire used the HoloNet as a potent military tool to link its fleets, enabling Emperor Palpatine to dominate the galaxy and quash virtually all resistance to his rule.

STARSHIP SENSOR ARRAY

CARBANTI UNIVERSAL TRANSCEIVER PACKAGE AND BERTRIAK "SCREAMER" ACTIVE JAMMER
FABRITECH ANq-51 SENSOR ARRAY COMPUTER
SIENAR FLEET SYSTEMS TXS-431 FLIGHT CONTROL CONSOLE

Sensor arrays, standard equipment aboard virtually every starship, use miniaturized processors to gather data from the ship's sensors. These data are compiled by the ship's main sensor computer, after which analysis aids pilots and crews in a broad spectrum of duties, such as plotting safe navigation routes and scanning for nearby vessels. In short, a ship's sensor array is one of its most essential systems.

Sensors, particularly those designed for fighters and other combat craft, must strike a delicate balance, packing the maximum data-gathering capacity into the smallest, lightest unit possible. Efficient energy use is also important with a sensor array since weapon, shielding, and drive systems receive priority with energy allocation. Speed and accuracy are critical, particularly in combat scenarios.

The New Republic's X-wing fighter features a Carbanti universal transceiver package coupled with a Bertriak "Screamer" active jammer. The Carbanti transceiver houses several standard sensor units, and interface ports accept supplemental sensors, making it one of the most flexible and easily upgraded starfighter array systems—one of the prime factors that has kept the X-wing competitive with newer starfighters.

The Bertriak "Screamer" sensor jammer disguises the ship's ion drive emissions, preventing long-range detection by enemy fighters and confusing homing computers aboard concussion

missiles and proton torpedoes.

Despite its battered appearance, the *Millennium Falcon* has one of the best sensor systems found aboard any small vessel. The dorsal rectenna dish is controlled by a Fabritech ANq-51 sensor array computer and includes a power-boosted electro-photo receptor, a subspace comm detector, and both active and passive long-range sensor arrays. Onboard jamming systems and short-range target acquisition programs also can be patched into the dish. Rounding out the *Falcon*'s sensor systems are signal-augmented jammers, an Imperial IFF ship identification transponder, and a Fabritech ANy-20 active sensor transceiver.

In contrast to the relatively primitive sensor suites maintained aboard starfighters and freighters, capital combat starships utilize sophisticated, integrated sensor systems that employ dozens of specialized sensor arrays for greater range and better sensitivity.

All sensor data are monitored by centralized com-scan computer systems, while specific sensors may be patched into specialized units such as the Txs-431 flight control console. The Txs-431, which was used aboard both Death Stars and is installed on many Star Destroyers, is used by hangar bay personnel to direct TIE fighter launches and handle docking and boarding duties.

A Txs-431 console normally can access a wide range of sensors—such as electro-photo and dedicated-energy receptors and full-spectrum transceivers—to identify incoming vessels and scan for evidence of damage or charged shields and weapons and to determine how many life-forms are aboard.

X-Wing Fighter and Its Sensor Array

STS: Short-Range Target-Acquiring Sensors
ALS: Active Long-Range Sensor Array
DER: Dedicated Energy Receptor
EPR: Electro-Photo Receptor

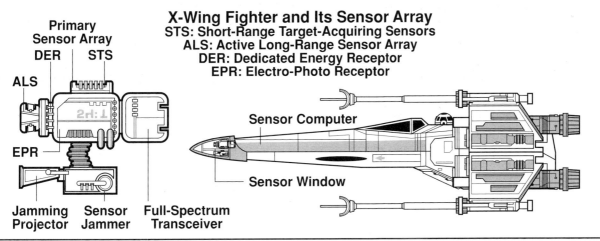

Primary Sensor Array
DER
STS
ALS
EPR
Jamming Projector
Sensor Jammer
Full-Spectrum Transceiver

Sensor Computer
Sensor Window

Millennium Falcon and Its Sensor Array

PLS: Passive Long-Range Sensor Array
ALS: Active Long-Range Sensor Array

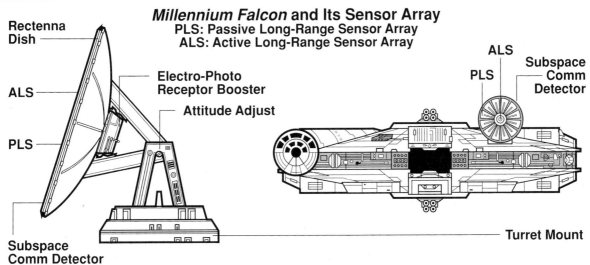

Rectenna Dish
ALS
PLS
Subspace Comm Detector
Electro-Photo Receptor Booster
Attitude Adjust

ALS
PLS
Subspace Comm Detector
Turret Mount

Imperial Sensor Console

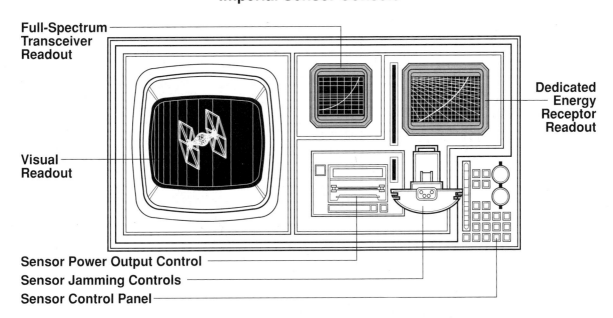

Full-Spectrum Transceiver Readout

Dedicated Energy Receptor Readout

Visual Readout

Sensor Power Output Control
Sensor Jamming Controls
Sensor Control Panel

COM-SCAN

MicroThrust OrC-19 Com-Scan Integrator Console

Com-scan computer systems control and integrate the complicated communications and sensors networks found aboard large capital ships such as Imperial Star Destroyers and Mon Calamari star cruisers.

Unlike starfighters, which have only a few sensors, large capital ships may have hundreds of specialized sensor arrays. Imperial Star Destroyers scan space with dozens of directional long-range electro-photo receptors and over a hundred full-spectrum transceivers and dedicated-energy receptors. A score of broadband transceivers monitor all communications—from comlink and subspace bands to radionics frequencies—searching for transmissions that are "hidden" under natural X-ray emissions or background static.

Com-scan computers instantly process and analyze this incredible volume of information. Indicators that match preprogrammed warning conditions—such as power fluctuations that might indicate the presence of a ship or an unexpected energy spike that could reveal a power generator hidden by a sensor-stealth system—automatically activate reserve sensor banks for a more detailed look.

By comparing data from both the sensor and communications networks, com-scan operators stand a better chance of detecting starships or hidden bases than do stand-alone sensor arrays. For example, upon emerging in the Hoth system, the com-scan systems aboard the Super Star Destroyer *Executor* confirmed the presence of the Rebel Alliance's Echo Base by detecting an energy shield around the sixth planet.

Com-scan control bays have rows of consoles for recording and analyzing data, while hologram projectors and flat-screen monitors display enemy fleet movements and run battle simulations. Droids programmed with complex data-sorting algorithms and highly skilled communications and sensors officers carefully evaluate the data to determine

which information is important enough to forward to the vessel's command staff.

Com-scan systems also are used to coordinate large-scale fleet actions, using encrypted subspace and HoloNet transmissions to direct strikes precisely against targets in several systems. This tactic was used successfully by both Grand Admiral Thrawn and the reincarnated Emperor Palpatine during their respective campaigns to topple the New Republic.

Similar systems are used at military bases. The Rebel com-scan system at Yavin Four remotely assisted the Alliance's pilots during the Battle of Yavin after the Death Star jammed the sensors aboard their X-wing and Y-wing fighters. At Hoth, the Rebellion's MicroThrust OrC-19 monitored Imperial forces and allowed General Rieekan to coordinate the ground defense of the base and the evacuation of transport ships.

Smaller systems, such as MicroThrust's CO-0012, sometimes are used aboard military command speeders such as the Imperial Uulshos QH-7 Chariot. The CO-0012 system helps theater commanders track enemy movements by compiling and analyzing information from troops, vehicles, and forward observer stations, while built-in comm encryption systems guarantee secure communications with widely dispersed units.

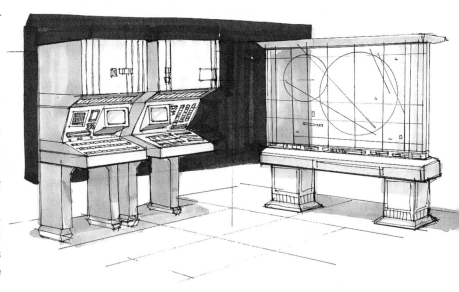

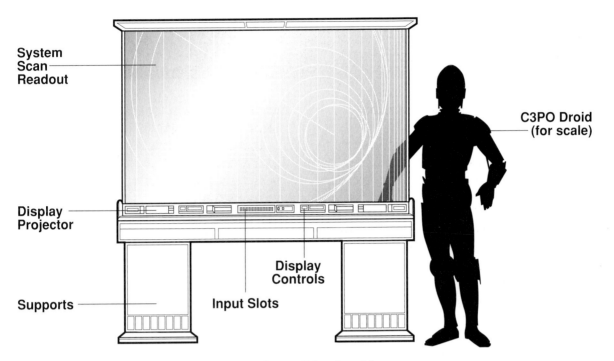

System Scan Readout

C3PO Droid (for scale)

Display Projector

Display Controls

Supports

Input Slots

Com-Scan Display Map

Com-Scan Computer Station

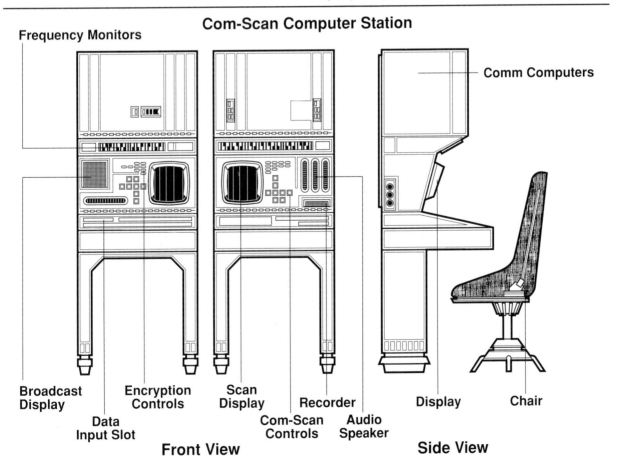

Frequency Monitors

Comm Computers

Broadcast Display

Encryption Controls

Scan Display

Recorder

Display

Chair

Data Input Slot

Com-Scan Controls

Audio Speaker

Front View

Side View

ELECTROTELESCOPE

NEURO-SAAV VXI-3 ELECTROTELESCOPE

Electrotelescopes are electro-optical devices used to observe nearby planets, moons, and asteroids. Similar in concept to electrobinoculars and macrobinoculars but much more powerful, electrotelescopes provide a tremendous degree of magnification through the use of optics and computers that electronically enhance existing light sources and reduce atmospheric haze and other sources of visual distortion. Electrotelescopes are equipped with sensors that scan for energy emissions or comm transmissions, making them capable of detecting small freighters at distances of up to five light-minutes. (This is more than adequate, since most starships are actually much closer to their destination worlds when they reappear in realspace.)

Electrotelescopes use a two-stage scanning system. The general scanning mode observes a large area, but with limited resolution and detail. When the control computer detects an anomaly or comes across energy emissions that might indicate nearby starships, the electroscope's detailed scan mode focuses on the specified area to gather as much information as possible.

Most models feature manual controls and standard datapad and astromech droid interfaces. External comm transceivers can transmit and receive data from a central base or link multiple units for composite imaging with tremendous detail.

Smaller units, such as the VXI-3 units used by the Rebels on Hoth, can weigh as little as

thirty-five kilograms, and their small repulsorlift generators allow them to be moved easily. Larger electrotelescopes provide much greater resolution but are so big that they must be stationed permanently at an observatory or placed aboard an orbiting satellite.

Electrotelescopes often are installed as sensor backups at starports and space stations and are used on deep-space observation stations for scientific research and to act as an early-warning system for inhabited planets. Smaller colonies use these devices to scan for asteroids and comets that may be on collision vectors.

Since these devices are passive—they only detect incoming light and energy emissions—they can be used without fear of detection by passing starships. They were perfectly suited for the Rebel Alliance's many hidden outposts, such as those on Tierfon, Thila, and Derra IV.

When the Rebel Alliance established Echo Base on Hoth, secrecy was vital to its survival. Active sensors or orbital satellites were out of the question; instead, the Alliance relied on nearly a dozen Neuro-Saav VXI-3 electrotelescopes positioned at the main base and at remote observation posts to provide an early-detection scanning system. Unfortunately, this network was hampered by the Hoth system's numerous asteroids and comets, and an Imperial probe droid managed to land on the planet undetected, alerting the Empire to the Rebels' presence.

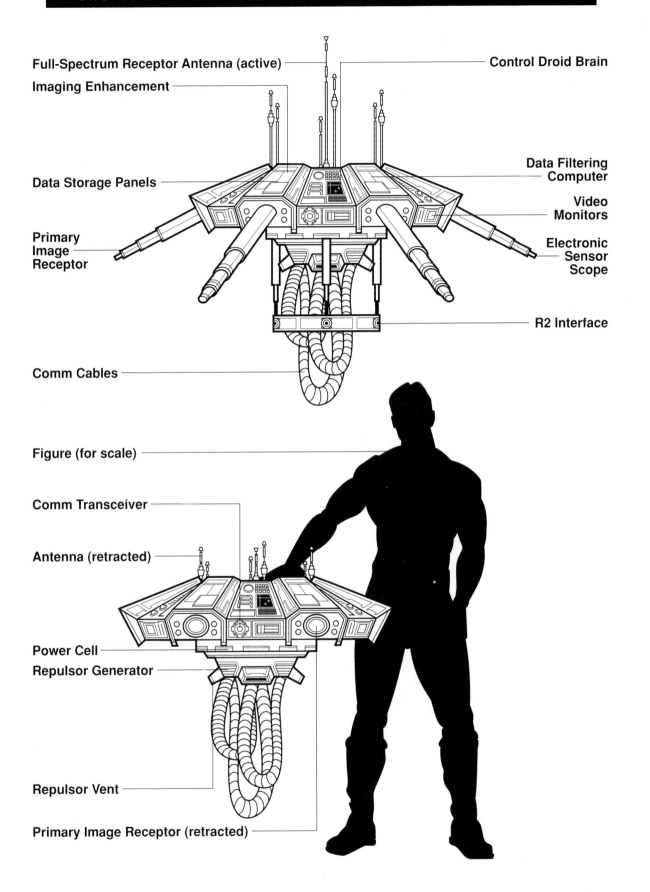

Full-Spectrum Receptor Antenna (active)

Imaging Enhancement

Control Droid Brain

Data Filtering Computer

Data Storage Panels

Video Monitors

Primary Image Receptor

Electronic Sensor Scope

R2 Interface

Comm Cables

Figure (for scale)

Comm Transceiver

Antenna (retracted)

Power Cell

Repulsor Generator

Repulsor Vent

Primary Image Receptor (retracted)

PORTABLE SCANNER

CRYONCORP. ENHANCESCAN GENERAL-PURPOSE SCANNER

While far less powerful and more specialized than the sensors found aboard starships and vehicles, portable scanners are relatively inexpensive handheld units that are perfect scouting tools for ground reconnaissance and exploration missions.

The Cryoncorp. EnhanceScan is a typical multipurpose sensor unit and was the portable scanner of choice for the Rebel Alliance's scouts, from those stationed on the frigid ice world of Hoth to the teams that patrolled Arbra's lush jungles and Thila's unforgiving mountains. An improved version of the earlier Lifedetec bioscanner, the EnhanceScan added communications, metal detection, and motion sensor modules to its attributes.

The bioscanner module can detect life-forms within 1,500 meters, and its computer memory banks can be preloaded with templates that allow the user to identify over three hundred different creatures. The communications scanner cannot transmit messages, but it automatically intercepts any standard-frequency comlink transmissions within three kilometers. Comlinks can be linked to the scanner through a data cable and configured to monitor any active frequencies.

The EnhanceScan's motion sensor module detects any movement within five hundred meters and can be programmed to sound an alarm, allowing the scanner to be used as an automated camp sentry. It can be programmed to search for concentrations of specific metals within a maximum range of approximately a hundred meters.

The unit's computer can control all four scanner modes simultaneously. Depending on the mode in use, the readout screen displays the shape and vital data of detected life-forms, the characteristics of intercepted comlink transmissions, or detected metal concentrations. In each mode the specific location and movement are also indicated. The EnhanceScan's data ports allow it to link with computers, datapads, and droids to exchange data. Six rechargeable power cells last for up to ten days of continuous operation.

While the EnhanceScan combines several distinct sensor arrays in one unit, single-purpose scanners are also popular because they offer good performance in an economical package. Specialized scanners may gather data about life-forms, comlink transmissions, energy emissions, electromagnetic or repulsorlift emissions, and geothermal activity. Sonic scanners can amplify sounds at long range or scan above and beneath the user's hearing range. Visual scanners may be equipped with long-range magnifiers or infrared or ultraviolet optics. Other specialized scanners include medical scanners, technical scanners (which examine repulsorlift drives and other common machinery), and geological scanners, which detect precious minerals and ore deposits.

These units vary widely in cost and performance. Durability is important, and it is often wise to spend a few extra credits to get a scanner with a sturdy casing so that the internal sensors are not easily knocked out of alignment or damaged.

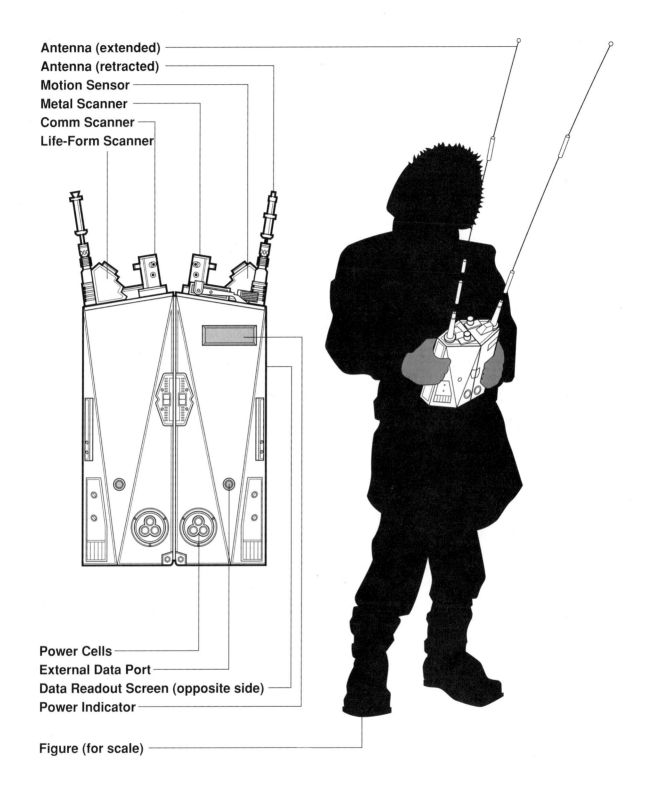

Antenna (extended)
Antenna (retracted)
Motion Sensor
Metal Scanner
Comm Scanner
Life-Form Scanner

Power Cells
External Data Port
Data Readout Screen (opposite side)
Power Indicator

Figure (for scale)

SENSOR TAG

RHINSOME TRACKING CORP. SURESNOOP

Sensor tags are tiny homing beacons that are secretly placed on a target or the target's belongings. The tracker, a handheld unit attuned to the tag's homing frequency, can then monitor the target's movements from a safe distance and with minimal risk of discovery. These valuable espionage tools are used by New Republic intelligence agents, corporate security officers, private investigators and skip tracers, bounty hunters, crime family enforcers, and just about anyone who needs to trail a target discreetly. Sensor tags also are used by some undercover agents to stay in touch with their backups since they are more secure and less likely to be detected than are hidden comlinks.

Rhinsome's SureSnoop is one of the more powerful sensor tags on the market. Locking on to the tag's comm pulse, the handheld tracker's display screen indicates its location, direction, and rate of movement. If maps are programmed into the tracker, it can display the tag's location relative to local landmarks. The tracker also sports a small hologram projector to display maps in three dimensions.

The SureSnoop sensor tag is less than three centimeters in diameter and can easily be hidden inside jewelry, comlinks, and other common items. When a detachable barb is used to clip the sensor tag to the tar-

get's clothing, it also can be disguised as a button or cuff link. A small magnetic plate allows the homing transmitter to be clipped to vehicles, droids, and other metal objects.

The SureSnoop's tag and tracker must be synchronized on the same frequency and pulse cycle for this system to work. Both the tag and the tracker can be reset for any of the millions of possible frequency and cycle combinations. The sensor tag has a broadcast range of five kilometers, while a thin layer of shielding blocks stray energy emissions, resulting in an extremely "tight" signal. The homing beacon has no encryption mode, but civilian comm scanners are unlikely to discover its homing transmissions. Unfortunately, though, most military-grade communications scanners are powerful enough to detect this type of sensor tag. The transmitter's energy cell lasts three days.

The Rhinsome SureSnoop costs three thousand credits, and its use is restricted on many worlds. Miniaturized sensor tags—some no more than a centimeter in diameter—command premium prices, although their broadcast ranges normally are limited to a few hundred meters. Cheaper beacons are available, including the Astroserver Industries Rover and Trailmaster and the MechBlaze Observer, but they tend to be much larger than the SureSnoop and have shorter broadcast ranges.

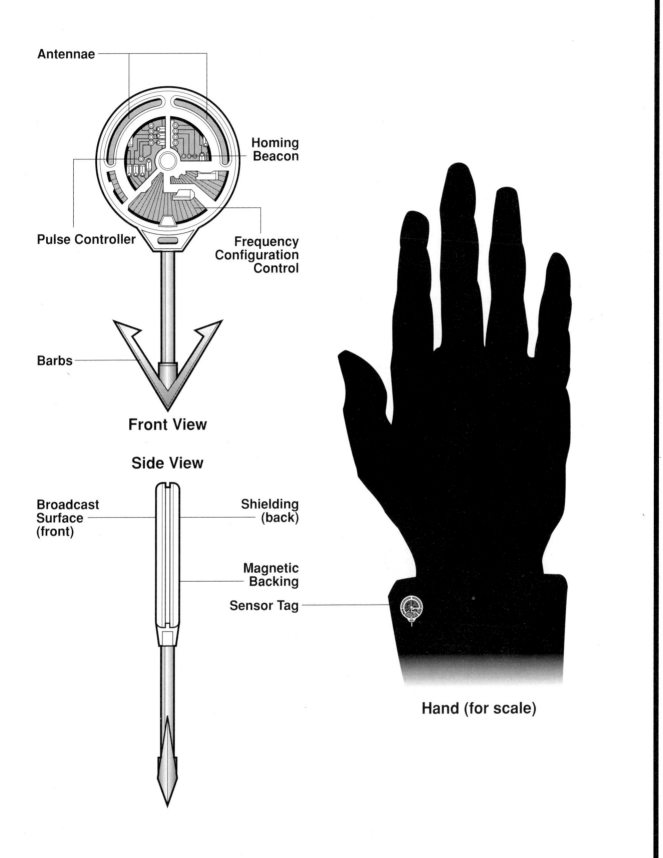

Antennae

Homing
Beacon

Pulse Controller

Frequency
Configuration
Control

Barbs

Front View

Side View

Broadcast
Surface
(front)

Shielding
(back)

Magnetic
Backing

Sensor Tag

Hand (for scale)

SENSOR BEACON

FABRITECH SE-VIGILANT AUTOMATED SENSOR BEACON

Sensor beacons are security scanners and alarm systems that can be deployed on agricultural facilities, moisture farms, parks, bases, and other areas too large to be marked off with energy fences or thoroughly patrolled by security guards. When properly positioned, sensor beacons provide nearly complete electronic surveillance and immediately alert command stations to intrusions of any kind.

The Rebel Alliance often used these types of automated scanners to guard wilderness areas around remote bases. In fact, Luke Skywalker was helping the Alliance place Fabritech SE-Vigilant sensor beacons near Echo Base on the ice planet of Hoth when he was attacked and nearly killed by a wampa ice creature.

The SE-Vigilant is a two-piece unit with low mass and a compact design. While its sensor packs are not as sensitive as those found on larger beacons, the SE-Vigilant is light enough that live mounts such as tauntauns, dewbacks, and banthas can carry nearly two dozen of these units on their backs, allowing easier deployment. Its lower main post, a small tube barely thirty centimeters long during transport, expands to 1.6 meters when deployed. The post is secured by a magnetic disk or anchoring rods that bore nearly fifty centimeters into the ground. For security, electrified stun strips deliver variable-intensity shock charges on contact—useful for driving off overly curious creatures.

The upper sensor pole holds twin sensor arrays, sensor analysis computers, and broadcast gear. The rotation joint makes four revolutions per minute, providing both sensor suites complete coverage of the surrounding terrain. Retractable solar energy collectors automatically recharge the power cells, offering three months of continuous operation. The cells are fully recharged during normal maintenance and recalibration adjustments.

The upper sensor array provides a general scanning system with a long-range, wide-angle visual recorder and a sophisticated motion sensor. Secondary components include light and heat sensors. The lower scanner shell is responsible for detailed scans and has a multipurpose visual recorder equipped with magnification, infrared, and heat emission adapters. Enhanced audio pickups supplement the visual records.

The sensor arrays feed data into their respective sensor analysis computers, which automate all basic scanning functions and direct continuous transmissions to the beacon's control station up to fifty kilometers away. Optional encryption modules can scramble data to ensure confidential transmissions.

When the SE-Vigilant is in detailed scan mode, the beacon's rotation ceases and careful adjustment of the scanner shells is controlled by the analysis computers.

The unit's modular design allows damaged sensor arrays to be replaced quickly. This standardization also allows other types of sensors to be mounted within the shells, including geothermal, life-form, communications, and radiation scanners.

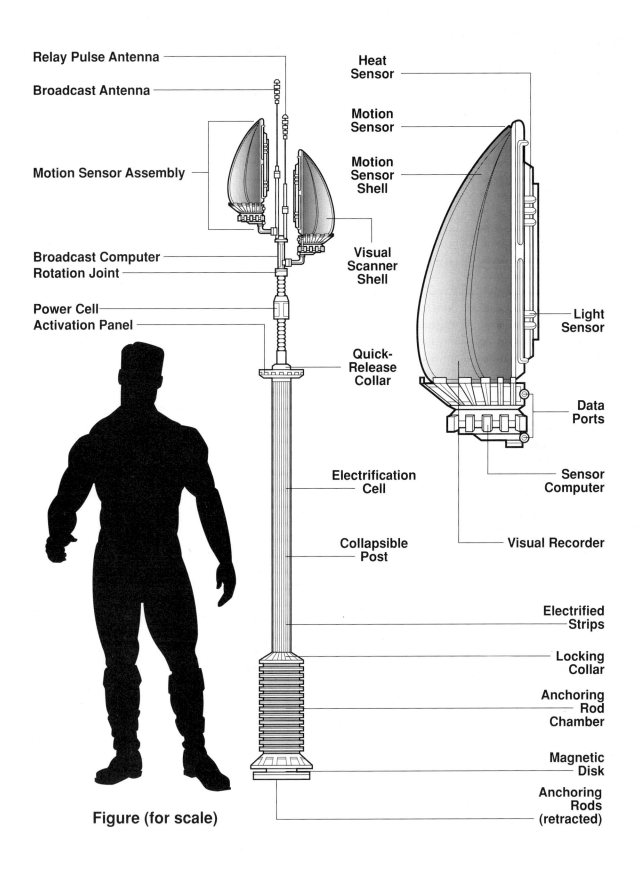

Relay Pulse Antenna

Broadcast Antenna

Motion Sensor Assembly

Broadcast Computer
Rotation Joint

Power Cell
Activation Panel

Heat Sensor

Motion Sensor

Motion Sensor Shell

Visual Scanner Shell

Quick-Release Collar

Electrification Cell

Collapsible Post

Light Sensor

Data Ports

Sensor Computer

Visual Recorder

Electrified Strips

Locking Collar

Anchoring Rod Chamber

Magnetic Disk

Anchoring Rods (retracted)

Figure (for scale)

SENSOR JAMMERS

MIRADYNE 4X-PHANTOM SHORT-RANGE SENSOR JAMMER
KUAT DRIVE YARDS 220-SIG TACTICAL COMBAT JAMMER

The ability to prevent the enemy from gathering intelligence about one's forces can be a significant factor in achieving victory. Sensor jammers accomplish this by producing broad-spectrum bursts that block sensor readings. While jammers affect all ships in the area—friendly and enemy vessels—they can provide a major obstacle for attacking enemy pilots, who often know little of the battle zone or the strength and composition of enemy forces.

Most starfighters carry small, short-range jammers designed to throw off concussion missiles and proton torpedoes, and the A-wing is one of the few fighters to carry a full-fledged jamming unit, a high-output Miradyne 4x-Phantom. The 4x-Phantom's main jammer is a dedicated-energy receptor (DER) projector that absorbs and blocks long-range sensor pulses, hiding the fighter as it closes in on its target. Once the enemy is engaged, the jammer's full-spectrum distortion projector uses broadband emissions to block *all* scanners and targeting computers.

Rounding out the 4x-Phantom's sensor suite is a row of static discharge panels that scramble comm and subspace frequencies, cutting off communications for all ships in the area. (A-wing squadrons normally preplan breaks in comm jamming to allow for their own periodic communications.)

The 4x-Phantom is perfectly suited for the A-wing's primary mis-sion profile: sudden interceptor strikes against cargo freighters and other light craft. By overlapping jamming fields, A-wings can completely block a target's distress signals.

Perhaps the most powerful jamming systems ever built were the hundreds of Kuat Drive Yards 220-SIG tactical jammers aboard the Death Star space stations. Each jamming emplacement's directional dish allowed concentrated jamming along specific vectors, creating narrow zones of interference while leaving most of the Death Star's sensor arrays clear to gather data.

During the Battle of Yavin, the Death Star's 220-SIG units interfered with the sensors and targeting computers aboard the Rebel Alliance's fighters, although they couldn't block Luke Skywalker, who used only visual targeting and scored the vital hit that destroyed the Death Star.

At the Battle of Endor the Second Death Star's jamming units blinded Alliance sensors, and only Lando Calrissian's last-second command to break off the attack prevented the Rebel fighter fleet from colliding with the battle station's invisible energy shield. The Death Star's jamming also prevented the Alliance's capital ships from detecting the Imperial fleet, which was orbiting on the far side of the forest moon. This allowed Star Destroyers to outflank the Rebels in a pincer movement that cut off their escape route during the last great battle of the Galactic Civil War.

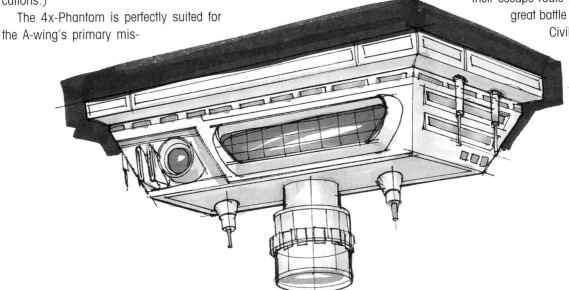

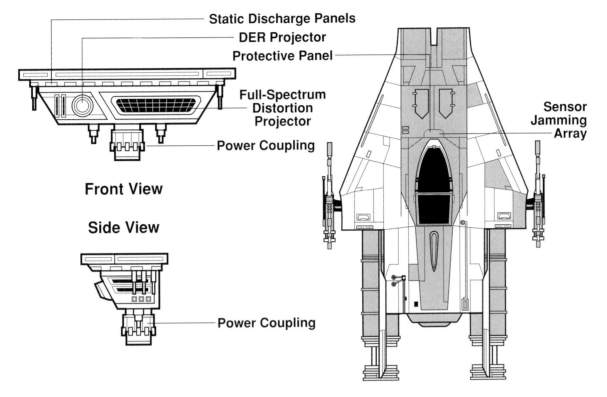

Static Discharge Panels

DER Projector

Protective Panel

Full-Spectrum Distortion Projector

Power Coupling

Sensor Jamming Array

Front View

Side View

Power Coupling

A-Wing Fighter with Sensor Jammer

Sensor Jamming Tower

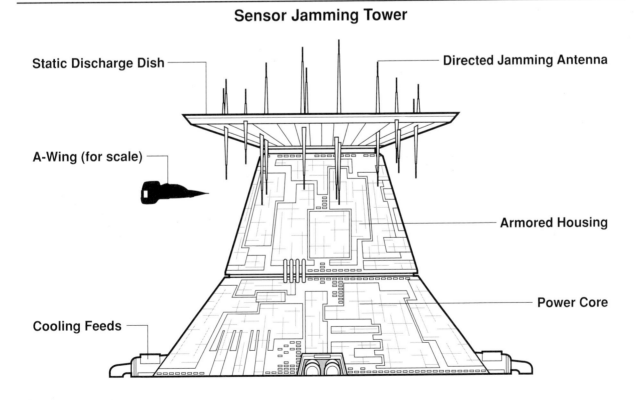

Static Discharge Dish

Directed Jamming Antenna

A-Wing (for scale)

Armored Housing

Power Core

Cooling Feeds

HOMING BEACON

NEURO-SAAV XXT-26 S-THREAD TRACKER

A military homing beacon is a small device that can be hidden aboard a starship. It emits a signal from its internal hyperspace transponder, allowing the "bugged" vessel to be tracked as it crosses the galaxy. While very expensive, a homing beacon can reveal the target ship's exact movements, which in turn can reveal the locations of enemy bases and fleet rendezvous points.

A homing beacon works by interacting with the HoloNet, a network that stretches throughout the galaxy and consists of hundreds of thousands of satellites that transmit messages through hyperspace. Each homing beacon's short-burst, coded hyperspace signal is recorded whenever it crosses a HoloNet communication signal known as an S-thread. Since a ship traveling in hyperspace normally crosses at least one S-thread per hour, a homing beacon can be used to track a ship to almost any system within the boundaries of the New Republic.

The signal is automatically logged into the HoloNet and forwarded to the beacon's control computer. After receiving the signal, the control computer knows the ship's location and can determine possible destination systems. When the ship leaves hyperspace, the beacon automatically broadcasts a location update that is accurate to within one parsec.

While extremely expensive, hyperspace homing beacons can play a vital role in intelligence gathering. After Rebel spies stole the

technical readouts of the Death Star battle station, an Imperial homing beacon hidden aboard Princess Leia Organa's Rebel Blockade Runner, the *Tantive IV*, allowed the Imperial Star Destroyer *Devastator* to follow the ship to Tatooine and capture it before Leia could deliver the plans to Obi-Wan Kenobi. After the *Millennium Falcon* was captured by the Death Star, Darth Vader had an Imperial XX-23 homing beacon hidden inside the smuggling freighter, and the beacon's signal led the Empire right to the main Rebel base on Yavin Four.

Like the Imperial XX-23, the Neuro-Saav XXt-26 is a small, lightweight homing beacon. Its narrow-beam hyperspace transponder signal is configured to blend into the ship's "background noise" (caused by drive emissions), making it virtually undetectable except by dedicated communications scanners. The assassin droid IG-88 hid two Neuro-Saav XXt-26 transmitters aboard Boba Fett's *Slave I* and tracked the ship to Tatooine. IG-88 sought to steal the carbonite-encased Han Solo, but Fett outsmarted the assassin droid and claimed Jabba the Hutt's bounty on Solo.

Subspace transmitters offer an alternative to the hyperspace-capable beacon, broadcasting a homing signal on standard subspace frequencies and allowing the targeted vessel to be tracked as it moves from system to system. While subspace beacons have transmission ranges of only twenty to fifty light-years, they are much cheaper and can be more easily tracked, since most vessels have subspace transponders as standard equipment.

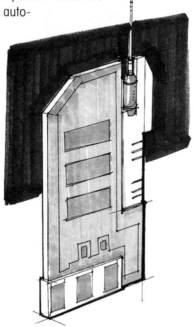

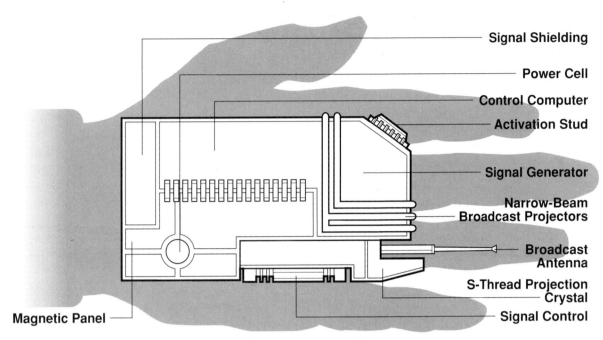

Signal Shielding

Power Cell

Control Computer

Activation Stud

Signal Generator

Narrow-Beam
Broadcast Projectors

Broadcast
Antenna

S-Thread Projection
Crystal

Signal Control

Magnetic Panel

Homing Beacon with Hand (for scale)

Slave I with Planted Homing Beacon

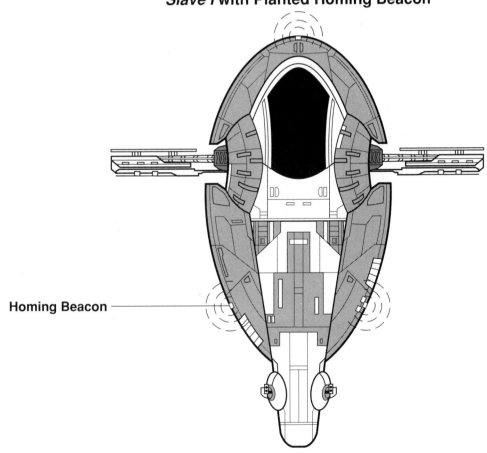

Homing Beacon

COMLINKS

SoroSuub C1 Personal Comlink
Crozo Industrial Products 3-MAL Personal Comlink
Fabritech PAC20 Visual Wrist Comm

Personal comlinks are standard communication devices used throughout the galaxy. Most vehicles and starships have long-range comlinks or comm units, and many planetary comm grids use similar technologies to provide entertainment and news, handle financial transactions, and carry personal messages and computer data transfers.

The two most popular personal comlink designs utilize small handheld cylinders and lightweight headset units. These audio-only communications devices have a range of fifty kilometers, enough to reach ships in low orbit under favorable weather conditions. Comlinks can be adjusted to operate on any of the millions of broadcast frequency and cycle combinations. They also monitor "Standard Clear Frequencies" (SCFs), which are used to broadcast civil defense warnings and provide information about pertinent local laws and nearby medical, educational, and governmental facilities.

Both the SoroSuub C1 and the Crozo Industrial Products 3-MAL are military-issue comlinks. Their features include limited encryption modules to prevent eavesdropping. The SoroSuub C1 was used widely by Imperial Army and Navy troops, while the 3-MAL was issued to the Rebel Alliance's naval troops and ground forces at Hoth, Yavin Four, and other bases.

Military comlinks are increasingly being mounted in lightweight headsets or inside helmets or sewn into wrist pads or chest panels for easier access and to reduce the odds of being dropped or crushed in battle. New comlink designs have better encryption systems, more reliable components, and greater tolerance for extreme conditions. Whereas Luke Skywalker and Han Solo nearly died on the frozen plains of Hoth because their comlinks were disabled by the severe cold, modern units are much more likely to survive this type of environment.

Stormtrooper helmets included sophisticated SoroSuub DH77 or Herzfall Corporation DH107 comlinks, which use linked encoding sequences to change frequencies every few seconds while keeping all soldiers in the unit synchronized. If a stormtrooper's helmet is removed without the soldier first hitting the comlink's control stud, the frequency coding routine is automatically deleted from that helmet.

The Fabritech PAC20, which was carried by the smuggler Dash Rendar, combines standard audio comlink functions with a screen for video transmission and data displays. The PAC20's internal computer can link to a datapad or droid, while the power cell allows a broadcast range of seventy-five kilometers.

Vehicle and backpack comlinks have larger energy cells and more powerful transmitters with broadcast ranges sometimes exceeding two hundred kilometers.

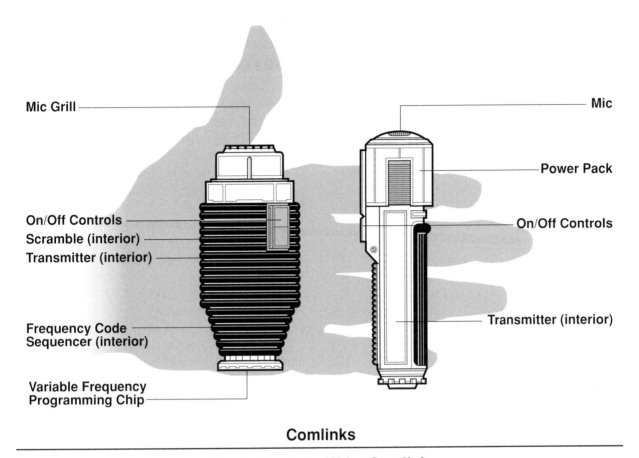

Mic Grill

On/Off Controls

Scramble (interior)

Transmitter (interior)

Frequency Code
Sequencer (interior)

Variable Frequency
Programming Chip

Mic

Power Pack

On/Off Controls

Transmitter (interior)

Comlinks

Dash Rendar's Wrist Comlink

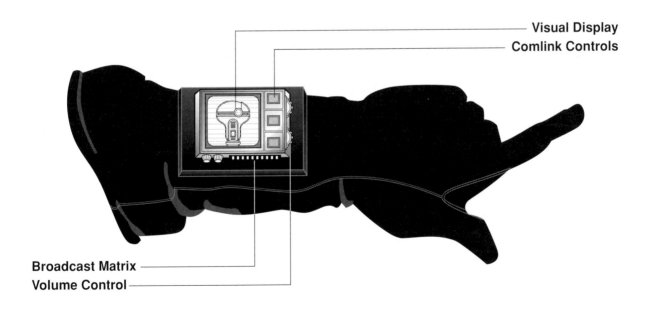

Visual Display

Comlink Controls

Broadcast Matrix

Volume Control

CYBERNETIC IMPLANT COMLINK/PAGER

CROZO INDUSTRIAL PRODUCTS AT-CYB HUSHER MIKE

Internal comlinks are among the most popular and practical cybernetic implants. Subdermal transmitters and receivers allow silent and unobservable comlink transmissions, making these tools useful for any number of activities, both legal and illicit.

The Crozo At-cyb husher mike is a small, self-contained comlink transmitter. The husher mike is surgically implanted near the subject's larynx, with additional microsensors placed inside the mouth. The user subvocalizes messages by subtly duplicating jaw, tongue, and vocal cord speech movements. This technique produces virtually no sound and minimal visible movement, and so observers are unlikely to notice the subvocalization process.

The husher mike translates these movements into electrical impulses, which are converted by short-range transponders into a standard comlink transmission. This signal can be received by any comlink within three kilometers that is set to the correct broadcast frequency. Although the user must carry a comlink or tiny audio transmitter to receive messages, the husher mike allows the user to circumvent audio surveillance systems, or "sound snoopers," such as those that were used to spy on local citizens during Imperial occupations. However, the comlink transmissions *are* susceptible to interception by military-grade communications scanners.

The basic At-cyb husher mike implant has externally visible transmitters and costs three thousand credits. For an additional two thousand credits an upgraded mike with an encryption module for scrambling messages can be placed entirely beneath the skin, making it detectable only with medical or weapons scanners.

Howzmin, former chief of palace security for the Falleen Prince Xizor, had a similar communications implant, a BioTech Com623. Howzmin was often regarded as seeming somewhat distanced, a quality that could be attributed to the fact that he was often silently receiving messages from his master via his one-way receiver implant.

Yet another standard comlink implant combines both broadcast *and* reception capabilities. Utilizing units such as the Traxes BioElectronics implant communicator, users can broadcast messages through subvocalization techniques, while comlink messages coded to the implant's frequency can be received automatically. Only medical scanners can detect this unit, which is implanted inside the user's head, completely hidden from view. This type of implant is just as susceptible to jamming as is any other comlink, and so users may suffer excruciating pain if their frequencies are jammed.

All such implants were originally designed for hands-free, noiseless communication to aid mining crews and space-dock repair techs, but they have been adopted for espionage and criminal enterprises. For example, a pair of gamblers and con men named Jaboth and Dereth made a fortune by using these devices to exchange messages illegally during high-stakes Helcos and sabacc tournaments.

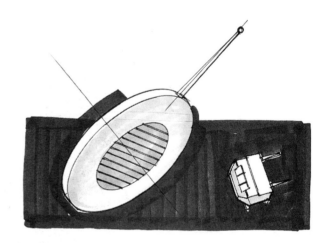

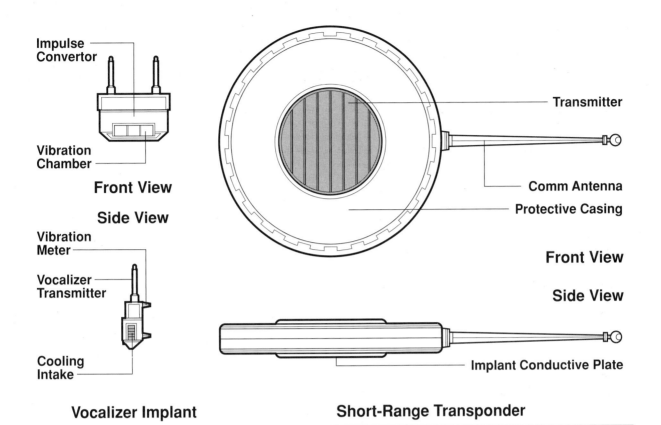

Impulse Convertor

Vibration Chamber

Front View

Side View

Vibration Meter

Vocalizer Transmitter

Cooling Intake

Transmitter

Comm Antenna

Protective Casing

Front View

Side View

Implant Conductive Plate

Vocalizer Implant

Short-Range Transponder

Cybernetic Implant Placement

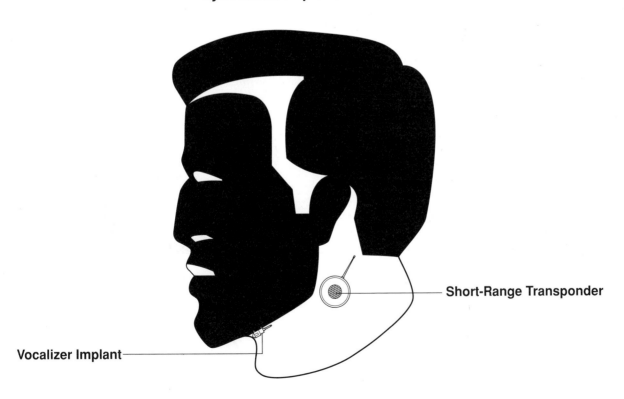

Short-Range Transponder

Vocalizer Implant

SUBSPACE TRANSCEIVERS

CHEDAK FREQUENCY AGILE SUBSPACE TRANSCEIVER

Subspace transceivers are standard devices used for instantaneous, faster-than-light communications between nearby systems. Starships carry these units to broadcast distress signals and other emergency messages. Planetary subspace transceivers normally are connected to sophisticated intersector communications networks.

The *Millennium Falcon* has a relatively common Chedak Frequency Agile subspace transceiver equipped with a Carbanti Whistler encryption module, although Han Solo uses this unit sparingly since subspace messages can be intercepted by any vessel within the transceiver's considerable broadcast range. The unit has audio and video pickups, while an interface port connects it to the *Falcon*'s three droid brain controllers and the heavily modified Hanx-Wargel SuperFlow IV computer, allowing for the transfer of navigation logs, recordings, and technical records.

The transceiver's subspace antenna has twelve kilometers of tightly wound, ultrathin superconducting wire that allows it to achieve a broadcast range of approximately forty light-years, and the receiver automatically monitors standard clear frequencies for distress signals and hailing messages from nearby vessels.

New Republic X-wings carry miniaturized Chedak Sprite subspace transmitters to broadcast distress signals up to a range of twenty-five light-years. In contrast, an Imperial Star Destroyer's Sienar Fleet Systems Ranger transceiver has a transmission range of one hundred light-years. The receiver can monitor more than three hundred different subspace frequencies simultaneously; by altering frequencies every tenth of a second, the Ranger scans the entire subspace spectrum in less than three hours. The powerful com-scan encryption computer can decode most intercepted messages within minutes.

Many planetary governments, large corporations, and wealthy individuals maintain private subspace transceivers. Most planets are integrated into local subspace networks that use subspace transceivers aboard deep-space satellites to link dozens of worlds in an instantaneous and continuous flow of data. These networks normally handle news, sports, entertainment, and educational programming. Individuals and corporations purchase broadcast time for private messages, with fees running anywhere from one to twenty credits per ten seconds of transmission time.

Hundreds of subspace networks are scattered across the New Republic, and so a message theoretically can be sent across the galaxy by bouncing it across multiple networks. While this process is much more affordable than using the HoloNet, subspace messages may be delayed for hours or days as they are routed through different networks. Because there are different communications protocols for each network, messages also may be corrupted or lost, and so it often is safer and cheaper to send long-distance messages by courier ships.

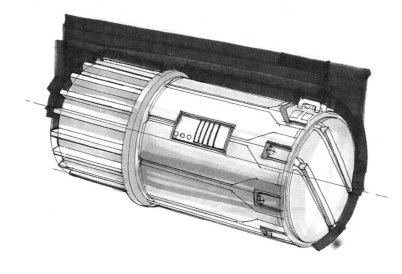

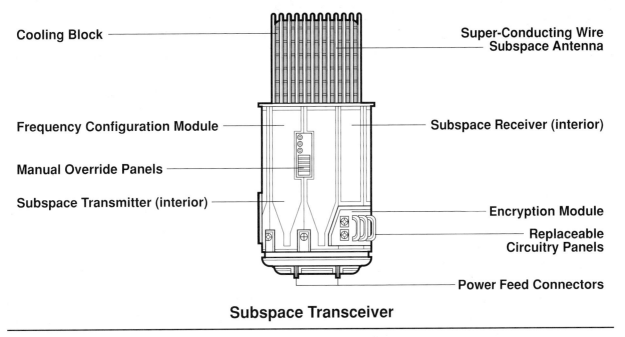

Cooling Block

Super-Conducting Wire
Subspace Antenna

Frequency Configuration Module

Subspace Receiver (interior)

Manual Override Panels

Subspace Transmitter (interior)

Encryption Module

Replaceable
Circuitry Panels

Power Feed Connectors

Subspace Transceiver

Millennium Falcon Cutaway

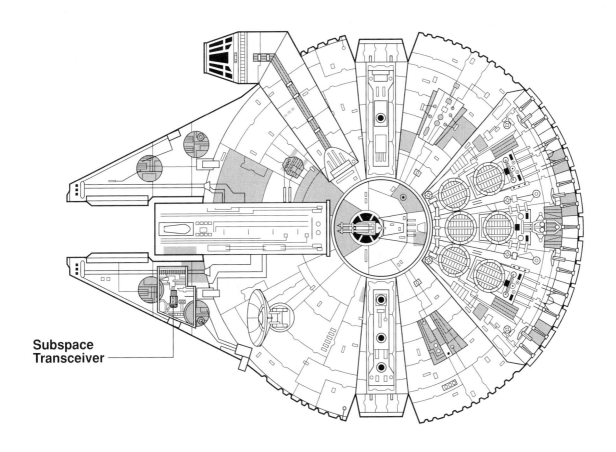

Subspace
Transceiver

HOLONET TRANSCEIVER

SoroSuub Hologram Projection Pod

The HoloNet is the most sophisticated communications system in the galaxy. HoloNet transceivers offer direct access to this network and enable users to broadcast instantly holographic messages to any world with its own transceiver.

All but the most remote New Republic planets have at least one HoloNet transceiver, and many capital ships, such as Star Destroyers and Mon Calamari Star Cruisers, carry their own transceivers for sensitive military communications. Standard hologram pods—such as the ones that were found aboard the bridge of the Super Star Destroyer *Executor* and in Darth Vader's private quarters—are used to broadcast and receive HoloNet messages.

The HoloNet itself consists of a network of hundreds of thousands of satellites that relay and boost messages through hyperspace. These signals are broadcast along channels called S-threads, which handle an incredible volume of data. The system is quite secure because of the very narrow bandwidth of HoloNet signals: it is almost impossible to intercept these messages while they are in transit, although tight security must be maintained around HoloNet transceivers themselves to prevent them from being bugged.

First built by decree of the Republic Senate, the HoloNet was regarded as one of the great achievements of the Old Republic. With the system in place, any citizen on any world could observe Senate pro-

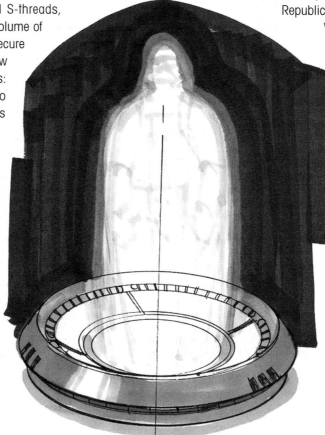

ceedings, view great works of art, or call up any information stored in the galaxy's great data libraries.

When Emperor Palpatine seized power, he knew that controlling the free flow of information would be essential. If he manipulated his citizens by allowing only official Imperial propaganda to reach them, his Empire would be welcomed. To achieve that objective, Palpatine quickly dismantled most of the HoloNet, limiting it to Imperial military use. During the war against the Rebel Alliance one of the Empire's greatest advantages was that its forces could instantly communicate with each other, while the Rebels had to rely on personal couriers to relay messages.

With the rise of the New Republic, one of the top priorities has been the restoration of the HoloNet system. Both a practical and a symbolic measure, the rebuilding of the HoloNet has proved to many member worlds that the New Republic truly stands for the ideals of the Old Republic, representing the needs of all.

While the HoloNet is an incredibly powerful communications medium, it is also staggeringly expensive to maintain. As a result of the ongoing war against Imperial remnants, most of the HoloNet's capacity is reserved for New Republic military and governmental use, although educational, cultural, and entertainment programming is carried as space becomes available. Fees for private users run into the thousands of credits per second, placing HoloNet access out of reach for all but the wealthiest citizens and corporations.

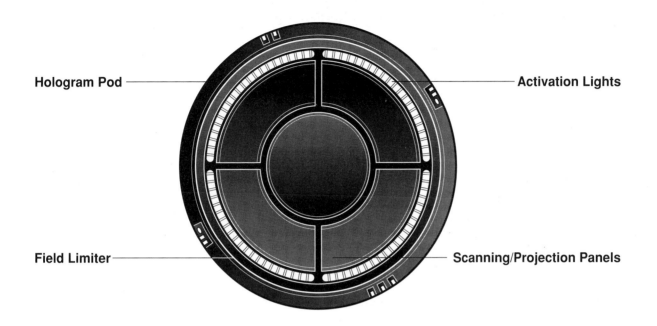

Hologram Pod

Activation Lights

Field Limiter

Scanning/Projection Panels

Top View

Side View

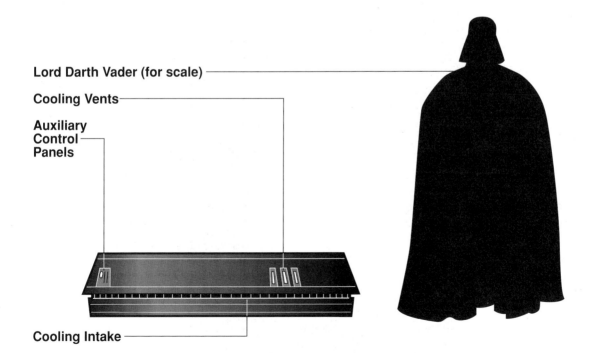

Lord Darth Vader (for scale)

Cooling Vents

Auxiliary Control Panels

Cooling Intake

SECURITY DEVICES

Security systems have advanced radically since the days when they consisted of armed lookouts, guard beasts, and simple mechanical locks. Modern governments, businesses, and private citizens can choose from a bewildering array of devices designed to protect property and sensitive information. Security measures are found in military bases, corporate complexes, prisons, research labs, government buildings, and personal residences.

Just as modern technology has been applied to develop more dangerous weapons and better sensor systems, advanced technical knowledge has been used to create more sophisticated (and often more deadly) security measures to frustrate the efforts of thieves, slicers, and other intruders. These systems are broken down into two primary categories: passive and active. A supplemental section concerns restraint systems for prisoner security. Finally, there are also specialty devices for *circumventing* even the most advanced security measures and for aiding espionage agents and criminals.

PASSIVE SECURITY SYSTEMS

"Passive" security systems take no direct physical action to restrain intruders. Since security systems must take into account the capabilities of a multitude of alien species, many facilities use a combination of sensors and devices to protect themselves.

A facility's most basic passive measure is its physical structure. Armor can negate attacks from vehicles, starships, and commando teams. Most often, this armor consists of permacrete or reinforced durasteel plating, and some buildings use extremely expensive molecularly bond-ed armor plating powerful enough to withstand sustained attacks from turbolaser batteries and proton torpedoes.

Some buildings supplement armor plating with force field projectors with dedicated power generators in order to thwart sabotage. Many buildings use reinforced walls and transparisteel windows as interior section dividers, thus requiring attackers to cut through several layers of security just to reach vital areas.

Complicated electronic security locks or identity passcode cards will control and regulate entry to secured buildings. Access is denied to those who cannot produce an authorized code. Scanners are commonly used to detect and record the actions of intruders. Infrared, visual, and audio scanners allow users to watch over a large area, and their control computers can sound alarms automatically if a trespasser is detected.

Other types of scanner alarms may be tripped by fluctuations in heat or movement within restricted areas. Communications scanners can be used to detect unauthorized comlink transmissions, while energy scanners are programmed to discover energy emissions indicative of weapon power packs. Some buildings also employ surveillance droids that conduct roving patrols or establish control checkpoints, although these droids cannot take direct action against intruders.

Most computer systems are protected by complex security programs designed to block intrusions by slicers while allowing *authorized* users to access confidential data. Most systems require legitimate users to enter a pass code or slide an identity card through a scanner upon logging in, although likely espionage targets—such as government computers and those of military contractors—may require retinal scans, voice recognition checks, or other confirmation scans before granting access to users. Even if a slicer does manage to force his or her way inside a computer system, antislicer programs can cut off access automatically as soon as the slicer trips any of the many "trip wires" programmed into the system.

ACTIVE SECURITY SYSTEMS

"Active" security systems take direct action to block or restrain trespassers. The most common approach is the use of guards who are armed with blasters and who may patrol corridors, supervise checkpoints, and maintain perimeter security. Guards customarily are given authorization to use any amount of force necessary to prevent the theft of goods or information. Armed security droids and trained guard beasts also may be employed.

Buildings also may be equipped with any of a number of permanent active security measures. Energy fences can be charged to zap intruders with the equivalent of a blaster rifle bolt. Automated laser traps may be placed at checkpoints and other sensitive areas. They activate as soon as an alarm sounds and can accurately target intruders and down them with blasters. Stun blasters may be used to fire nonlethal stun blasts; the stunned targets are then rounded up by living security guards.

Like laser traps, gas dispensers activate as soon as unauthorized personnel are detected in a secure area. They can release a wide variety of agents, ranging from relatively harmless stun gases to lethal nerve agents that can kill within seconds.

Less dangerous capture methods may include electrified floor and wall panels, tangle traps, stun fields, and reversed repulsorfields (also known as man traps). These measures normally are left activated at all times; they shut down only when an authorized pass code has been punched in by authorized personnel. To improve their effectiveness, these systems often are hidden.

PRISONER CONTROL MEASURES

Prisoner control measures range from conventional binders to high-security energy cages, such as those used by the Empire to hold captive Jedi Knights. Most prisons employed a number of traditional passive and active security measures to keep prisoners secured.

Many prisons employ sophisticated scanners to control access to different portions of the facility and to protect personnel from attacks by prisoners. Most prisons have computerized control systems with emergency overrides, allowing officials to lock down an entire facility when the need arises.

Commonly used personal restraint devices include binders, stun cuffs, and slaving collars. These units can be linked to remote controllers. The Empire was particularly fond of implanting explosives or poisons in remotely controlled collars so that escaped prisoners could be "dealt with" in short order.

Facilitywide confinement tools often include tamperproof security locks, reinforced walls and windows, and weapons scanners. Armed guards and security droids often are equipped with portable scanners during their regular patrols. Most prison security checkpoints are built to include hidden shock panels, force field projectors, and automated laser traps.

Despotic governments such as the Empire and the Corporate Sector Authority often coerced prisoners into revealing sensitive information through the use of intimidation and torture. They had many tools at their disposal, including energy prods, interrogation and truth drugs, torture droids, and nerve disrupters. While the New Republic has taken a firm stand against the use of such methods, these goods are still manufactured in secret and often are used by criminals and Imperial remnant worlds. These organizations also employ brainwashing and indoctrination, sometimes programming instructions into a prisoner's subconscious through the use of hypno-imprinting. This technique was used on many captured Rebel agents, who were released and then found their way back to Rebel bases. The hypno-imprinting forced those Rebels to spy for the Empire without knowing that they were betraying the Alliance.

SECURITY COUNTERMEASURES

For those who want to evade a building's security systems, there are many countermeasures devices available to those with enough credits. Perhaps the greatest factor brought into play for bypassing security systems is reliable intelligence. Agents can review plans and surveillance data, plant hidden transmitters, or bribe personnel to detail a building's security systems. With the right information an intruder will often slip undetected around scanners and other security measures.

Security scanners also can be bypassed via stolen authorization codes and falsified access cards. A number of devices can falsify retinal, dermatoglyphic, or genetic samples. Agents can use electronic lock breakers to defeat computerized locks, while portable scanners and infrared imagers can detect invisible scanning beams. By accessing a facility's computer network, an intruder may knock sensors off-line to allow unrestricted movement. Portable computers and slicing spikes are used to disable computer security programs for a few moments at a time, allowing slicers to get inside a computer network, steal the desired data, and get out before anybody realizes what has happened.

STUN CUFFS

Locris Syndicated Securities SC-401 Stun Cuffs

Binders, magnacuffs, and stun cuffs are common and cost-effective prisoner restraint devices used throughout the galaxy.

Binders are standard durasteel cuffs equipped with simple mechanical locks, key-code chip readers, or identity scanners. When Luke Skywalker and Han Solo staged their reckless attack on Death Star Detention Block AA-23, they restrained Chewbacca with durasteel binders, leaving the lock open so that the Wookiee could "break free." As planned, this ploy caused considerable confusion, giving the trio time to dispatch the Imperial guards and destroy the holocam monitors, automated laser cannons, and other security devices in the detention block.

Magnacuffs are similar to standard binders, but with added micromagnetic fields that lock the restraining bands in place. Magnacuff locks normally are controlled with coded data chips or use scanners that are programmed to recognize authorized fingerprints.

Stun cuffs are reserved for prisoners who are considered severe security risks. They have all the features of standard magnacuffs, plus a remotely controlled electrical stun system used to restrain and control detainees.

Locris Syndicated Securities SC-401 stun cuffs are made of reinforced durasteel that can contain a Wookiee's remarkable strength. The variable-size binders can be adjusted to accommodate a wide variety of species and automatically tighten if the prisoner tries to maneuver his or her hands out of the binders; they can cut off the prisoner's circulation completely if he or she persists in escape attempts. The restraints and locks are reinforced by channeled magnetic fields that effectively triple the strength of the durasteel. Stun filaments lining the interior of each cuff release paralyzing jolts of energy when activated via the remote control unit. Low-power settings merely cause pain, but a full-power blast can knock a prisoner unconscious.

The remote control unit has a keypad and a small read-out screen and can direct up to forty pairs of stun cuffs. The unit has a broadcast range of fifty meters, although stun cuffs often are set to shock the prisoner automatically if he or she moves more than ten meters away from the controller. The control unit allows the user to adjust both the intensity of the stun charge and the tension control used to determine the acceptable amount of resistance permitted from the prisoner before the cuffs tighten.

A seven-digit master code must be entered into the remote control before the stun cuff locks can be opened, and command codes can be reprogrammed on an as-needed basis. With a price of one hundred credits per pair of cuffs and five hundred credits for the remote controller, stun cuffs offer a high level of security at a very modest price.

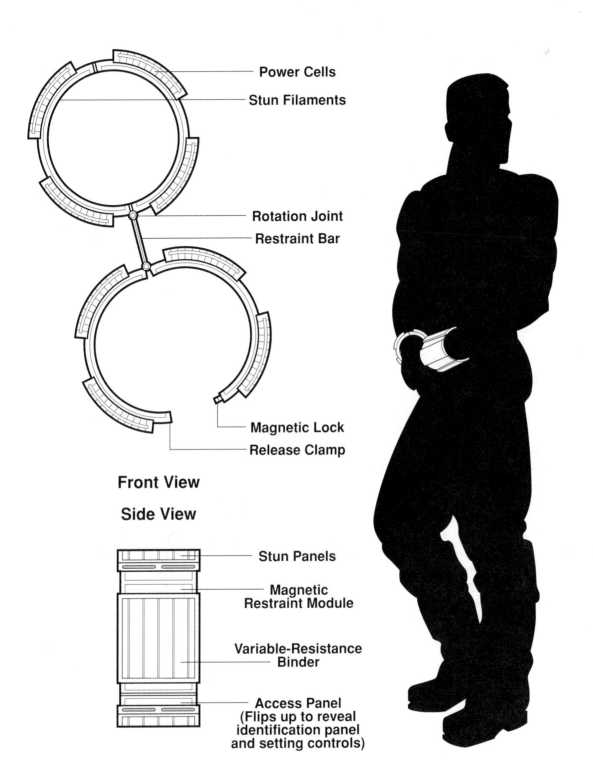

Power Cells

Stun Filaments

Rotation Joint

Restraint Bar

Magnetic Lock

Release Clamp

Front View

Side View

Stun Panels

Magnetic
Restraint Module

Variable-Resistance
Binder

Access Panel
(Flips up to reveal
identification panel
and setting controls)

STUN NETS

GOLAN ARMS RL-40 STUN NET LAUNCHER

During the Republic Scouting Service's many exploration missions—from Halka Four-Den's ill-fated expedition to Dagobah to the perilous cataloging of life-forms native to Kashyyyk's lower levels—stun nets were the preferred method of allowing the explorers to capture newly discovered animals for study with minimum risk to the scouting team.

Since that time these tools have been adopted for less admirable applications. Big-game hunters use them to capture trophy animals without marring their pelts, and the nets can be rigged as security devices to protect military encampments. Slavers and kidnappers use them to capture sentient targets—uninjured, so as to not reduce their market value—while bounty hunters often carry one or two stun nets for postings that offer a bonus for live delivery.

Stun nets are made of tough duracord covered with a conductive liquid adhesive. Stun threads and beads woven throughout the netting deliver paralyzing electrical shock charges, while the adhesive traps the target within the net. The net can be set to activate its charge upon contact with any creature, or a handheld control unit with a range of fifty meters can be used to handle all functions, including the adjusting of the shock charge's intensity.

Stun nets sometimes are

packed in canisters for use with specialty net launchers such as the Golan Arms RL-40 pistol. The net automatically activates upon launch and quickly unfurls to its full 2.5-meter diameter, traveling its thirty-meter range in less than half a second. The net wraps around the target on contact, forming a tight stun cocoon that is almost impossible to escape from. The stun charge ceases as soon as the target stops moving. (It is believed that this weapon inspired the development of Stokhli spray sticks, which deliver similar electrical stun charges but use a spraynet mist to achieve a much greater range.)

The stun net's intensity ranges from a light charge for subduing small game to full-power jolts that can down gundarks and dewbacks or kill humans. The RL-40 commands a price of five hundred credits, while canisters with ten nets cost fifty credits each, making this tool a relatively inexpensive but potent nonlethal capture device.

A larger version of the RL-40 is the Golan Arms RGL-80A electronet grenade launcher, which has an optimum range of 350 meters and a maximum range of 500 meters. Its small magazine holds five electronet grenades. Each net's stun intensity is adjusted by a remote control unit.

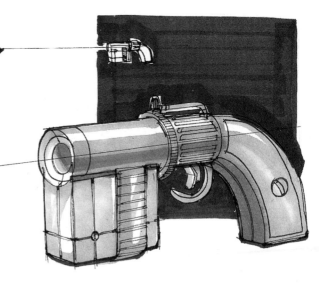

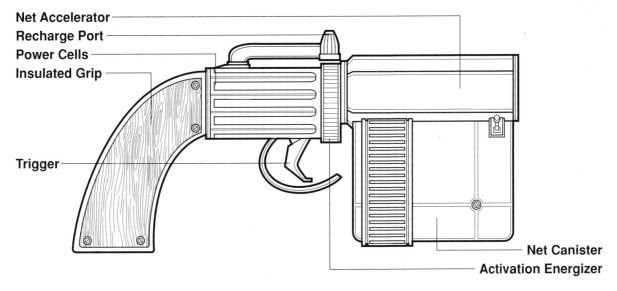

Net Accelerator

Recharge Port

Power Cells

Insulated Grip

Trigger

Net Canister

Activation Energizer

Stun Net Launcher

Stun Net

Anchors

Stun Threads

Figure (for scale)

Stun Bead

Stun Field
Generator
(in center)

SLAVING COLLARS

MODIFIED THALASSIAN SECURITY COLLAR

Slaving collars are the tools of a despicable trade in which living beings have no value beyond the number of credits they can command on the auction block. In the past, these devices were widely used in slaving rings and Imperial labor camps to shackle the millions of Wookiees, Mon Calamarians, and other aliens who bore the brunt of the Empire's cruelty. Though the New Republic has outlawed slaving, the vile commerce continues in dangerous criminal havens. Remnants of the infamous Thalassian and Zygerian slavers' guilds provide a steady stream of victims to the Hutt crime families and other ruthless groups. Since slaving collars are illegal in most systems, they must be purchased on the black market or built in back-alley shops.

Slaving collars consist of adjustable neck, arm, or leg braces. Heavy chains or conductive cables link multiple collars together and can be used to confine the slaves to a specific area. Most slaving collars are made of reinforced durasteel and may include shock panels that deliver painful electrical charges.

Jabba the Hutt was fond of using slaving collars and chains to keep his dancing girls within easy reach. For a time, even a captive Princess Leia Organa endured the gangster's affections, knowing that she would be fed to the rancor or subjected to painful shock charges delivered through her slaving collar if she resisted. Leia's chance to escape finally came during the mission to rescue Han Solo. While most of Jabba's minions battled Luke Skywalker, Leia took advantage of the confusion and strangled Jabba with her slaving chain, all the while preventing him from reaching the collar's shock controller. No one noticed her treachery until after she was cut free by R2-D2 and escaped.

Han Solo encountered slavers using these devices when he agreed to a contraband pickup on the planet Lur. It had been kept from him that the "cargo" was a group of Lurrian slaves, and Zlarb, the lead slaver, threatened Solo and Chewbacca with death if they did not cooperate. The Lurrians themselves knew they would suffer excruciating shocks from their collars if they offered the slightest provocation.

However, Zlarb underestimated the resourcefulness of Han Solo's two companion droids, Bollux and Blue Max, who surreptitiously activated the *Falcon*'s fire control system. While gouts of fire-suppressing foam sprayed the freighter's interior, Solo, Chewbacca, and the slaves subdued Zlarb and his men, although many Lurrians died during the struggle. As Solo and Chewbacca blasted off from Lur, Zlarb and his henchmen discovered the other side of the slaving trade when they were bound in their own collars and left in the hands of the newly freed and rather vengeful Lurrians.

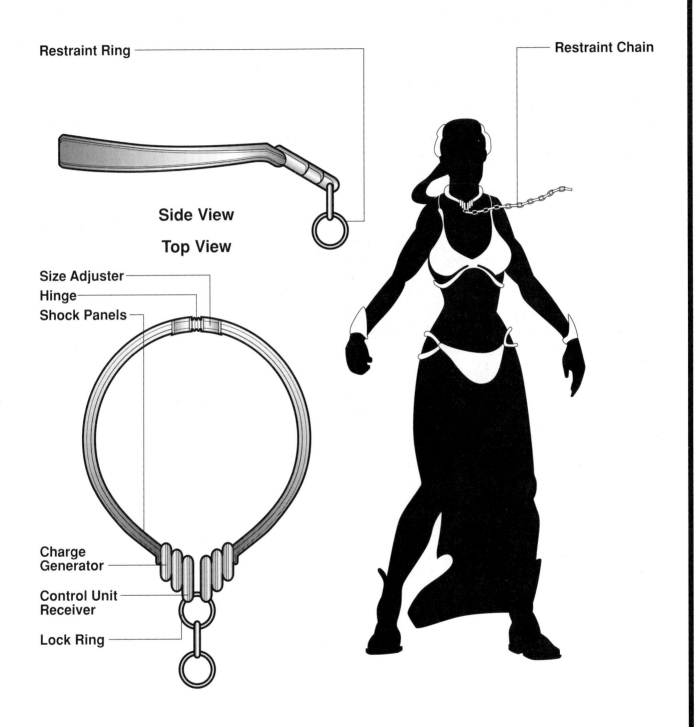

Restraint Ring

Restraint Chain

Side View

Top View

Size Adjuster

Hinge

Shock Panels

Charge
Generator

Control Unit
Receiver

Lock Ring

NERVE DISRUPTOR

ARAKYD AGONIZER-6 NERVE DISRUPTOR

Whereas the Old Republic was founded on the principles of justice and the rule of law, the Empire was concerned only with holding power by any available means, including intimidation and torture. Under Imperial rule, there was intense demand for interrogation droids and torture units of all kinds. The Arakyd Agonizer-6 nerve disruptor was one of many such devices.

The Agonizer-6 is a small device sporting a Cybot Galactica AI-4 droid brain and several microfilament injectors. The AI-4 droid brain is fully functional, with a vocoder for speech, audio sensors, and a data port for linking with

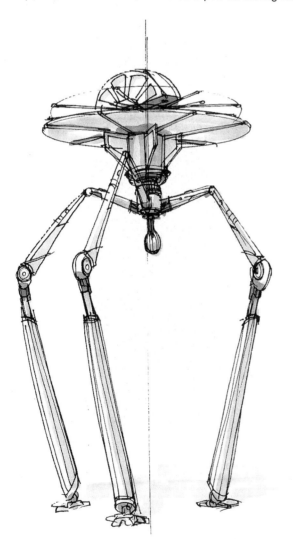

other droids and computers. Unlike other droids, which often have rather elaborate personality modules, the AI-4 is coldly impersonal and is interested only in completing its duties. This contrasts with droids in similar positions, such as Imperial interrogation units, which tend to have decidedly sadistic temperaments.

In each assignment, the Agonizer-6 assesses the current subject's condition, taking into account any distress or injuries remaining from previous interrogation sessions. During questioning sessions, the droid brain closely monitors heartbeat, respiration, nerve functions, and other life indicators, but instead of extending life, it pushes the victim to his or her physical and mental limits. Microfilament injectors dispense pain and truth drugs, while stimulators trigger particularly sensitive nerve clusters, causing tingling, aches, pain, or uncontrollable spasms.

Other nerve stimulation methods can be used to induce altered states of consciousness, ranging from euphoria, relaxation, and bliss to panic, fear, and uncontrolled terror. By artificially enhancing these emotional states, the torturers attack and eventually destroy the victim's mental defenses. Once the will is broken, not only is the victim more likely to reveal everything, but the droid brain can then begin hypno-indoctrination and imprinting sessions to implant subconscious orders and posthypnotic commands. Naturally, the droid implants a suicide command that will activate if this subconscious brainwashing is discovered.

While the Agonizer-6 is no longer manufactured under New Republic law, this nerve disruptor has been found in Imperial prisons and labor camps across the galaxy. Jabba the Hutt acquired one of these devices and used it to coax information from spies his men had captured. He nearly uncovered vital Rebel Alliance intelligence when he captured the agent Barid Mesoriaam, but the Rebel withstood repeated torture sessions without breaking. Held in Jabba's townhouse in downtown Mos Eisley, Mesoriaam slipped a hidden datadot to two thieves, Kabe and Muftak, promising them a huge reward if they delivered it to another Rebel agent. The two completed their end of the bargain, and this vital information was soon delivered to the Rebel's high command instead of falling into Jabba's clutches.

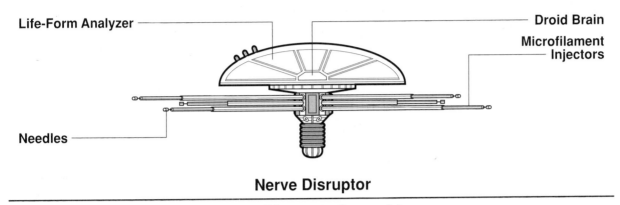

Life-Form Analyzer

Droid Brain

Microfilament Injectors

Needles

Nerve Disruptor

Nerve Disruptor Assembly

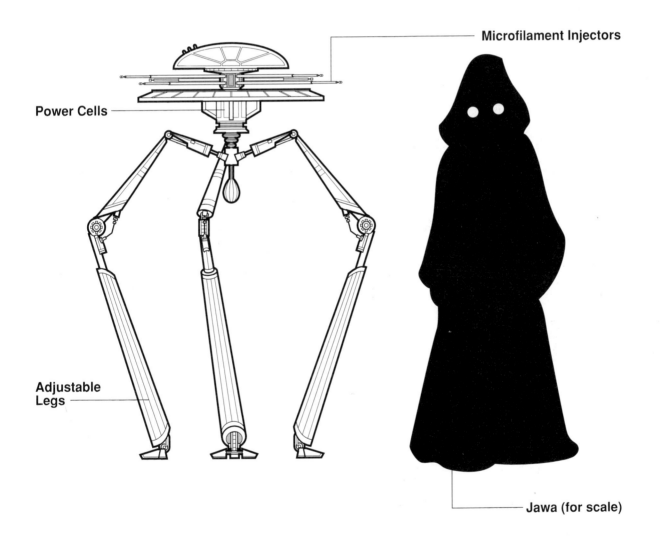

Microfilament Injectors

Power Cells

Adjustable Legs

Jawa (for scale)

UNIVERSAL ENERGY CAGE

IMPERIAL UNIVERSAL ENERGY CAGE

During Emperor Palpatine's rise to power, he orchestrated the capture and extermination of nearly all the hated Jedi Knights. One of the potent tools used by his servants during this great purge was the universal energy cage, a trap designed to hold a Jedi Knight immobile and block his Force powers. The universal energy cage consists of a floating confinement sphere approximately three meters in diameter and is ringed by reinforced durasteel bars.

No physical object, no matter how strong, is a match for Force powers that bestow on the user the ability to levitate objects or affect the thoughts and perceptions of others. Accordingly, the Imperial engineer Umak Leth, who later would design the infamous World Devastators, devised an elaborate system of overlapping superconductive coils that cloaked the containment sphere in an energy force field. That field would effectively seal the captive Jedi within the cage.

The cage's force field interrupts the Jedi's ability to manipulate the Force, preventing him from moving items that lie outside the cage or from tricking guards into releasing him. The force field's intensity is variable and automatically increases as the Jedi applies more energy against it. In theory, it is capable of containing even the most accomplished Jedi Masters. A contact shock field is projected along the

cage's interior to further prevent the Jedi from escaping, and the guards can increase the shock field's intensity to fill the entire cage and knock the Jedi unconscious if he appears to pose a threat.

For loading and unloading prisoners, additional energy projection coils and repulsorlift generators are placed near the sliding access bars to allow the force field and the repulsorfield to be projected as much as ten meters beyond the cage's perimeter. The cage's small repulsorlift unit can achieve a top speed of forty-five kilometers per hour. A handheld controller unit with a range of one hundred meters handles all the cage's functions: setting the intensity of the force fields and stun charges, opening the access bars, and directing the cage's movement.

Universal energy cages are extremely rare, and it is believed that only a handful of them were ever manufactured. Luke Skywalker first learned of these devices when he traveled to the reincarnated Emperor's capital world of Byss. There, Imperial Sovereign Protectors used one of these cages to transport Luke and Artoo to Palpatine's towering Imperial Citadel.

It is unknown how many of these energy cages survive—perhaps hidden in the Emperor's abandoned treasure vaults scattered across the galaxy—but in the wrong hands they could represent a major threat to Luke Skywalker's efforts to rebuild the Jedi Knights.

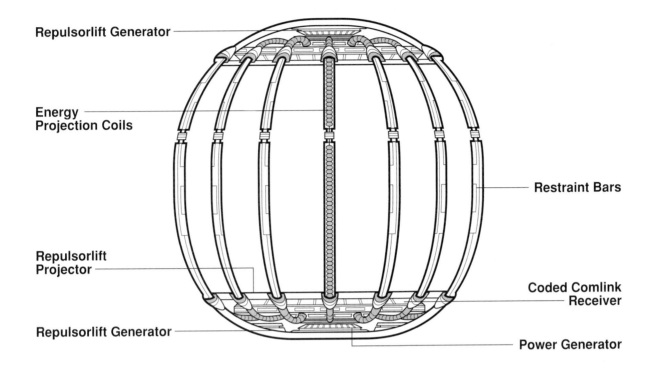

Repulsorlift Generator

Energy
Projection Coils

Repulsorlift
Projector

Repulsorlift Generator

Restraint Bars

Coded Comlink
Receiver

Power Generator

Universal Energy Cage Cutaway

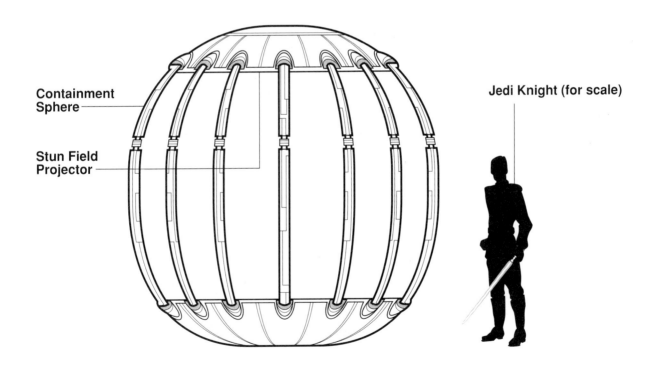

Containment
Sphere

Stun Field
Projector

Jedi Knight (for scale)

MAN TRAP

UBRIKKIAN R-TechApp MAN TRAP

A favorite of slavers and bounty hunters, the man trap is a nearly perfect incarceration tool. Its powerful reversed repulsorfield captures targets by producing an intense gravity field and often leaves them undamaged for delivery to customers.

The man trap's reversed repulsorfield intensifies a planet's gravity, creating a very strong field that is localized over the trap's projection plates. Settings are measured as multipliers of the local gravity, ranging from one—which equals the planet's gravity—up to an eightfold increase in gravity. When a high enough gravity setting is selected, anyone who steps over the trap will be pulled down, immobilized by his or her own mass. With the target helpless, the captor can stun, tranquilize, or interrogate the prisoner.

The man trap consists of a one-meter-square metal plate that is barely five centimeters tall; there is no external machinery, which makes the unit easy to move and set up. It is placed flat on the ground and may be camouflaged easily with a covering of leaves, topsoil, and other ground clutter. Since many species can see farther into the infrared spectrum than humans can, infrared bafflers are used to hide a man trap's slight heat emissions.

A remote activator, linked to the plate via a ten-meter-long activation line, controls all functions. Additional activation lines can be used to allow the operator to control the man trap from a more remote hidden position. Normally, the man trap is

charged, but the gravfield generators are left inert and activated by the operator only at the precise instant when a target steps over the device.

The man trap is designed to facilitate nonlethal captures, but sprains, dislocations, and even broken bones are possible since victims may fall at an odd angle. Precise calibration of the gravity field is necessary for this device to be effective: On an average one-gravity planet, a setting of four or five gravities is more than enough to restrain an average human but would barely slow down a Wookiee. By contrast, the maximum eight-gravity setting (on a one-gee world) will trap an angry Wookiee, but this level is strong enough to crush the bones of a hollow-boned avian, such as a Mrissi.

At eight thousand credits the man trap is somewhat expensive, but it weighs only eight kilograms and can be set up in less than two minutes. The power cells supply energy for up to three hours of continuous operation.

Bounty hunters are most commonly associated with the use of these devices, but man traps also can be very effectively utilized in most security systems, since they can be hidden in floors and linked to remote security scanners, automatically activating when an intruder is detected. Traps can be used to block entire corridors, and perhaps the greatest advantage becomes evident when intruders, preoccupied with avoiding security scanners and automated blasters, stumble right into man traps and are promptly captured.

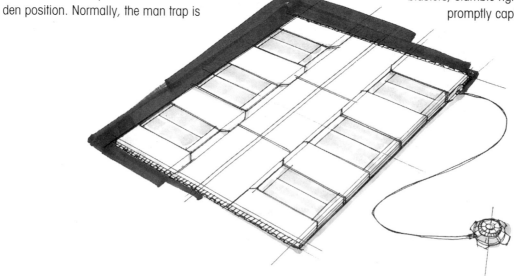
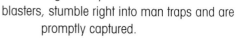

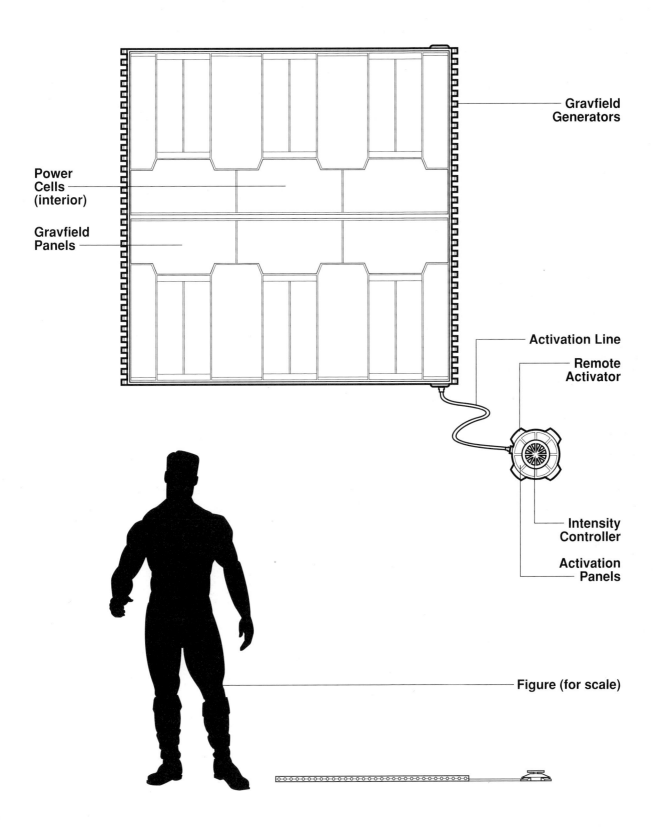

Gravfield
Generators

Power
Cells
(interior)

Gravfield
Panels

Activation Line

Remote
Activator

Intensity
Controller

Activation
Panels

Figure (for scale)

AUTOMATED LASER TRAP

BLASTECH CLASS VI AUTOMATED LASER PROJECTOR

When Luke Skywalker suggested breaking into Death Star Detention Block AA-23 to rescue Princess Leia Organa, he naively hoped to find metal bars and mechanical locks like those used in Mos Eisley's primitive lockup. Unfortunately, the Death Star's detention blocks were protected by some of the most sophisticated security systems employed by the Empire, including several BlasTech Class VI automated laser projectors.

These automated blasters—nicknamed laser traps—often are used at security checkpoints, where they may be activated by guards assigned to the designated area or controlled by officers who keep watch through security monitors operated from remote control stations. Laser traps also provide a common security measure at prisons and labor camps, where they can be used to put down inmate uprisings. These units often are installed as part of an overall security system that may include force fields, security cameras, weapons scanners, and even laser force fields.

The complete Class VI laser projector unit consists of a control computer, a sensor suite, and a small blaster cannon. When responding to an alarm, security guards may control and fire the blaster manually or activate the unit's onboard combat computer, which can use the sensor system to track up to two dozen targets simultaneously.

The laser projector's blaster rotates up to forty-five degrees in any direction and has an optimum range of ten meters and a maximum range of twenty-five meters. The blaster bolts have as much stopping power as a blaster

rifle, and the weapon can be set to fire high-energy stun blasts that pack enough of a punch to stop a full-grown gundark in its tracks. Internal power cells supply enough energy for fifty shots, or the weapon can be connected to a power generator to give it unlimited firepower.

Most security stations—particularly prison blocks—use multiple laser projectors, which may be wall-mounted or placed on rotating turrets that hang down from the ceiling. To surprise attackers, laser traps also may be mounted on retractable platforms and hidden behind false panels. Security cameras often are linked to the projectors to feed additional targeting data to the laser trap's combat computer.

Many facilities supplement their security systems by issuing coded identification chips to all authorized personnel. The laser trap's sensor suite automatically scans anyone entering the established security checkpoint area, alerting control officers if anyone lacks the identification chip.

Automated laser traps were used throughout Imperial security stations and detention blocks and remain a standard security measure in many New Republic facilities, providing emergency backup for guards. In the private sector, automated laser traps often are used to protect high-security research labs, museums, executive offices, and sensitive corporate facilities. Wealthy individuals often use laser projectors to guard their residences. Remotely controlled hidden laser projectors also are used by criminal bosses who desire unquestionably loyal backup in case ambitious henchmen try to move up in the organization through assassination.

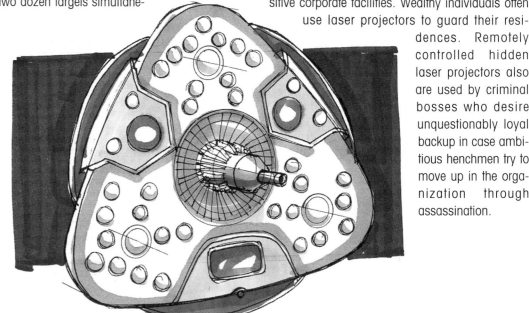

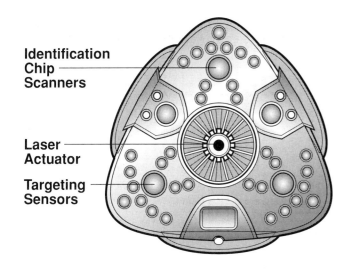

Identification Chip Scanners

Laser Actuator

Targeting Sensors

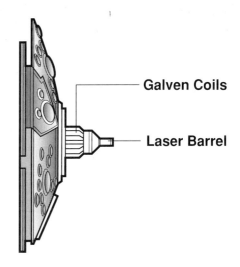

Galven Coils

Laser Barrel

Front View

Side View

Laser Projector Placement

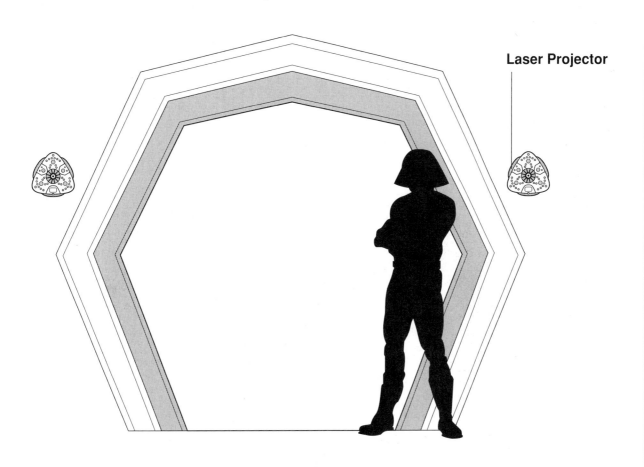

Laser Projector

RANK CYLINDER

IMPERIAL RANK CYLINDER

Rank cylinders, standard-issue security encoding devices, were used throughout the Imperial Army and Navy. Each military officer carried one or more of these cylinders, which could be used to control entry into restricted facilities and sensitive portions of the Imperial computer network. This allowed the Imperial military to operate in an efficient manner while keeping confidential data secure from Rebel spies. Rank cylinders are still used in many Imperial remnant systems, and some New Republic member governments employ similar measures, such as issuing coded identification cards and electronic keys, while using scanners to confirm an individual's identity.

Each rank cylinder contains a combination scomp link and data terminal that allows interfacing with computers, droids, and security locks. Custom-programmed coding and identification chips list each officer's identity and overall security clearance as well as special clearances for specific departments, research labs, and prototype testing facilities. The cylinder also contains the individual's voice, retinal, and dermatoglyphic records for further verification via specialized scanners.

Whenever an officer tries to access a computer network or enter an area protected by a security lock, he will be required to slide his personal command cylinder into a security terminal or data port and enter his personal access code. An incorrect pass code or any attempt to access unauthorized facilities or computer data automatically sounds a security alarm.

Each command cylinder's clearances must be confirmed by the computer network before access will be granted. This automated system controls the flow of information and limits access while minimizing the number of living security guards needed to protect a facility.

During the Galactic Civil War the Empire issued updated command cylinders with new pass codes at least once a month to prevent Rebel agents from using stolen cylinders to infiltrate Imperial bases and computer databases. Additionally, the Imperial computer network kept a detailed log of each cylinder's activity, noting all facilities entered and any data files that were accessed. This electronic record was a valuable tool for Imperial Intelligence and Imperial Security Bureau (ISB) agents, who often relied on access records to locate suspected Rebel spies. Imperial security officers used these records to covertly observe a suspect's behavior; when illegal activity was detected, the target's authorization codes were blocked and the suspect was detained for interrogation.

Low-ranking officers or technicians were issued one cylinder, but high-ranking officers with access to multiple facilities carried several command cylinders. Imperial regulations called for high-level officers to display their cylinders on their front shirt pockets, adjacent to the rank insignia. Technicians and engineers often carried their rank cylinders in other pockets, on their belts, or on chains hanging around their necks.

Rank Command Cylinder

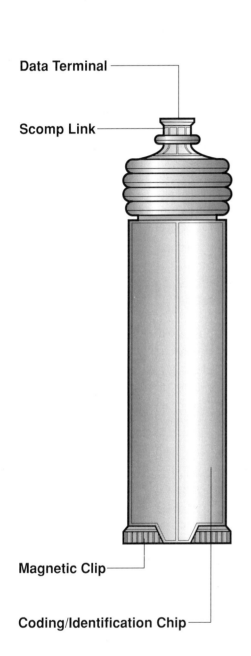

Data Terminal

Scomp Link

Magnetic Clip

Coding/Identification Chip

Side View

Figure with Rank Command Cylinder

ELECTRONIC LOCK BREAKER

OutlawTech Lock Breaker

The electronic lock breaker is an antisecurity slicing system that can override alarms and open all but the most sophisticated computerized locks. Obviously designed for undertakings of dubious legality, this contraband device is a valued tool among criminals, espionage agents, and computer programmers known as slicers.

Security systems often use computer-controlled electronic locks that are supposed to be tamperproof. Heavy-duty magnetically reinforced durasteel bolts—sometimes coupled with miniature force fields—keep locks secure even if outside communications, alarms, and power supplies are cut off. Access is granted only through systems that require a password or identity code; most sensitive facilities add secondary identity verification methods, such as scanners that check genetic samples or retinal, voice, or dermatoglyphic patterns and match them against stored records.

The most advanced locks have computer-control systems that use rapidly changing coding sequences to block slicing attempts by droids and portable computers.

Such locks often are used to protect items of immense value, and this provides more than enough motivation for computer slicers to develop ways to nullify advanced security systems. The result: the electronic lock breaker.

Each lock breaker's high-capacity portable computer has more processing power than do most starships' navigation systems and is available only through black market channels, with a price of twenty-five thousand credits per unit. The slicer takes the lock breaker's key-code replicator input/output jack and plugs it into the lock. The lock breaker's primary program spikes a complicated polynomial computation into the lock's security monitor programming to keep it occupied and prevent it from noticing the secondary slicing program. This program randomly flashes access code combinations in an attempt to match an authorized code and open the lock.

Considerable privacy is needed in using the lock breaker, since its hum can be heard up to ten meters away. The slicing effort can take hours unless the lock breaker is preprogrammed with the target lock's computer architecture and code sequencing, in which case the device may need only a few minutes to determine an acceptable entry code and open the lock.

During Grand Admiral Thrawn's campaign against the New Republic, a team of Imperial agents attempted to kidnap Princess Leia Organa Solo and her twin infants. They used an electronic lock breaker to defeat the Imperial Palace's gene-code sequencer locks. The agents nearly succeeded but were foiled by Mara Jade, Han Solo, and Princess Leia.

Soon after this attack, New Republic programmers developed better countermeasures by adding "flagged" genetic codes to the locks' computers: Any lock breaker could accidentally flash one of these codes, and this would automatically trip an alarm.

Lock breaker programmers soon developed subroutines to counter these flagged codes. As with all forms of warfare, technological competition continues unabated, with the New Republic's best security programmers pitting their locks against lock breakers designed by the most talented slicers in the galactic underworld.

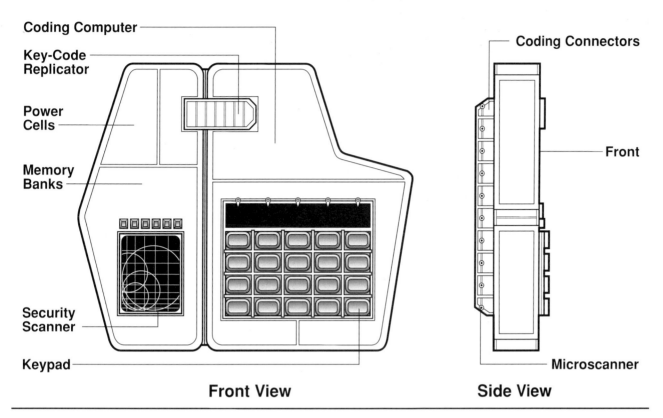

Coding Computer

Key-Code Replicator

Power Cells

Memory Banks

Security Scanner

Keypad

Coding Connectors

Front

Microscanner

Front View

Side View

Lock Breaker Placement

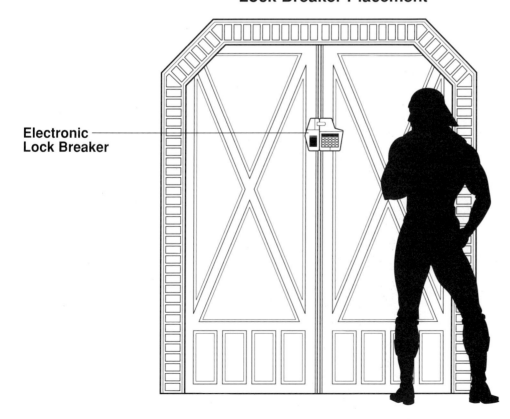

Electronic Lock Breaker

SECURITY SCANNERS

MERR-SONN MUNITIONS 57C HOLOCAMERA

Scanners and observation cameras are standard-issue security items. They range from simple visual scanners such as the Merr-Sonn 17C to advanced holographic recorders such as the military-issue 57C unit. While inexpensive two-dimensional video scanners are used almost everywhere—from retail shops to private residences—the more advanced holographic units are used primarily for high-security applications and supplement guards in starports, detention blocks, and other facilities likely to be targeted for armed attacks, sabotage, or terrorism.

All but the cheapest scanners record images and sound, storing them on standard data disks and tapes. Most units have motion-sensor tracking programs that allow them to automatically follow the movements of individuals within the scanner's range. Security scanners normally feed their visual data to centralized guard stations and often have automated functions to alert personnel. At military installations scanners often provide targeting data for automated blasters.

Scanners vary widely in size: Larger monitors generally offer greater range and detail—often employing macrobinocular functions—but are readily visible. Miniaturized scanners may be small enough to fit inside a comlink or data stylus, but they have limited range and their image resolution is often poor. Smaller scanners normally have transmitters used to relay images to nearby recorders and often utilize scramblers to hide the signal.

Merr-Sonn 57C holographic scanners were used in all Imperial military bases, and a number of the units were installed in Death Star Detention Block AA-23. After Han Solo, Luke Skywalker, and Chewbacca staged their famous rescue of Princess Leia Organa, Imperial officials used security recordings to identify the intruders.

Many security scanners are equipped with special magnification lenses or infrared and ultraviolet spectrum optics, making them useful for nighttime observation. Long-range scanners can record the activities of individuals dozens of kilometers away, while paired audio sensors using precisely focused unidirectional pickups can record distant conversations. These devices were deployed routinely during Imperial planetary occupations. During the subjugation of the planet Ralltiir, Darth Vader's troops used scanners to eavesdrop on members of the population and identify thousands of Rebel sympathizers, who were rounded up and taken to interrogation centers and labor camps.

There is also a wide variety of specialized short-range security scanners. Weapon scanners used in starport security systems look for key clues that indicate hidden weapons: metal, composite ceramics, power cells, and blaster-gas residue. Computerized card or chip scanners provide standard clearance systems for security checkpoints. Particularly sensitive facilities also may verify an individual's identity through retinal, voiceprint, and dermatoglyphic scans or by examining a skin sample.

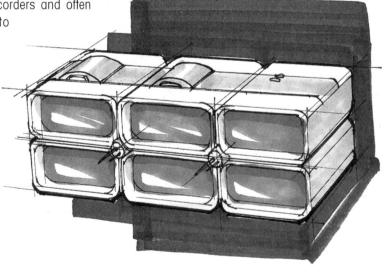

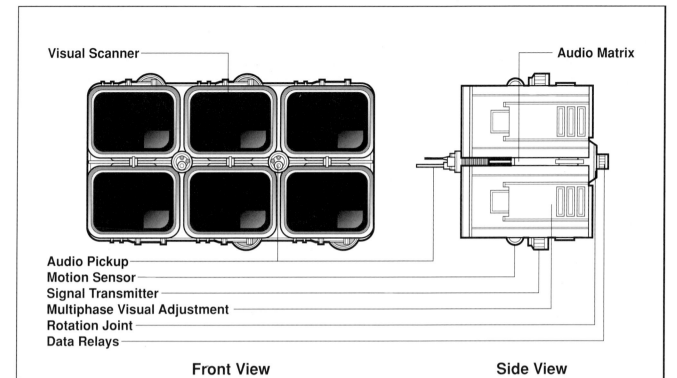

Visual Scanner

Audio Matrix

Audio Pickup
Motion Sensor
Signal Transmitter
Multiphase Visual Adjustment
Rotation Joint
Data Relays

Front View

Side View

Security Station

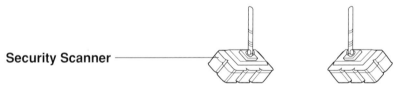

Security Scanner

Control Panels

BIOSCAN

ATHAKAM/RSMA BIOSCAN UNIT

The Athakam/RSMA bioscan system is a detailed medical scanner that combines a sensitive broad-spectrum sensor suite with a very powerful analysis computer. While originally designed to allow surgeon droids and doctors to examine a patient's biofunctions and to quickly diagnose injuries and diseases, this system's detailed scans have made it a perfect tool for espionage.

The bioscan's analysis computer is small enough to be carried in a briefcase and has a flat-screen monitor and a holographic projector. The sensor suite is slim for mounting on an examination bed but also can be hidden above ceiling panels or below deck plates or mounted adjacent to a door frame. Its only limitations are that the six-centimeter-wide scanning surface *must* be located within forty centimeters of the subject and the unit must be firmly secured, since the slightest vibrations can foul the sensor readings.

The sensor suite includes a full-range scanner, a vaprosampler, a doppraymagno scanner, and a medtox detector. A comprehensive scan can be completed in less than two seconds, and the results then can be compared to the bioscan computer's data library, which contains physiological templates for more than eighty-six thousand alien species. An operator also can input data for newly encountered species.

Scan results are astoundingly comprehensive, listing the subject's species, sex, heartbeat and respiration rate, muscle-tone index, height, weight, and temperature. The unit automatically highlights any anomalies in metabolism and chemical and hormone levels as well as diseases and viral infections. More detailed data are gathered during the scan and can be called up for a more elaborate assessment. The operator may make a permanent record for later reference—an outstanding feature for ongoing medical care and one that's extremely useful during espionage operations, when an agent's identity may need to be verified through genetic scans or similar measures.

The full-range and doppraymagno scanners instantly detect cybernetic implants, energy cells, weapons, and even comm transmissions, making it virtually impossible

for the subject to hide a transmitter. The sensors can detect encoded chips or datadots less than a millimeter in diameter. The bioscan's data library also stores template specifications for identifying three thousand different types of droids.

The bioscan computer has standard data ports used to exchange data with computers, droids, and datapads. The internal power supply operates for a full year between recharges. While the bioscan unit costs thirteen thousand credits, its efficiency and the level of detail make it exceptionally useful.

During one of her missions for the Rebel Alliance, Princess Leia Organa secretly used a bioscan unit to scan Guri, the mysterious Black Sun operative who met her on the planet Rodia. Leia barely contained her surprise when the bioscan units indicated that Guri was not the normal human woman she appeared to be. Guri was actually a human-replica droid, a custom-built engineered organism who served Prince Xizor, leader of Black Sun, as his personal adjutant and messenger.

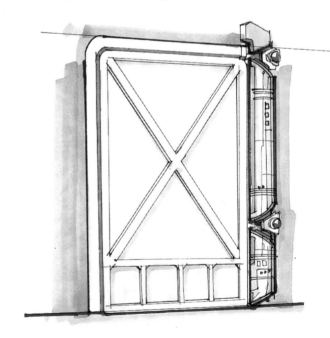

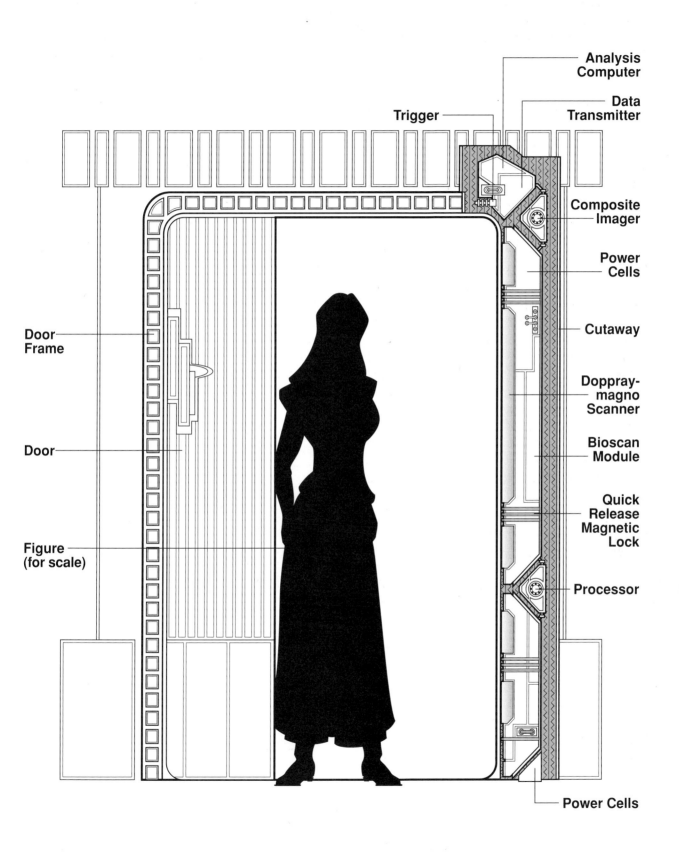

Analysis
Computer

Data
Transmitter

Trigger

Composite
Imager

Power
Cells

Door
Frame

Cutaway

Doppray-
magno
Scanner

Bioscan
Module

Door

Quick
Release
Magnetic
Lock

Figure
(for scale)

Processor

Power Cells

HOLOGRAPHIC IMAGE DISGUISER

CORELLIDYNE CQ-3.9X HOLOGRAPHIC IMAGE DISGUISER

While the widespread use of holograms is taken for granted by the average galactic citizen, holographic image disguisers—also known as holoshrouds—use cutting-edge hologram technology to create stunning visual illusions. Yet such a device is small enough to be worn on the belt.

Corellidyne's CQ-3.9x holographic image disguiser uses a miniaturized Corellidyne CP-3.3 hologram projector, which originally was developed for the entertainment industry and for use in military simulations. The projector incorporates remarkable advances in image output, projection density, and light manipulation to create a lifelike hologram image that appears absolutely real; that is, until someone tries to touch the hologram and that person's hand passes right through the image!

The holoshroud projects the prerecorded likeness of another person, hiding that person underneath the hologram. Obviously, the dimensions of the projected image must be greater than those of the flesh-and-blood person hidden beneath. The projector's computer is sophisticated enough to match the hologram's movements perfectly to those of the operator so that the image is utterly convincing to the unaided human eye, although droids and security scanners can detect a telltale visual "flicker."

The projector drains its high-energy power cell in less than two minutes; a warning tone sounds when the power cell's charge is down to fifteen seconds.

The CP-3.3 hologram projector contains no recording apparatus. The image of a person or object must be scanned by Corellidyne's high-density CX-3.1 hologram recorder, which has data intake capability nearly a thousand times greater

than that of standard hologram recorders. The CX-3.1 perfectly replicates every element of the subject's appearance and movement.

The CP-3.3 projector has enough memory to hold the image of only one subject, yet each unit commands a price of twenty-five thousand credits.

Though their energy cells run down quickly, portable holoshrouds provide excellent short-term disguises. It was an assassin using a holoshroud who gained entry to the heavily guarded fortress of the infamous Doctor Evazan, the psychotic surgeon who'd once boasted to Luke Skywalker that he faced the death sentence in twelve systems.

Despite such dramatic examples, hologram image disguisers are most often used in amusement park rides, called immersion holographic environments, featured at entertainment parks such as Hologram Fun World. There, holoshrouds are connected to power generators that permit long-term use and are programmed to present fanciful characters and creatures. Attractions use holographic simulations to re-create exotic environments faithfully and provide total sensory feedback in a make-believe environment that is almost indistinguishable from reality.

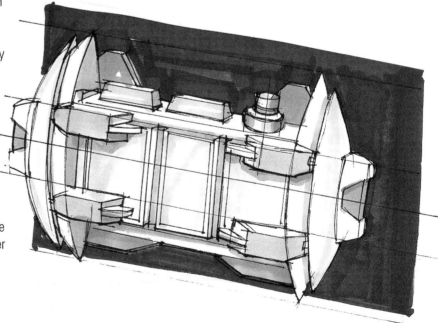

Front View

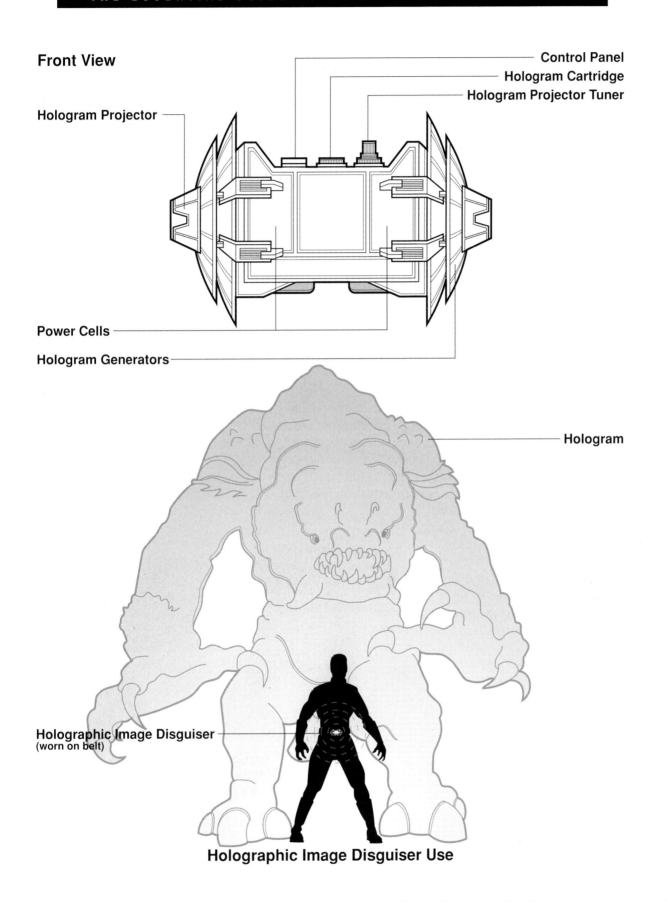

Control Panel

Hologram Cartridge

Hologram Projector Tuner

Hologram Projector

Power Cells

Hologram Generators

Hologram

Holographic Image Disguiser
(worn on belt)

Holographic Image Disguiser Use

MOLECULARLY BONDED ARMOR AND ANTICONCUSSION FIELD

CSA MOLECULAR-BOND ARMOR SHEATH AND
CSA *RAMPART*-CLASS ANTICONCUSSION GENERATOR

The Corporate Sector Authority built the top-secret Stars' End prison facility to withstand virtually any attack. The prison, situated on the remote planetoid Mytus VII, had turbolasers, combat and patrol ships, and powerful deflector shields. However, the key defensive system was Stars' End itself, a forty-story tower cloaked in a seamless sheath of molecularly bonded armor and supplemented by an anticoncussion field.

Molecularly bonded armor is extremely expensive and normally is used to protect vaults, bunkers, and containment cells designed to store priceless treasures or secret military prototypes. This armor was selected for Stars' End because the prison's tenants had to be held under the tightest security measures possible.

In manufacturing the armor, texture-molding tractor fields hold dense metals in place. These metals are softened—even liquefied—by ion fusers. While the resulting alloy cools, it is bombarded with charged-particle vibrating waves. This dramatically improves each molecule's subatomic bonding strength and gives the armor incredible resiliency. At Stars' End, this bonding process was performed across the tower's entire surface, resulting in a nearly indestructible shell that could withstand barrages from a Star Destroyer's turbolasers.

A complete anticoncussion field complemented the armor coating. Numerous anticoncussion projectors honeycombed the prison's interior to strengthen the integrity of floors, ceilings, walls, and other internal surfaces. The projector's umbrella-shaped magnetic fields created a single cohesive anticoncussion field that absorbed and dispersed kinetic energy and was powerful enough to render blasts, collisions, and other impacts inert. This anticoncussion system consumed as much energy as did a Star Destroyer's ion engines, but it was needed to preserve the integrity of the thousands of stasis booths that stored prisoners in a state of limited hibernation. Any disruption of the stasis system would bring the prisoners out of hibernation.

Of course, no amount of technological innovation could account for the craftiness of an angry Corellian smuggler named Han Solo. He came to Stars' End hoping to find his friend and copilot, Chewbacca. Solo found Chewbacca—and thousands of other criminals and political opponents of the Authority—being held in the prison's stasis booths.

Solo initiated a desperate rescue plan, rerouting energy from key systems and feeding it back into the prison's power generator to trigger an overload spiral that detonated the power core. The anticoncussion field, armor, and deflector shields channeled the core explosion, so that the Stars' End tower was launched into a high-altitude trajectory that almost achieved orbit! The explosion also shut down the stasis system, freeing the prisoners. Solo evacuated them before the tower plummeted back to the surface of Mytus VII.

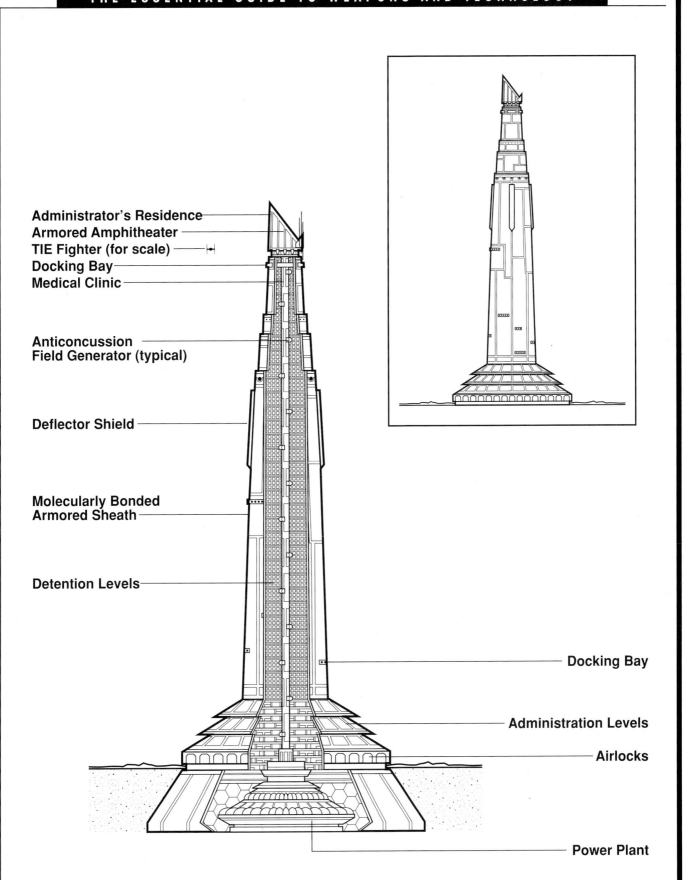

Administrator's Residence

Armored Amphitheater

TIE Fighter (for scale)

Docking Bay

Medical Clinic

Anticoncussion
Field Generator (typical)

Deflector Shield

Molecularly Bonded
Armored Sheath

Detention Levels

Docking Bay

Administration Levels

Airlocks

Power Plant

GENERAL EQUIPMENT

The quality of life across the galaxy is enhanced by an incredible variety of goods manufactured by various companies. These range from the datapads and glow rods needed by almost everyone to specialized products such as cyborg units and bacta tanks.

Without the widespread application of technology, there would be no scanners and breath masks to aid scouts and explorers. Thanks to the availability of beamdrills, molecular sifters, and automated refinery systems, miners can retrieve precious metals in a fraction of the time it once took. Advanced tools and computer applications help mechanics and engineers build, repair, and improve the starships that sustain galactic trade. In fact, every industry depends on high-technology products.

THE GALACTIC ECONOMY

The spread of technology and civilization led to the development of a so-called galactic economy. Few worlds are entirely self-sufficient. Some specialize in manufacturing high-tech goods yet depend on neighboring agricultural worlds for food. Those agricultural worlds rely on manufacturing worlds to produce the machinery for efficiently harvesting and processing the foodstuffs as well as supplying the chemical industries that make pesticides to kill insects and provide nutrient sprays to speed crop growth.

This galactic economy has allowed megacorporations to accumulate tremendous economic and political power. Companies such as the SoroSuub Corporation produce goods for hundreds of fields, while the Tagge Company controls thousands of star systems and owns dozens of subsidiaries, making it one of the galaxy's most influential organizations. Even small businesses, such as Bespin's Figg and Associates, may have tremendous influence on their homeworlds, while others, such as Pretormin Environmental, are specialized interests that are satisfied to produce a small number of products for very limited markets.

THE SPREAD OF TECHNOLOGY

The spread of high-technology goods came about because of the ready exchange of information, the widespread availability of compact energy sources, and the development of sophisticated miniaturized computers.

As each society progressed, it developed its own means of generating energy, processing information, and propelling starships. As cultures conducted trade with their neighbors, they shared their knowledge, and almost inevitably, new and better technological devices were invented as different approaches were compared, refined, and integrated.

Virtually all high-tech products require some form of energy. The perfection of safe, high-yield fusion supplied virtually unlimited energy and allowed the development of starships. Smaller fusion generators were soon developed as portable units for use during remote scouting missions or on isolated homesteads. Technological innovation led to the invention of high-capacity rechargeable power cells, and this allowed all manner of goods—from personal datapads to industrial beam cutters—to operate for extended periods without having to be linked to a bulky power source.

The development of miniaturized computers has led to their incorporation in many tools, including ordinary items such as glow rods and breath masks. These computers control all functions and are easy to employ, allowing users to program even the most complex tools to meet their needs.

EXOTIC TECHNOLOGIES AND THEIR APPLICATIONS

Many species and cultures have applied their unique forms of knowledge and ingenuity to develop an astounding variety of items specifically suited to their needs. The Verpine, an insectoid species inhabiting the Roche Asteroid Field, have refined repulsorlift technology to develop advanced mining equipment and high-output repulsor generators that shield their massive asteroid colonies from collisions. The Vratix of Thyferra developed bacta as a medicine for themselves, but its remarkable properties have led to its use across the galaxy. Meanwhile, the Ho'Din and the Ithorians (or "Hammerheads") use their highly developed technology for plant gene-splicing and selective cross-fertilization to develop hardier foodstuffs and potent medicinal herbs.

Despite the proliferation of advanced technologies, some items still awe and amaze even the most cynical galactic citizens. Items such as cybernetic replacement limbs can perfectly replicate the function of their organic counterparts, and many can take human performance to astounding levels. The ancient technology used in the Jedi Holocron and the famed Jedi lightsabers is similarly amazing to the layperson.

Some technologies remain a secret to most of the galaxy's population and are prohibitively expensive. These devices include the teleportation system found in Magwit's mystifying hoop and human-replica droids that to all appearances seem to be normal human beings but are actually machines with incredible strength and genius-level intelligence.

TECHNOLOGICAL STANDARDIZATION

An important aspect of New Republic society is that most technology is standardized. Even though there are thousands of different blasters, most of them have similar parts and rely on essentially the same technology. This standardization applies to and enhances most types of goods, from datapads and droids to vehicles and starships. Because of their similarities, high-tech goods are easier to repair and maintain.

An interesting consequence of this is that truly revolutionary technological discoveries—such as Magwit's portable teleportation disks—have proved to be rather rare. Instead, most engineers and scientists have devoted their work to steadily improving existing technologies. For example, modern breath masks feature better filters than those used during the Clone Wars, but the underlying technology is the same. Modest improvements over long periods of time are more common, and as a result, items such as electrobinoculars and Han Solo's BlasTech DL-44 heavy blaster pistol may still be widely used even though their designs are well over two decades old.

The result is the same, though. Technological breakthroughs have touched nearly every known sentient, improving the quality of life from one planet to the next.

COMMON HAND TOOLS

SoroSuub F-187 Fusioncutter
Udrane Galactic Electronics ReliaCharger
Power Calibrator
Regallis Engineering FastTurn-3 Hydrospanner

Countless high-technology devices sustain the New Republic. These devices range from datapads and hologram projectors to starships that allow travel between systems. Maintaining and repairing these technological wonders require the use of specialized tools that are, in their own way, quite amazing. These tools include macrofusers, plasma welders, power prybars, vibro-cutters, powerdrivers, and powerlifters.

SoroSuub's F-187 fusioncutter is a handheld cutting torch that's invaluable in making starship and vehicle repairs. Its high-energy plasma beam is capable of slicing through dense metals, duraplast, and other reinforced materials. The F-187's cutting beam can be adjusted so that it extends anywhere from one to twenty centimeters long, with a swath up to six centimeters wide or as narrow as a millimeter. An extendable "drill bit" is used for punching holes. The fusioncutter can be mounted on a jig with a droid-brain control unit for automated cutting. Fuel canisters last for one hour, although larger fuel cylinders can be attached.

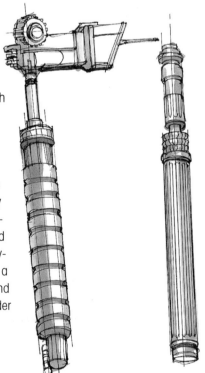

Another common tool is the ReliaCharger power calibrator, which can serve as an emergency energy source to power small appliances such as datapads and hologram projectors for several days. It can energize a droid for up to ten hours and can even keep a landspeeder running for up to half an hour. The calibrator has a circuit tester, connector rods, and a control computer used to analyze and repair electronic circuitry, making it exceptionally useful for maintaining droids, vehicles, and starship computer systems.

Hydrospanners are socket and bit drivers used to tighten and loosen all types of fasteners, including nuts, fusion bolts, fuse pins, and molecular screws. They are useful for many types of mechanical work, from assembling droids to performing major repairs aboard starships.

The Regallis FastTurn-3 hydrospanner's hydraulic compression cylinder greatly increases its torque, allowing the user to fasten bolts with minimal exertion. The variable-size socket fits nuts as small as two millimeters across, while an extending attachment can brace around fasteners up to twenty-five centimeters in diameter.

The FastTurn-3's rotary driver accepts any standard drive bit and delivers enough torque to drive screws and bolts into duraplast and transparisteel. A special universal bit uses seventy retracting durasteel pins to fit around any screw, bolt, or fastener. A tiny fusioncutter attachment cuts through molecular adhesives and fusion welds to loosen bolts before their removal.

The socket driver's hinge twists up to 180 degrees in any direction for use around tight corners and at unusual angles. For working inside complex machinery, a flexible thirty-centimeter-long extension cable twists around any obstructions; the cable's vid receptor line connects to any standard datapad for a real-time video feed so that the technician can see his or her work. The cable accepts standard drive bits and sockets.

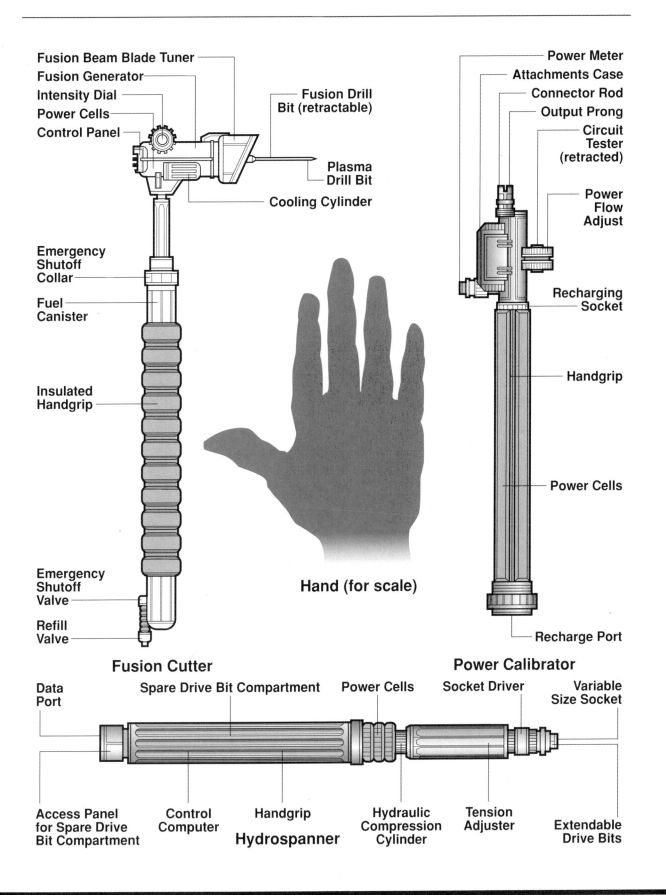

Fusion Beam Blade Tuner
Fusion Generator
Intensity Dial
Power Cells
Control Panel

Fusion Drill
Bit (retractable)

Plasma
Drill Bit

Cooling Cylinder

Power Meter
Attachments Case
Connector Rod
Output Prong
Circuit
Tester
(retracted)

Power
Flow
Adjust

Emergency
Shutoff
Collar

Fuel
Canister

Recharging
Socket

Insulated
Handgrip

Handgrip

Power Cells

Emergency
Shutoff
Valve

Refill
Valve

Hand (for scale)

Recharge Port

Fusion Cutter

Power Calibrator

Data
Port

Spare Drive Bit Compartment

Power Cells

Socket Driver

Variable
Size Socket

Access Panel
for Spare Drive
Bit Compartment

Control
Computer

Handgrip

Hydrospanner

Hydraulic
Compression
Cylinder

Tension
Adjuster

Extendable
Drive Bits

BREATH MASK

GANDORTHRAL ATMOSPHERICS ROAMER-6 BREATH MASK

Breath masks are portable and inexpensive air purifiers that filter a planet's atmosphere for the wearer, blocking harmful compounds while providing life-sustaining gases. These devices are designed for use in harsh environments, as occurred when Han Solo, Chewbacca, and Princess Leia exited the *Millennium Falcon* to chase away mynocks who were feeding on the ship's power cables.

The Roamer-6 breath mask allows the wearer to operate in a wide range of environments, from near vacuum to poisonous atmospheres. The mask fits over the user's nose and mouth, while the small gas filter can fit in a pocket or be clipped onto the user's belt. The filter's computer can be programmed to handle the needs of any number of species, and filter controls can be adjusted manually in the field.

The purifier has six layers of atmospheric scrubbers that filter out dangerous gases, dust particles, pollen, and other microscopic contaminants. The power-driven intake compresses thin atmospheres and can dilute very thick atmospheres, while the temperature adjuster heats or chills the air to a comfortable temperature. When there is an inadequate supply of breathable gas, the scrubbers can break down compound gases, for example, converting carbon dioxide into breathable oxygen. The

filters are spent after one hour of use, but replacements can be snapped into place in seconds. The filtration unit also has a compressed gas tank with a ten-minute supply of air.

The Roamer-6's tank coupler can be connected to larger air tanks (normally carried on the back) or to filters with microfine scrubbers that block unusual trace gases. The mask has a small programmable-frequency comlink. Small molecular hooks clip the mask to protective goggles or blast helmets.

Breath masks are standard equipment aboard all starships and escape pods and are included in most survival packs. Emergency and medical crews use them to prevent smoke inhalation, and they also can be used in emergency relief camps to stop the spread of contagious, sometimes deadly, airborne diseases.

While breath masks are useful for producing a breathable air supply, they offer no protection from a total vacuum and do not shield users from corrosive atmospheres and those containing toxins or bacteria that penetrate the skin, where a sealed space or environmental suit is required.

For those who need to stay in a hazardous atmosphere for extended periods, long-term filter breathers offer more sophisticated computers and finer filtration systems. The Ubese bounty hunter named Boushh used one of these filters to supply vital trace gases when he traveled on human-compatible worlds such as Tatooine and Coruscant.

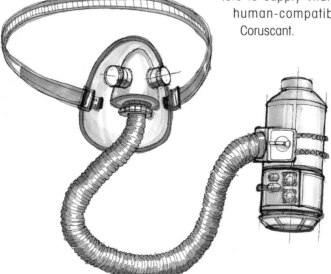

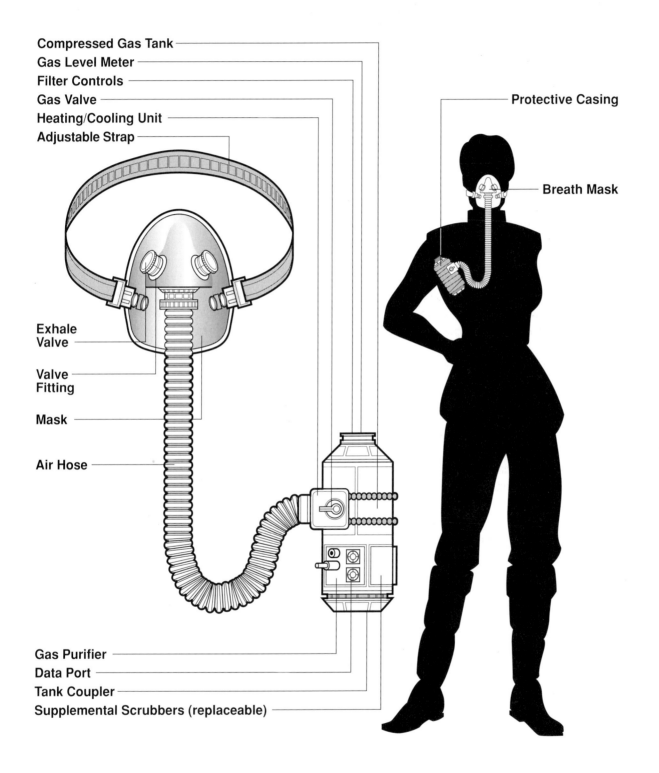

Compressed Gas Tank

Gas Level Meter

Filter Controls

Gas Valve

Heating/Cooling Unit

Adjustable Strap

Protective Casing

Breath Mask

Exhale Valve

Valve Fitting

Mask

Air Hose

Gas Purifier

Data Port

Tank Coupler

Supplemental Scrubbers (replaceable)

VAPORATOR

PRETORMIN ENVIRONMENTAL GX-8 WATER VAPORATOR

Fresh water is essential for survival, but on some worlds it is so scarce that it must be coaxed from the air by devices known as vaporators. Found on many worlds, these devices are best known for their use on the planet Tatooine's moisture farms, where five-meter-tall Pretormin GX-8 vaporators are used to gather water vapor from the arid desert atmosphere.

The GX-8 projects a low-power ionized field and uses refrigerated cylinders and chilling bars to cool the surrounding air. This causes condensation even in barren environments where the humidity is as low as 1.35 percent. The moisture condenses on the vaporator's chilled surface and trickles down into a collection chamber, where it is pumped into the vaporator's large underground storage tanks. The GX-8's control computer automatically adjusts ionization and refrigeration levels to account for wind speed and external temperature, while energy for the refrigeration units is stored in energy cells that are charged by retractable solar panels.

On Tatooine, vaporators set 250 meters apart can be expected to gather 1.5 liters of water per day. In more arid areas, such as near the Dune Sea, moisture farmers must place their vaporators at least five hundred meters apart to achieve the same water yields.

Since their functions are quite limited, vaporators often use binary programming languages. C-3PO's previous experience programming similar binary load lifters encouraged Owen Lars to purchase the fussy protocol droid.

The moisture farmer's greatest foe is

blowing sand, which gets into a vaporator's lubricants and can disable the refrigeration machinery unless it is removed promptly. Luke Skywalker spent much of his adolescence maintaining and repairing his uncle's dozens of aging vaporators.

Single-family moisture farms, each with a range of several square kilometers, are the norm on Tatooine. These businesses are risky propositions, since even minuscule water loss can mean the difference between survival and bankruptcy. One notable exception is the sprawling ranch of Huff Darklighter, which covers hundreds—maybe thousands—of square kilometers.

As the demand for water grows, moisture farms steadily spread into unexplored territory, and clashes with Sand People become increasingly common. Most vaporators on Tatooine are protected by security locks or voice recognition scanners that discourage attacks. The harvested water often is stockpiled in huge underground tanks adjacent to the family's farmhouse so that the farmer can personally fend off Tusken Raider attacks.

Moisture farmers may take their water directly into Mos Eisley spaceport for sale, ship it into the city by pipeline, or sell it to a broker. Some farmers also maintain underground hydroponics labs where vegetables are grown for later sale in Mos Eisley.

Many of Mos Eisley's streets have vaporators set up to reclaim water vapor exhaled by the city's residents. Scouts often carry small vaporators in their survival kits, while most escape pods have personal vaporators to provide fresh water to stranded pilots and crew members.

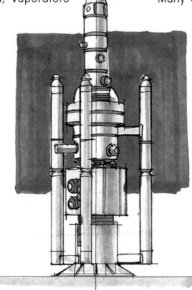

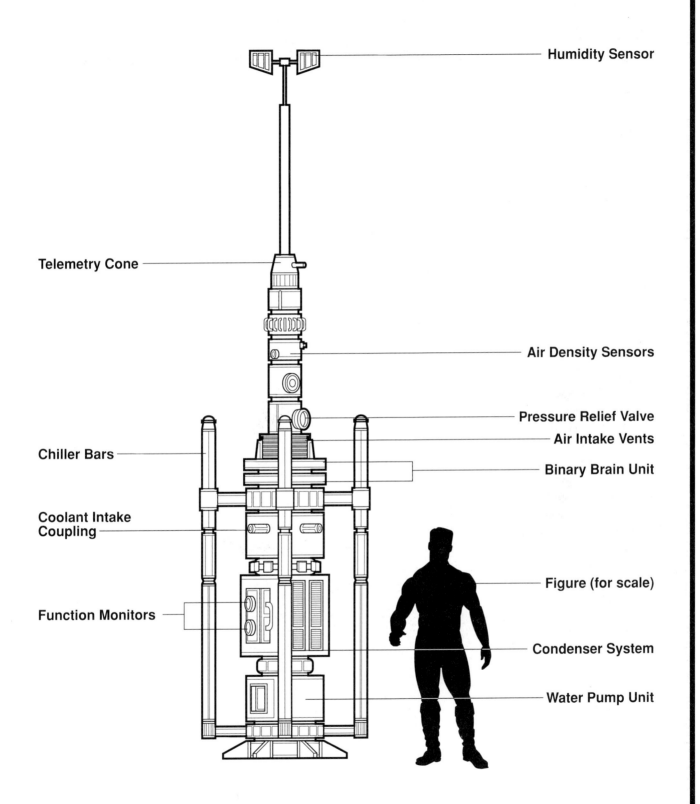

Humidity Sensor

Telemetry Cone

Air Density Sensors

Pressure Relief Valve

Air Intake Vents

Chiller Bars

Binary Brain Unit

Coolant Intake
Coupling

Figure (for scale)

Function Monitors

Condenser System

Water Pump Unit

ELECTROBINOCULARS

NEURO-SAAV MODEL TD2.3 ELECTROBINOCULARS

Electrobinoculars such as the Neuro-Saav TD2.3 utilize stereoscopic sights and computer-enhanced magnification to view images of distant objects with great detail and clarity. These devices normally cost about a hundred credits, have durable plastic casings that protect the optics modules, and use rechargeable energy cells that last up to six months.

The TD2.3's instant-focus functions allow the user to shift quickly between objects at varying distances. Screen readouts indicate the distance to the object, the relative elevation, and the relative and true azimuths.

Computer-enhanced telescopic lenses provide up to five hundred times magnification, while imaging chips adjust and enhance visible light to allow for observation in full daylight or near darkness. Dampeners automatically negate potentially blinding bursts of light, such as those from flash grenades or spot lumas.

Control dials are used for general zoom adjustment and allow for manual focusing and light compensation. The focus studs set between the viewers permit precise incremental adjustment to the telescopic magnification. The user can preprogram up to eight zoom settings and can activate them by hitting the reset switch, which cycles through the settings. The electronic imagers run a self-diagnostic when the user hits the calibration switch. The nonelectronic secondary lens offers one hundred times magnification and can be used if the electronic lens unit fails or provides suspect readings.

Most electrobinoculars have data ports that accept linking cables and feed images to hologram recorders, datapads, or recording rods. Some electrobinoculars, including the TD2.3, are preprogrammed with software that links and synchronizes them with blasters for long-range attacks. An electronically generated crosshair image corresponding to the blaster's fire vector appears on the electrobinocular readout screen.

A limited number of electrobinoculars, such as Neuro-Saav's TT-4, have internal hologram and visual recorders that can be used to store up to three hours' worth of images on a standard data card. These units can cost over two thousand credits.

As a youth, Luke Skywalker often carried a pair of electrobinoculars so that he could quickly survey the vast ranges of his uncle's moisture farm; he even used them to view the final exchanges of turbolaser fire between the Rebel Blockade Runner *Tantive IV* and the Imperial Star Destroyer *Devastator*. Luke also used his electrobinoculars to spot Sand People while searching for R2-D2 in Tatooine's Jundland Wastes.

Similar devices, called macrobinoculars, offer many of the features of electrobinoculars but lack image enhancement chips. This yields a truer but less detailed image. They lack the sophisticated light-adjustment circuitry as well, and this limits their utility in darkness, but their optics are much less likely to be damaged or thrown out of calibration.

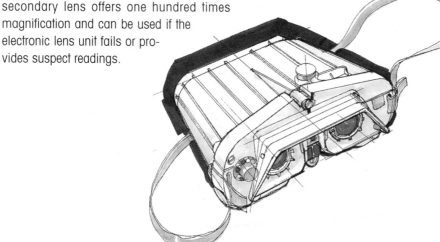

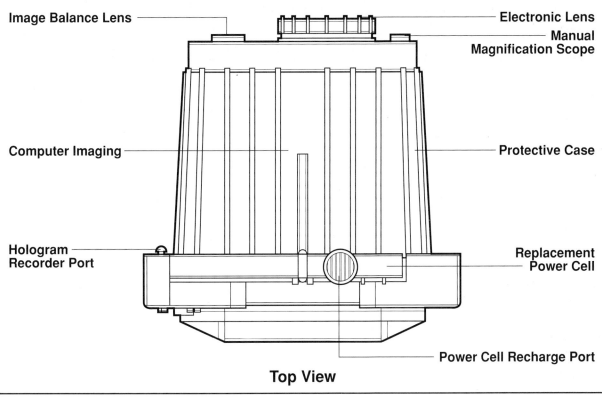

Image Balance Lens

Electronic Lens

Manual
Magnification Scope

Computer Imaging

Protective Case

Hologram
Recorder Port

Replacement
Power Cell

Power Cell Recharge Port

Top View

Front View

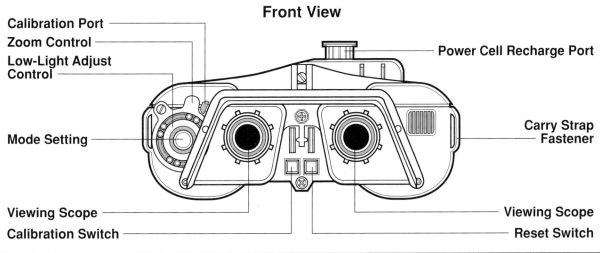

Calibration Port
Zoom Control
Low-Light Adjust
Control

Power Cell Recharge Port

Mode Setting

Carry Strap
Fastener

Viewing Scope

Viewing Scope

Calibration Switch

Reset Switch

Scope View

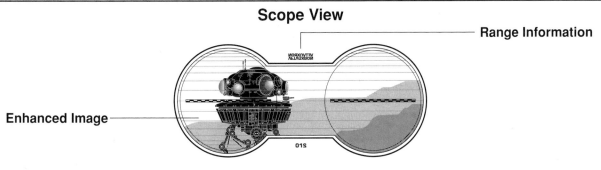

Range Information

Enhanced Image

BEAMDRILL

KARFLO CORPORATION G2-GE BEAMDRILL

Beamdrills are powerful, short-range cutting tools that produce intense plasma-beam pulses that can slice through almost any material, including stone, rock, duracrete, reinforced durasteel, and armor plate. They are used for mining and construction and are found in starship yards and other large industrial operations.

Karflo Corporation's G2-GE is a typical medium-size beamdrill that's designed for handling by a single worker. It is mounted on a small repulsor platform that offers a top speed of fifteen kilometers per hour. The beamdrill's technology base is similar to that used in blasters: Power cells charge the catalysts, which ignite the fuel slugs and cause an intense energy conversion reaction. The energy flows into the drill's beam actuator, which produces an energized plasma beam used for cutting.

The plasma beam's length can be varied from one centimeter to one and a half meters in length. At low intensity the beam slowly melts reinforced plastics. At the full-energy setting it is commonly used in mining operations to vaporize waste material. The beamdrill is mounted on a rotating joint that allows a 180-degree arc of movement. It can be programmed to follow sensor strips for more precise cutting along a specific path.

The G2-GE's three fuel slugs supply enough energy for up to ten hours of continuous operation. As with many high-energy tools, heat buildup is a major concern, and so the beam-

drill has several internal cooling units and multiple emergency cutoff switches. As an added safety feature, the beamdrill automatically shuts off if the operator leaves the repulsor sled.

The beamdrill has a built-in comlink unit so that teams of workers can coordinate their actions. A small visual scanner with a range of twenty meters warns the operator of nearby objects and individuals in order to prevent worksite collisions.

A beamdrill also can be used as a deadly impromptu weapon, as Han Solo observed when a group of war robots attacked a mining camp on the planet Dellalt. While Solo's DL-44 heavy blaster pistol couldn't penetrate the armor on the attacking robots, a stocky Maltorran seized one of the camp's beamdrills and used the plasma beam to cut through the robot's armor plate. Unfortunately, the beam also hit the war robot's power core, causing a tremendous explosion that killed the Maltorran.

There are a number of other types of beamdrills designed for different environments. These include the G2-GS, a modified G2-GE unit with a life-support bubble and small ion engines for starship yard operations. Karflo's TS-Titan is a heavy-duty drill unit used for large construction projects, such as building starships, highways, and buildings. Mounted on a repulsorlift platform, this beamdrill mechanism itself is over ten meters long and produces a plasma beam that is ten meters long and up to three meters in diameter.

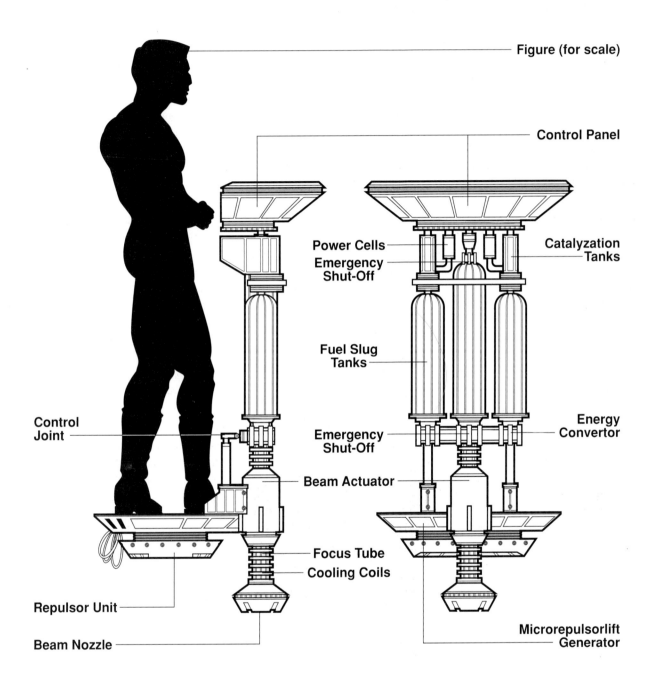

Figure (for scale)

Control Panel

Power Cells

Emergency Shut-Off

Catalyzation Tanks

Fuel Slug Tanks

Control Joint

Emergency Shut-Off

Energy Convertor

Beam Actuator

Focus Tube

Cooling Coils

Repulsor Unit

Beam Nozzle

Microrepulsorlift Generator

Side View

Front View

GLOW ROD

Lerrimore Contracting Industrial Glow Rod

Glow rods—also known as lumas—are inexpensive portable light sources that provide illumination through the use of phosphorescent chemicals or small power cells and bulbs.

Chemical reactant glow rods cost about ten credits and provide up to fifty hours of illumination per rod. The glow rod is discarded when the reactant is used up. A simple intensity dial determines how much reactant is used, controlling the illumination, which can reach as far as twenty meters away. These tiny stylus-shaped instruments weigh only twenty grams each and may be as short as six centimeters long. Most have clips that attach them to clothing or can hook onto belts. Some soldiers affix glow rods to the barrels of their blasters, where they serve as impromptu torches, although this makes the soldiers excellent targets for enemy snipers.

Glow rods that run on power cells cost up to twenty-five credits but have longer illumination ranges and provide light for up to one hundred hours. The power cells can be recharged in less than an hour and accept up to fifty charges before burning out. These glow rods range from tiny personal units—similar to the chemical reactant glow rods, with a range of thirty-five meters—to portable spot-lumas, which emit intense beams of light up to a range of three hundred meters.

Heavy-duty work glow rods such as the Lerrimore Contracting industrial glow rod are used commonly in construction and mining operations. This rod emits a high-intensity beam of light that reaches up to fifty meters away; a twist dial controls the amount of light emitted. An eight-section light shield can be used to create a directional spotlight; fully retracting the shield allows light to radiate in all directions. This glow rod also has movable tint filters for projecting red, green, blue, and yellow light.

A sliding platform allows the glow rod to be placed upright and stationary to illuminate a path or serve as a marker. The glow rod has a control panel, and its input ports can be linked with a datapad or comlink for remote control functions. The small control computer can be programmed so that the glow rod rotates on the platform and flashes in certain sequences for marking remote landing strips or sending coded messages. This function is invaluable for miners and scouts, but it is also quite handy for smugglers and pirates, who frequently use coded light-flash systems to signal incoming ships.

Each Lerrimore glow rod weighs only three hundred grams and has a retractable fastener to hook it onto belt loops or to clip it to cloth, metal, wood, and other solid materials. This rod is made of sturdy duraplast that will withstand numerous falls and bangs, and its eight power cells provide an operational time of fifty hours between recharges. It also can be connected to a small power generator for indefinite operation.

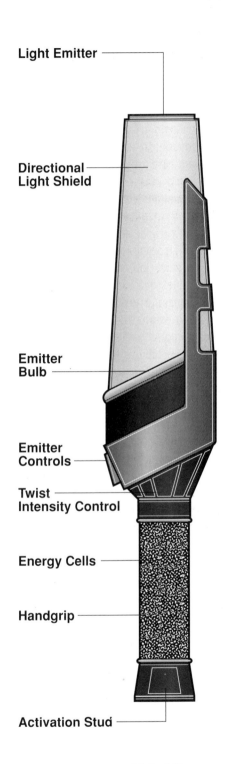

Light Emitter

Directional
Light Shield

Emitter
Bulb

Emitter
Controls

Twist
Intensity Control

Energy Cells

Handgrip

Activation Stud

Side View

Figure (for scale) with Glow Rod

RECORDING ROD

TaggeCo. PersonalAssistant-4x Recording Rod

Recording rods are personal recording devices that can store hundreds of hours of audio and two-dimensional video data on chips or storage crystals. Recordings can be played back on any standard audio, two-dimensional video, or holographic player. Most datapads also have vidprojector modules.

The TaggeCo. PersonalAssistant-4x is a typical consumer-grade recording rod that combines high-quality visuals and audio recording with a compact unit that costs only thirty credits. The rod's visual-recording lens has a range of fifteen meters, with computerized automatic focus, zoom, and light-adjustment features. With one-touch recording and simple adjustment controls, even the most intimidated technophobe can get good results. A small playback screen and a speaker grille allow instant review of recordings, although the screen's image quality is primitive compared to that of a full-size two-dimensional vidprojector or hologram projector.

The PersonalAssistant-4x stores data on a dozen removable storage crystals, offering a total continuous recording time of one hundred hours. The time meter displays the remaining recording time. Power cells supply energy for two hundred hours of operation between recharges.

The recording rod's interface ports accept more sophisticated microphones and enhanced lenses, such as those with long-range imaging or infrared and ultraviolet wavelength sensitivity. The PersonalAssistant-4x's data port can be used to connect the unit to datapads, droids, and computers to exchange data. While this unit cannot record in true holographic mode, it uses interpolation coding that allows computers and hologram projectors to extrapolate the two-dimensional data into nearly authentic holographic images.

While most recording rods are aimed at the mass market, with impulse-purchase prices and good-quality recording, there are specialized recording rod designs to suit every need and budget. Miniaturized units—some as small as a comlink—can cost over one hundred credits and use miniaturized data chips or small laminated cylinders for data storage, with a recording time of up to twenty hours.

Professional-grade recording rods for the entertainment and news industries are two to three times the size of the personal recording rod and cost several hundred credits each. They have much more sensitive lenses, greatly enhanced recording ranges, and built-in infrared and ultraviolet optics. Audio pickups offer longer ranges as well as high- and low-range sensitivity. Enhanced storage crystals hold up to a thousand hours of data.

Recording rods are used commonly for scouting surveys and police investigations as well as to make transcripts of government and corporate meetings. During the Galactic Civil War the Rebel Alliance used these types of tapes to hide secret coded messages for its agents. Personal uses range from recording family celebrations to making personal logs and diaries. There is also a thriving two-dimensional recording industry that supplies entertainment to the countless travelers and students who carry cheap, miniaturized two-dimensional vidprojectors. These two-dimensional productions tend to offer unsophisticated, lurid storytelling but are extremely affordable.

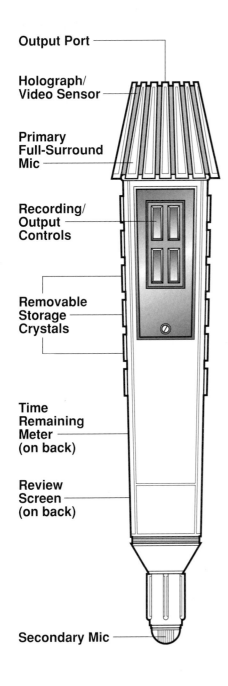

Output Port

Holograph/
Video Sensor

Primary
Full-Surround
Mic

Recording/
Output
Controls

Removable
Storage
Crystals

Time
Remaining
Meter
(on back)

Review
Screen
(on back)

Secondary Mic

Side View

Figure (for scale) with Recording Rod

HARPOON AND TOW CABLE

UBRIKKIAN POWER HARPOON LAUNCHER

Across the galaxy, power harpoons and tow cables are bolted onto tugs and airspeeders. These cables are affixed to loaded cargo skiffs, which can then be maneuvered through bustling, often mazelike freight yards.

When towed by another vehicle, a cargo skiff can carry considerably larger cargo loads because the skiff's repulsorlift generator can be applied for the sole purpose of providing lift—the landspeeder or airspeeder pulling the skiff provides the forward momentum. Since specialized cargo skiffs were always in short supply, the Rebel Alliance frequently added power harpoons to its T-47 airspeeders. They were then used for transferring cargo modules during base deployments. When these devices were first installed, few of the Alliance's technicians suspected that ordinary cargo-hauling tools would prove to be practical weapons capable of toppling the Empire's fearsome All Terrain Armored Transport (AT-AT) walkers.

The Ubrikkian power harpoon is a simple device that consists of a magnetic accelerator, multiple fusion disks, and spools of high-tension cable. Power harpoons typically are mounted facing backward, though a swivel mount increases flexibility for targeting in tight spots. The unit has its own simple electronic sight and can link to standard targeting computers.

When fired, the harpoon's magnetic accelerator propels each fusion disk as far as two hundred meters; the optimum range is a hundred meters. The fusion disk, trailing a tow cable, automatically adheres to any metal surface. Once the disk is securely attached to its target, the harpoon operator takes in any slack and locks the high-tension tow cable in place.

The harpoon may have an attached fusioncutter that can be used to sever the cable at any time. When this is done, the cable can be allowed to drift free, or a second fusion disk can be connected to the cable's loose end. This procedure can be followed for linking multiple barges simultaneously or for transferring barges to other tow vehicles. Normally, the Ubrikkian power harpoon holds three two-hundred-meter-long spools of cable and three fusion disks.

Such harpoon launchers turned out to be potent weapons at the famous Battle of Hoth. Although the Empire's walkers proved impervious to the Alliance's artillery and snowspeeder blasters, Luke Skywalker and the Alliance tactician Beryl Chiffonage devised a plan that would allow them to entangle the walkers by using specially reinforced tow cables. The daring attack plan required that the snowspeeder circle the walker, eluding its moving legs. Pilots had to carefully avoid exhausting the two-hundred-meter-long spool of cable.

Pilot Wedge Antilles and gunner Wes Janson aboard Rogue Three were the first to complete this dangerous maneuver, toppling a walker only moments before it was to destroy Echo Base's power generators. This spectacular success boosted morale among ground troops and pilots alike, encouraging them in their valiant fight to delay the Imperials while the Alliance's high command rushed to evacuate the base.

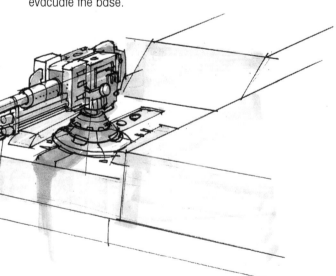

Top View of Snowspeeder with Harpoon Gun Placement

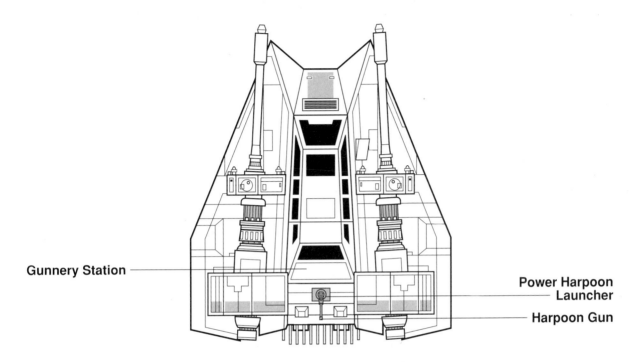

Gunnery Station

Power Harpoon
Launcher

Harpoon Gun

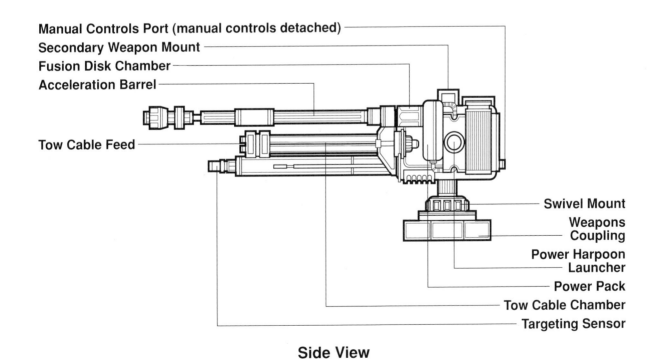

Manual Controls Port (manual controls detached)
Secondary Weapon Mount
Fusion Disk Chamber
Acceleration Barrel

Tow Cable Feed

Swivel Mount

Weapons
Coupling

Power Harpoon
Launcher

Power Pack

Tow Cable Chamber

Targeting Sensor

Side View

HOLOGRAM PROJECTOR

PLESCINIA ENTERTAINMENTS CS-MARK 12

Hologram technology provides the basis for the galaxy's most common communications medium. For example, miniaturized holographic players and recorders can be mounted inside datapads and astromech droids, while hologram communicators—also known as hologram pods—can be found almost everywhere for use in local communications. Starship hologram pods generally are patched into a ship's comm or subspace transceiver for broadcasting to other vessels, while many military and government hologram pods are connected to the HoloNet for instantaneous transmission of messages across the galaxy.

When a holographic recording is made, the recorder scans the subject via two synchronized imagers, while an internal computer combines those recordings to construct a three-dimensional light image complete with color, sound, and motion. The hologram can be stored on crystals, data tapes, or data disks for playback on any standard hologram projector. Miniaturized units, such as those installed in R2 units, produce images plagued by flickers, sudden color shifts, and other technical glitches.

A larger unit designed for public presentations, the CS-Mark 12 hologram projector produces images up to five meters in diameter. Input slots accept data disks, data dots, and other storage media, and interface ports accept direct feeds from droids and computers. The CS-Mark 12's operators can control sound, playback speed, projection size, and image rotation speed. An alternative flat-screen data display system can be used for two-dimensional images.

The CS-Mark 12 can call upon specialized programs to edit, enhance, and manipulate the recordings. The computer-generated holographic images contained in the plans to the Second Death Star were enhanced by Rebel technicians, allowing the techs to illustrate key locations aboard the battle station and demonstrate the flight path that would be best for fighters entering the Death Star on the mission to destroy its main reactor.

Holograms also are used for entertainment and are predominantly broadcast through planetary and subspace networks. Holographic films, three-dimensional sculptures, and three-dimensional paintings are also extremely popular. The holographic strategy game dejarik is a favorite of Chewbacca, and the Wookiee had a gameboard installed aboard the *Millennium Falcon*.

Public holographic theaters on cosmopolitan Core Worlds—such as Coruscant and Corulag—exhibit entertainment programming, documentaries, sporting events, and news. Most of these arenas have a central hologram unit that can project images over thirty meters tall. Even more advanced holographic systems create total immersion environments for use at amusement centers such as Hologram Fun World.

Military simulators also use holographic technology. Luke Skywalker earned clearance to fly in the Battle of Yavin after having completed an X-wing simulator mission, and many New Republic pilots enjoy flying simulated missions. A favorite scenario re-creates the Battle of Yavin and adds an Imperial perimeter fleet with several cruisers.

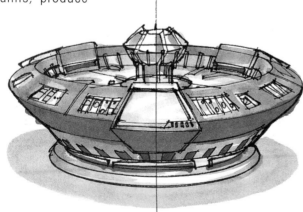

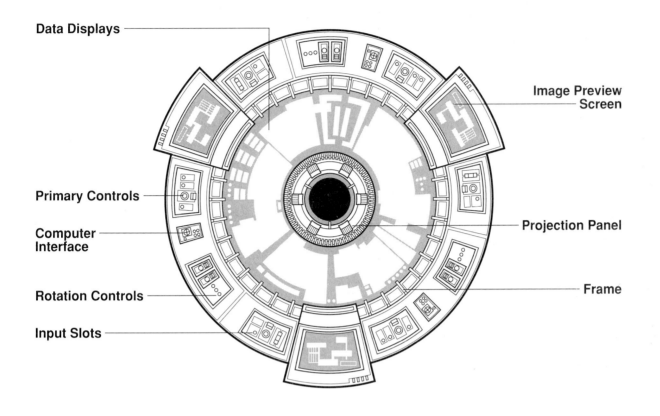

Data Displays

Image Preview Screen

Primary Controls

Computer Interface

Projection Panel

Rotation Controls

Frame

Input Slots

Top View

Side View

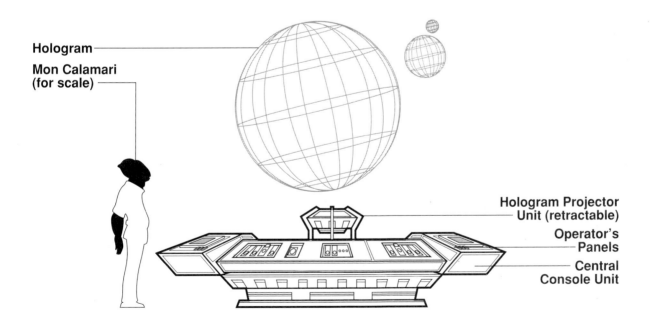

Hologram

Mon Calamari (for scale)

Hologram Projector Unit (retractable)

Operator's Panels

Central Console Unit

JET, ROCKET, AND REPULSOR PACKS

MITRINOMON Z-6 JET PACK

While portable rocket and jet packs are considered outdated for transportation, they will always be romanticized because of the Old Republic's famous Rocket-jumper troops, which played such a prominent role during the great battles of the Sith War, four thousand years before the Battle of Yavin. Even today, backpack devices provide enough thrust to transport users over vast distances in a few seconds. This can make them quite useful in certain circumstances. The bounty hunter Boba Fett uses his Mitrinomon Z-6 jet pack as he charges into battle, hiding his movements under a cloud of exhaust. He often captures and whisks away his targets before anyone can muster a response.

When activated, the jet pack's intake system forces a mixture of air and fuel into miniaturized turbines. There the mixture is ignited, and each three-second ignition provides enough thrust to propel Fett up to one hundred meters horizontally or seventy meters vertically. Directional exhaust

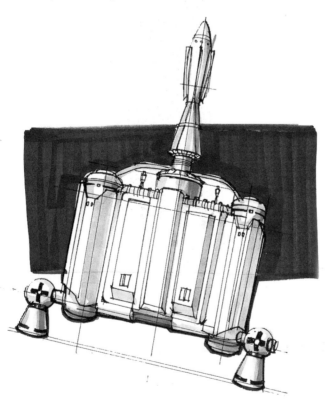

nozzles are used for midflight course adjustments, while the pack's gyro-stabilizer automatically applies counterthrust for safe landings.

This model weighs about thirty kilograms, carries enough fuel for twenty bursts, and costs three hundred credits. It can lift the user and up to a hundred kilograms of additional cargo. The jet pack's control panel is mounted on Fett's forearm, and a secondary verbal interface system has been run through his helmet's control computer.

Unfortunately, jet packs can misfire if struck—this occurred at the Great Pit of Carkoon when Han Solo clobbered Fett's jet pack with a vibroblade. The blast sent Fett careening into Jabba the Hutt's sail barge, and the stunned bounty hunter quickly tumbled into the Sarlacc pit. Fett's armor protected him and the hunter was able to escape eventually.

Jet packs tend to be lighter and less bulky than rocket packs because they draw in oxygen from a planet's atmosphere for combustion. However, they are useless underwater, in a vacuum, and in low-oxygen atmospheres. Alternatively, rocket packs use premixed fuels that require no added oxygen and can work in any environment, including the vacuum of space. Despite their additional bulk, rocket packs offer performance comparable to that of jet packs, although they are more expensive.

Repulsorlift packs are used rarely since their miniaturized repulsorlift generators offer slow movement, although they are incredibly maneuverable and the user can apply steady thrust to hover in place. Like all repulsorlift generators, repulsor packs operate by propelling the wearer away from any object with a substantial gravity field. Thus, they do not work in zero-gravity environments. Repulsor packs use rechargeable energy cells, each offering about ten minutes of flight time and top speeds of around forty kilometers per hour.

Some rocket and jet packs incorporate a secondary repulsorlift unit that offers stability, greater maneuverability, and hovering capability. These combination packs normally cost over a thousand credits and tend to be much heavier, but many users indicate that the added versatility counters any disadvantages.

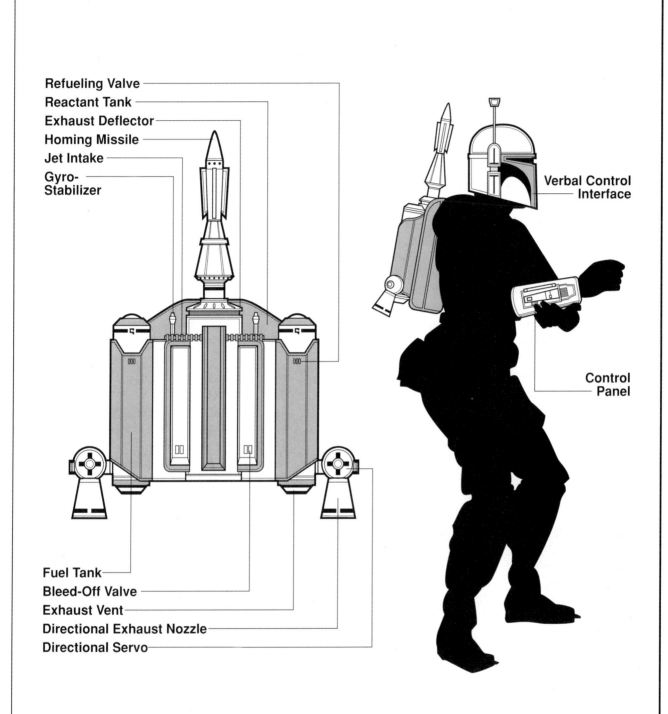

Refueling Valve

Reactant Tank

Exhaust Deflector

Homing Missile

Jet Intake

Gyro-Stabilizer

Verbal Control Interface

Control Panel

Fuel Tank

Bleed-Off Valve

Exhaust Vent

Directional Exhaust Nozzle

Directional Servo

Front View

Figure (for scale) with Rocket Pack

MEDPAC

BioTech FastFlesh Medpac
Chiewab GLiS Emergency Medpac

Medpacs are emergency medical kits used in the field to treat minor injuries and stabilize badly injured patients until they can be taken to advanced medical facilities. These inexpensive kits cost only about a hundred credits each but carry a wide variety of medicines and emergency-care tools. Internal diagnostic computers offer the user complete descriptions of essential procedures, and so persons with no medical training can use them effectively.

The Chiewab GLiS (General Life-Sustaining) is a basic medpac and carries supplies for treating contusions, broken bones, burns, and traumatic injuries. Its computer can store treatment procedures for one species at a time—typically humans—although program modules can be purchased for thousands of other species. Its limited diagnostic scanner allows the user to monitor a patient's vital signs constantly.

Standard medicines include coagulants to stop bleeding, healing salves and sterilizers used to treat burns, and antiseptic irrigation bulbs and disinfectant pads that cleanse wounds and prevent infections. Small bacta patches can be applied to promote the healing of traumatized tissues. Stim-shots and adrenaline boosters keep the patient alert and prevent him or her from going into shock, while painkillers and localized nerve anesthetics reduce discomfort. General-use antibiotics, countertoxins, and immunity boosters can be used to treat patients subjected to poisons, animal venoms, diseases, and infectious microbes, thus stabilizing a patient until he or she arrives at a health facility where more potent countertoxins can be administered.

All medicines can be applied through patches or painlessly injected with a spray hypo. The GLiS also has a bone stabilizer and several spray splints that immobilize and protect broken bones; when the patient arrives at a hospital, bone fusers can repair the damage completely.

More advanced and expensive medpacs such as the BioTech FastFlesh are designed for use by trained medics and include a much larger assortment of medicines. These medpacs are excellent for battlefield use, offering multiple spray splints, large supplies of stimulants and body boosters, and advanced synthe-nutrient replicators that sustain patients with vital nutrients. Specialized medicines can counteract the effects of radiation, biological poisons, and nerve agents. The FastFlesh medpac also includes a canister of chromostring, which offers deeper penetration of healing agents without causing nerve damage. This medpac has several instruments for emergency field surgery, including a sonic scalpel, a laser cauterizer, and nerve and tissue regenerators.

The FastFlesh diagnostic computer's database covers five hundred different species and is linked to the unit's remote scanner and a sample analyzer that can identify poisons, toxins, and unknown compounds. The computer automatically stores a record of the patient's condition for later reference. This medpac costs five hundred credits and is widely used by emergency-care technicians, including many New Republic medics.

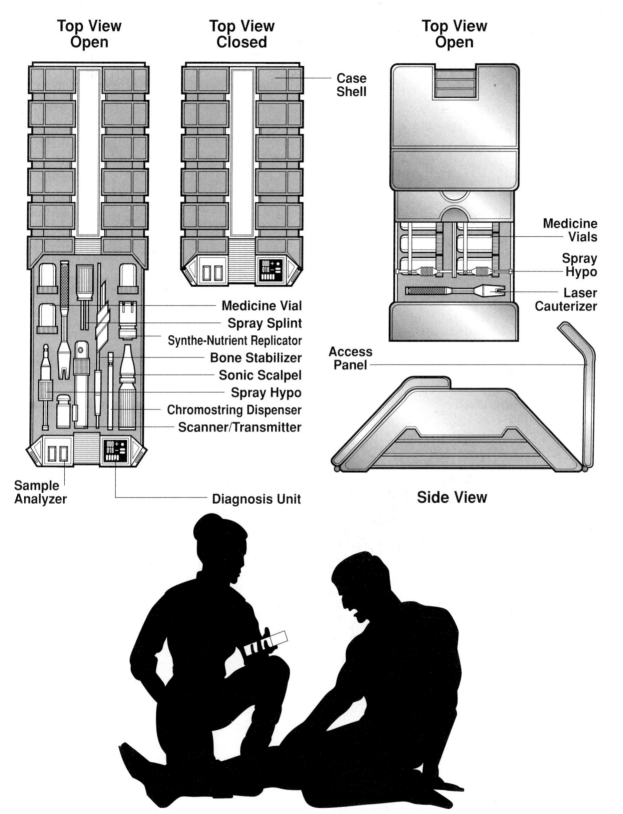

Top View Open

Top View Closed

Top View Open

Case Shell

Medicine Vial
Spray Splint
Synthe-Nutrient Replicator
Bone Stabilizer
Sonic Scalpel
Spray Hypo
Chromostring Dispenser
Scanner/Transmitter

Sample Analyzer

Diagnosis Unit

Medicine Vials
Spray Hypo
Laser Cauterizer

Access Panel

Side View

Figures (for scale) with Medpac

BACTA TANK

ZALTIN BACTA TANK

One of the galaxy's medical miracles, the liquid known as bacta is a powerful healing agent that allows patients to recover from life-threatening injuries in a matter of days. To receive treatment, the patient is fitted with a breath mask and is immersed in an enclosed rejuvenation tank known as a bacta tank. The mask has a microphone and audio speakers that allow the patient to communicate with doctors and surgical droids.

The bacta tank is filled with a clear synthetic fluid that mimics the patient's vital fluids and acts as a nutrient and disinfectant bath. This fluid also treats and preserves the bacta, which is otherwise prone to spoiling when exposed to open air.

When the bacta—a red, translucent fluid—is injected into the tank, it interacts with traumatized tissues to promote rapid healing while blocking infections. The bacta triggers the rapid regeneration of muscle, nerves, tendons, skin, and other tissues without permanent scarring. Patients often recover from nearly fatal injuries after less than a week of bacta immersion. Medicines, stim-shots, adrenaline boosters, and immunity enhancers can be released directly into the fluid mix or can be injected into the patient via retractable spray hypos.

Industrial Automaton's 2-1B surgeon droids and similar units constantly attend to the patient and link directly to the tank's medical computers, which constantly monitor the patient's condition and can provide complete internal scans. At Echo Base on Hoth, the 2-1B droid worked with a Medtech Industries FX-7 medical assistant droid.

Bacta tanks cost three thousand credits each and can be set up in a matter of hours. Most hospitals maintain several tanks for treating patients who are in critical condition, while smaller partial-immersion tanks are used to treat less serious injuries.

The Vratix, a species of insectoid aliens native to the planet Thyferra, created bacta by mixing alayhi salve with a synthetic liquid chemical known as kavan. The result was a universal healing agent that could be used to treat thousands of different species. Two companies—Zaltin and Xucphra—soon came to dominate bacta production and distribution. When the Empire rose to power, it forged an agreement with them to restrict bacta sales; as a result, the Rebel Alliance suffered continual bacta shortages during the Civil War. Two and a half years after the Battle of Endor bacta shortages became so critical that the New Republic staged a campaign to liberate bacta production, and that conflict became known as the Bacta War.

In addition to bacta tanks, most hospitals offer specialized treatment centers that include surgery suites, recovery wards, and quarantine units. Many large hospitals have prosthetics units to produce cybernetic replacement limbs and organs. Also, patients can supply genetic samples for use in growing replacement organs, eyes, muscles, and skin tissues in cloning tubes. This cloning process can take up to three weeks, but it greatly reduces the odds of the patient's body rejecting the replacement.

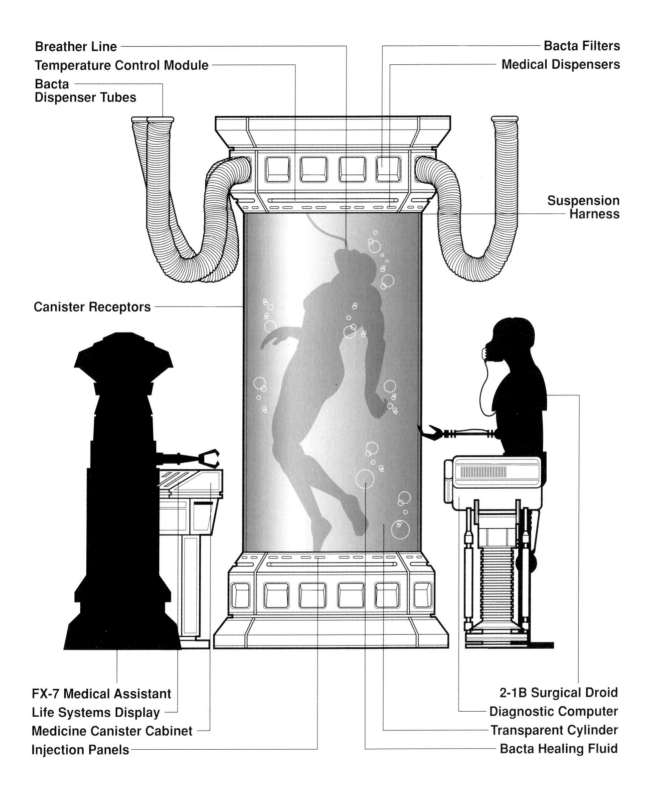

Breather Line

Temperature Control Module

Bacta
Dispenser Tubes

Bacta Filters

Medical Dispensers

Suspension
Harness

Canister Receptors

FX-7 Medical Assistant

Life Systems Display

Medicine Canister Cabinet

Injection Panels

2-1B Surgical Droid

Diagnostic Computer

Transparent Cylinder

Bacta Healing Fluid

REMOTE

INDUSTRIAL AUTOMATON MARKSMAN-H COMBAT REMOTE

The term "remote" applies to an entire class of restricted automatons. These automatons have no independent initiative, acting only on orders given by their owners. Like droids, remotes possess a degree of intelligence—although it is quite limited—and draw on a library of preprogrammed instructions and past experience to complete their tasks.

Han Solo keeps an Industrial Automaton Marksman-H combat remote aboard the *Millennium Falcon* for target practice. During their ill-fated trip to Alderaan, Obi-Wan Kenobi used it to train Luke Skywalker in the fundamentals of lightsaber combat. This remote is a fifteen-centimeter-diameter sphere that is covered with maneuvering thrusters, laser emitters, and sensors.

The remote's onboard computer is programmed with numerous combat drills. Each ends after a preset time or after a specific number of hits has been scored. The trainee sets his blaster to emit light only—no destructive energy—and the remote's sensors automatically detect when a hit has been scored. For novice drills, the remote moves slowly and the stun blasters are disabled. However, at expert settings the remote weaves around the opponent at top speed, filling the air with stinging stun blasts. Marksman-H remotes are excellent for lightsaber combat drills: Since the remote's stun blasts have a much greater reach than does the lightsaber's blade, the Jedi must deflect numerous stun blasts while patiently waiting for an opportunity to strike back.

Stun blast intensity is variable, ranging from light discharges that merely tingle to full-intensity stun beams that can numb an arm or leg for several minutes. The selected difficulty level determines the remote's fire rate, which may be as fast as twice per second. The remote's firing accuracy also is variable, although advanced drills feature *very* precise targeting so that the trainee gets excellent practice at dodging attacks.

Beneath the remote's lightly armored casing there is a small repulsorlift generator that can achieve a top speed of twenty-five kilometers per hour. Eight maneuvering thrusters make the remote exceedingly nimble, with surprisingly fast acceleration and deceleration and instantaneous turns and altitude adjustments.

A handheld signaler controls the Marksman-H through high-pitch coded bursts, and there is a verbal emergency override code. Some droids can replicate the coded signals, and this allows them to seize control of the remotes. This came in handy when the droid named Blue Max summoned Han Solo's remote and used it to bowl over several goons who were about to terminate the Corellian smuggler and his Wookiee copilot.

Other common remotes include cargo lifters, baggage carriers, and remotely controlled drones such as the Krystallio Detection Plus RMD-20 Eye in the Sky. The Eye is a long-range surveillance unit that can be used by police forces to track criminal suspects.

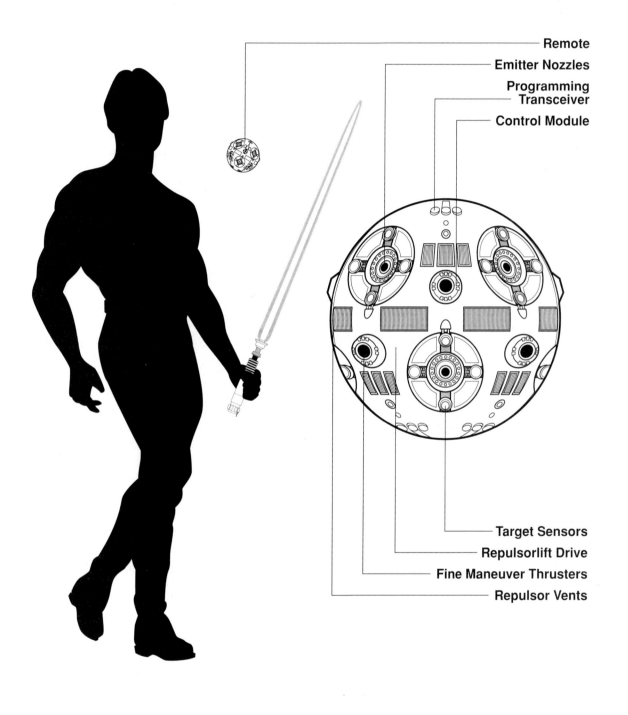

Remote

Emitter Nozzles

Programming
Transceiver

Control Module

Target Sensors

Repulsorlift Drive

Fine Maneuver Thrusters

Repulsor Vents

Figure (for scale)

Side View

SEEKER

ARAKYD MARK VII INQUISITOR SEEKER

Seekers are specialized hunting remotes that track and capture or kill their targets. Arakyd's Mark VII Inquisitor was used throughout the Galactic Empire, and many criminals and outlaw Imperial-sympathizer governments still use seekers even though they have been outlawed by the New Republic.

The Mark VII's small repulsorlift generator produces a top speed of forty kilometers per hour, with a maximum altitude of fifty meters. This seeker has a high level of artificial intelligence and cunning and typically hovers out of sight while tracking suspects. After confirming the target's identity, the seeker moves in and completes its task with merciless efficiency.

Internally, the Mark VII carries an Arakyd BXT-4 central processing computer and an AA-1 Verbobrain that understands fifty thousand languages. The seeker's vocoder system can replicate organic languages and transmit the high-density electronic languages that are used by droids. The seeker's data probe can interface with computers, security monitors, and communications networks. Imperial seekers often invoked emergency overrides to compel droids to reveal information or used data probes to review and download memory banks and files.

The Mark VII seeker has an incredibly sophisticated sensor suite. Four visual sensors provide full 360-degree vision, and electrobinocular functions can focus on objects up to two hundred meters away. Directional audio sensors can record any conversation within a hundred meters, and their frequency range extends far above and below the threshold of human hearing. Heat sensors with infrared scopes can locate footprints and other heat sources, while the unit's genetic sampler can analyze hair, blood, and skin, comparing the results with stored records to identify the sample's source. The seeker's internal transceiver can monitor all comlink frequencies.

The Mark VII carries a pair of blasters, each with an optimal range of twenty-five meters and a maximum range of fifty meters, and with an energy output that matches that of a standard blaster rifle. They can be set to stun or to kill, and the power cells store enough energy for one hundred shots.

Seekers were developed by the Old Republic to serve as nonlethal trackers, investigation drones, and emergency bodyguards. With the rise of the Empire, seekers were armed with lethal weaponry and given increased autonomy; missions often specified "shoot-to-kill" orders. Imperial officers often used seekers to track and eliminate "enemies of the state," including Rebels, political opponents, and even rival officers who stood in the way of their career advancement.

While the New Republic has banned lethal seekers, restricted units with stun blasters are legal and often are used by local police forces to supplement security checkpoints and for discreet surveillance of criminal suspects. Seekers can be programmed for use as practice remotes, since they can handle complex drills and can use comlink transceivers to synchronize their actions. During his Jedi training on the planet Dagobah, Luke Skywalker often drilled against Yoda's seekers, sometimes battling as many as four of the remotes at a time.

Figure (for scale) with Seeker

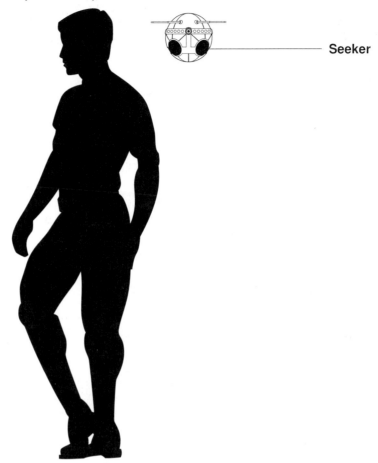

Seeker

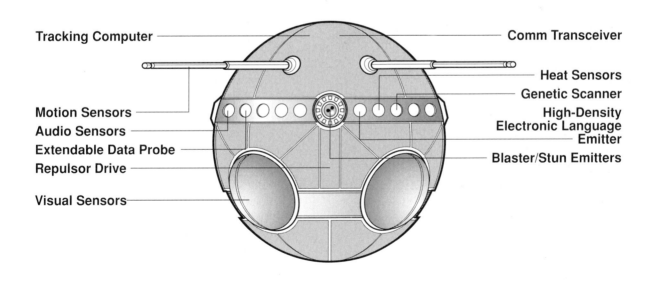

Tracking Computer

Comm Transceiver

Heat Sensors

Genetic Scanner

High-Density
Electronic Language
Emitter

Motion Sensors

Audio Sensors

Extendable Data Probe

Repulsor Drive

Blaster/Stun Emitters

Visual Sensors

Front View

DATAPAD

MicroData Companion2000 Datapad

Datapads are handheld computers designed to offer general computer functions such as data gathering and storage. They also can be customized to provide specialized programs. MicroData's Companion2000 is a standard datapad with a weight of less than one kilogram and a cost of one hundred credits.

Standard uses include information organizing, writing, data processing, and reviewing recording rod crystals. The unit's processing power is backed up by a storage capacity of five million data screen units (DSUs), and automated instruction sequences allow users to initiate complex processing tasks with only a few keystrokes.

The Companion2000 has several standard features that are common to most datapads, including its touch-sensitive color readout screen, audio pickups, headphone ports, and power cells that operate for three months between recharges. Data can be inputted via the keypad or by using a data stylus. Users can attach readout glasses that scroll information across transparent lenses so that the wearer can perform other tasks while simultaneously calling up data.

The Companion2000's standard data ports and interfaces allow linking with datapads, droids, and computers. Special programs permit linking with computerized tools, weapons, and vehicles. The datapad's input slot enables the user to read and record to data cards, disks, and microdots, while internal software can recognize dozens of different computer formats. An additional program called the Galactic Universal Translator (GalUT) analyzes and interprets unknown computer systems and develops pro-

grams to allow the exchange of data. The Companion2000 also interfaces with recording rods and hologram projectors, while its small built-in hologram projector can produce images up to twenty centimeters tall.

Some datapads include miniaturized hologram recorders or visual recorders to scan text and data images. Voice and retinal-motion controllers provide hands-free operation. Many datapads also have built-in comlinks for exchanging data across local comm networks or for open-air broadcasts on comlink frequencies. As might be expected, encryption programs block the legions of slicers, criminals who are dedicated to illegally intercepting, stealing, or destroying data.

Customized programs allow the Companion2000 to be used for specialized tasks in any number of fields. For example, starship engineers can store maintenance and repair manuals, analysis programs, and performance specs. Medics often use datapads to store databases that contain diagnosis and treatment information for thousands of species.

One step up from datapads, portable computers provide the processing power and memory of a mainframe. While they originally were designed for traveling executives, they are used frequently by slicers for espionage and data theft. Portables are quite expensive—ranging anywhere from five hundred to fifty thousand credits—but can analyze and manipulate data at fifty times the speed of a standard datapad. They also utilize a form of artificial intelligence called holistic data transfer (HDT) to compress and store data in an information shorthand, thus increasing storage capacity by a factor of at least one hundred.

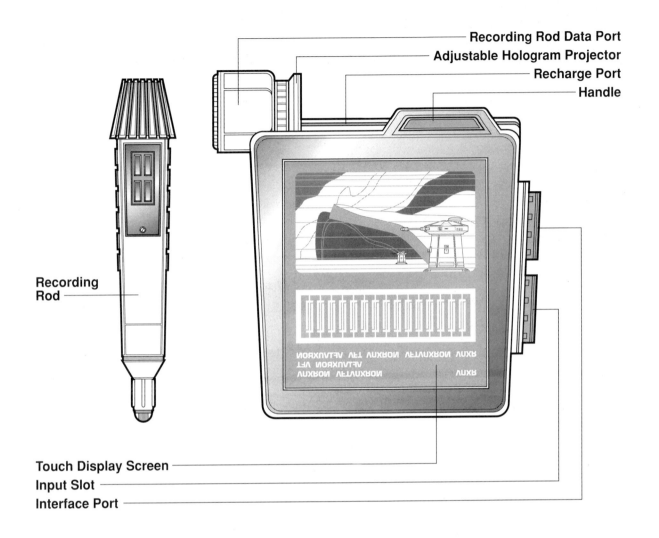

Recording Rod Data Port

Adjustable Hologram Projector

Recharge Port

Handle

Recording Rod

Touch Display Screen

Input Slot

Interface Port

Top View with Recording Rod

Left Side View

Computer Processor

Cooling Vents

Power Cells

CYBORG UNIT

BioTech Borg Construct Aj^6

Technology has produced many wonders, but perhaps the most remarkable and most feared and misunderstood advances have appeared in the field of cybernetics, where the result has been the part man, part machine known as the cyborg. Applications run the gamut from the production of lifelike replacement limbs to enhancements that can make people run faster or give them better reflexes.

Advanced cybernetic implants such as BioTech's Borg Construct Aj^6—as used by Lobot, Cloud City's administrative aide—allow recipients to control computer systems directly. The Aj^6 construct brain/biocomputer interface connects the user to a sophisticated cyborg computer, dramatically enhancing his or her logic and reasoning capabilities. The user can control any linked computer system via mental commands, and the cyborg's computer simultaneously analyzes data, resulting in a twentyfold increase in speed compared to computer operators lacking these enhancements.

The Aj^6's memory can store millions of data screen units (DSUs) for instant access. Several external ports accept knowledge cartridges that provide exhaustive additional information on any given subject. Thus, the cyborg can load a specific procedure as needed and proceed with the assuredness of an expert who has performed the task thousands of times.

The cyborg construct's utility will depend on the computer systems to which it is linked. At Cloud City, Lobot can instantly check any data within the massive computer core and adjust all operations, from altering the output of the city's massive repulsorlift generators to sounding a citywide general alarm. He can access the city's communications scanners to listen in on comlink and subspace transmissions. Lobot supervises the Wing Guard, Cloud City's police force, and can instantly dispatch officers to deal with security concerns. Lobot is responsible for keeping the Baron Administrator fully informed of any important developments that may affect Cloud City's safety and relays important data directly to the Baron Administrator's comlink or datapad.

Cyborg implants are tremendously expensive. The Aj^6 cyborg implant itself costs eighty thousand credits, while the implantation surgery procedure costs seventy thousand credits, and a mistake can result in brain damage or death. Cyborgs face prejudice because people know they go psychotic. Expressions of emotion and personality gradually disappear as the recipient begins to think in terms of pure logic, machine codes, and mathematics. There have been several recorded instances in which implant subjects have suffered cybernetic psychosis, whereby they go insane when their minds lose the ability to maintain control of the cyborg computer.

Cyborgs also sacrifice many of their rights. Under Imperial law, they weren't considered citizens, and cyborging surgery had to be sponsored by a corporation or local government to which the cyborg was indentured. The New Republic has adopted a more enlightened attitude, but cyborgs are still considered "special-class" citizens and are required to submit to periodic neural scans that ensure that the cyborg unit is operating properly.

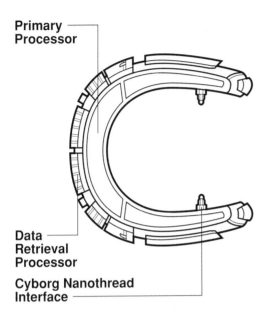

Primary
Processor

Data
Retrieval
Processor

Cyborg Nanothread
Interface

Top View

Side View

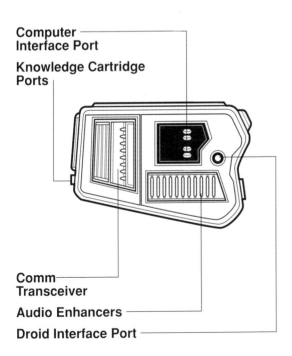

Computer
Interface Port

Knowledge Cartridge
Ports

Comm
Transceiver

Audio Enhancers

Droid Interface Port

Figure (for scale) with Cyborg Unit

CARBON-FREEZING CHAMBER

FIGG AND ASSOCIATES CLASS THREE CARBON-FREEZING CHAMBER

Cloud City's many carbon-freezing chambers are an important part of the city's economy because they prepare Tibanna gas, the mining colony's main export, for shipment to other worlds. They are hot, uncomfortable, and dangerous places to work, with mazes of machinery and conduits that pump Tibanna gas, freezing agents, and molten carbonite into each chamber's freezing pit.

Tibanna gas is harvested from the lower levels of Bespin's atmosphere via a giant tractor-beam tube found at the base of Cloud City. The gas is pumped through the city's refineries and stabilized at high pressure in press-chem tubes. In the final step before shipment, the gas is pumped into a carbon-freezing chamber pit, where it is suspended by miniature magnetic fields. A control casing slides into place, providing a frame for the scalding liquid carbonite that floods the pit and wraps around the Tibanna gas molecules, locking them in place. Then liquid cooling agents flash-freeze the carbonite, instantly forming an airtight solid block.

The carbonite blocks—which weigh over one hundred kilograms each—are raised to the carbon-freezing chamber's floor by hydraulic lift, and retrieval tongs are used to place the blocks on repulsor sleds for transport to processing and shipping stations. The frozen carbonite yields high-quality durable metal alloy shells that provide outstanding protection and can withstand radiation and temperature extremes.

Tibanna gas is used as a hyperdrive coolant. However, the initial survey of Bespin revealed that the planet's atmosphere naturally produces spin-sealed Tibanna

gas. The spin-sealing process greatly compresses the Tibanna molecules at the atomic level, storing a tremendous amount of energy and making the gas an outstanding fuel for turbolasers and other energy weapons. Instead of being shipped off-world, the blocks containing spin-sealed Tibanna gas are shipped to panning chambers where high-powered microporous energy fields scrape off the Tibanna gas atoms. These atoms are processed and packed in canisters for shipment to waiting customers.

While carbon-freezing chambers were designed for industrial use, Darth Vader intended to employ one to capture and freeze Luke Skywalker so that he could be delivered to the Emperor. When Baron Administrator Lando Calrissian suggested that carbon-freezing might kill Luke, Vader tested the process on Han Solo.

Solo survived, suspended in hibernation within the carbonite block, but when he was freed by Princess Leia, he experienced many of the symptoms of hibernation sickness, including disorientation, temporary blindness, and painful hypersensitivity to sensory input. Dreams and hallucinations flooded his mind. Such side effects have been known to cause insanity, but Solo soon recovered.

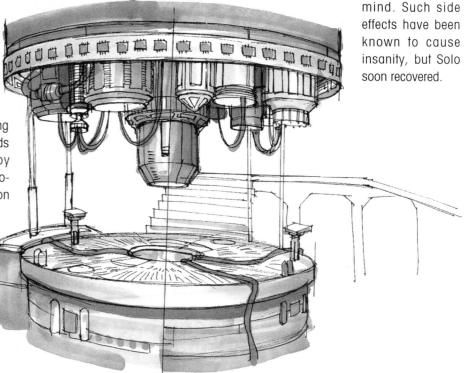

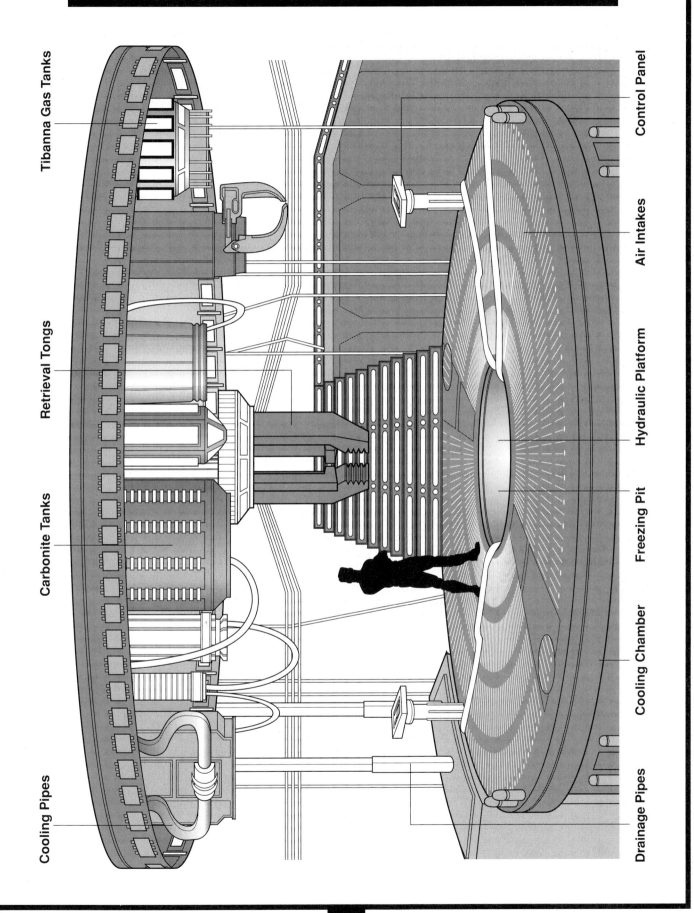

Tibanna Gas Tanks

Retrieval Tongs

Carbonite Tanks

Cooling Pipes

Control Panel

Air Intakes

Hydraulic Platform

Freezing Pit

Cooling Chamber

Drainage Pipes

HOLOCRON

JEDI HOLOCRON

Holocrons are the custom-built instructional tools used by Jedi Masters. These small crystalline cubes store volumes of holographic records documenting the history and lore of the Jedi Knights.

Some Holocrons are simple cubes, while others have unusual geometric shapes or ornate symbols etched into their crystalline faces. Each Holocron has its own different access method, such as touching a specific panel or speaking a certain phrase aloud. The Holocron built by the famed Master Bodo Baas automatically activated as soon as it was grasped by anyone who was attuned to the Force.

Holocrons use what seems to be a forgotten technology through which many crystals form a complex latticework that serves to record and reproduce holographic images and sound. They appear to have unlimited storage capacity and have no visible energy source.

Holocron records depict important historical events, such as the struggle to defeat Dark Lord of the Sith Exar Kun, or document a Master's training and meditation techniques. Jedi Knights used their Holocrons to explain newly formulated Force abilities and record their theories about the nature of the Force. These devices provided a means of passing Jedi knowledge from generation to generation to ensure that the lessons of the past—both heroic and tragic—would never be forgotten.

However, a Holocron is more than a collection of static recordings. It is an interactive teaching tool, an intuitive logic module that faithfully re-creates the images and personalities of past Jedi Masters, who act as hosts. The Jedi who built the Holocron is the primary host, while other contributors add their images and personalities to host their sections.

The hosts guide Jedi students through specific lessons, imparting information, and also testing their abilities. They pose philosophical challenges about the nature of the Force to help Jedi students master their new abilities while remaining in harmony with the light side of the Force. These guides restrict access to sensitive information—particularly techniques related to advanced Force powers—until students have proved their ability to use the knowledge responsibly.

Unfortunately, the ancient Jedi Holocrons have all but disappeared from the galaxy. Emperor Palpatine destroyed many as part of his plan to obliterate the Jedi Knights. Luke Skywalker first learned about these devices during his tutorials with Obi-Wan Kenobi, but he didn't actually see one until nearly a decade later, when he confronted the reincarnated Emperor Palpatine, who possessed the Holocron of Master Bodo Baas. Luke and Princess Leia Organa Solo liberated this device, and Luke used it to greatly improve his knowledge of the Force. Unfortunately, it was destroyed during the struggle against the Emperor's forces.

It is believed that other Holocrons may still survive, hidden in the isolated huts of long-dead Jedi Knights, awaiting a time when those strong in the Force will rediscover the old ways.

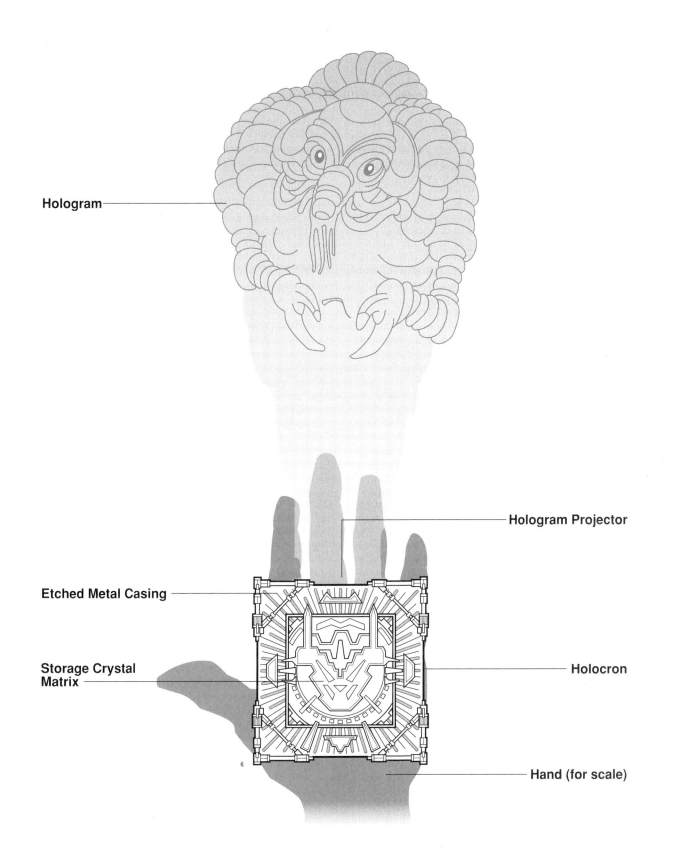

Hologram

Hologram Projector

Etched Metal Casing

Storage Crystal
Matrix

Holocron

Hand (for scale)

SSI-RUUVI ENTECHMENT RIG

SSI-RUUVI ENTECHMENT RIG

The aliens known as the Ssi-ruuk rely on a horrifying power-conversion process known as entechment, through which a being's life energies are drained to supply energy that is used for powering technological devices.

Each victim is captured and strapped into an entechment chair, where a catchment rig is strapped into place. A magnetic solution, or magsol, is injected into the subject's carotid artery. The catchment arc applies an intense magnetic field that charges the magsol and drains all the victim's life energy in an excruciatingly painful procedure that kills the subject. The life energy is stored in battery coils, then charged into Ssi-ruuvi paddle beamers, battle droids, and other devices.

The Ssi-ruuk originally developed this technology for use on a species of small reptilians known as P'w'ecks but

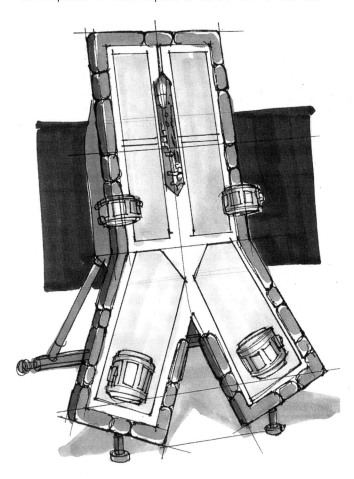

soon discovered that humans provide a superior quantity of entechment energy. However, an echo of the human's memory accompanies the electricity into the catchment arc. This echo perceives itself as being conscious and often suffers psychosis triggered by the entechment process. This reduces the life energy's sustainable period to a span of only a few days.

The Ssi-ruuk solved this problem when they captured and brainwashed a young human named Dev Sibwarra, who quickly demonstrated an ability—a manifestation of the Force—to soothe entechment subjects so that their life energies wouldn't degrade as quickly. When the Ssi-ruuk attacked Bakura, Dev detected Luke Skywalker and theorized that Luke's Jedi abilities would allow him to entech subjects from vast distances.

In anticipation of Luke's capture, the Ssi-ruuk built a special reclining entechment bed equipped with locking arm and leg bands. Twin tubes would puncture the victim's throat and pump magsol and nutrients into his or her bloodstream, orienting the victim's nervous system toward the bed's catchment circuitry. The nutrient stream would allow the Ssi-ruuk to leave the subject in the entechment bed for several days. To limit the subject's resistance, an upper spine beamer could numb his or her body for up to two hours and thirty-five minutes. Finally, the Ssi-ruuk developed a mind-control drug that would force a Jedi to entech subjects against his or her will in a process that's incredibly painful for both the Jedi and the entechment victim.

This bed was tested on Dev Sibwarra, who enteched a subject kept a few meters away from him. It was believed that Luke's Jedi abilities would allow him to entech subjects from up to thousands of kilometers away. The Ssi-ruuk captured Luke and began preparing for their ambitious scheme, but Dev overcame the Ssi-ruuvi brainwashing. Together, he and Luke escaped, forcing the aliens to evacuate their flagship and retreat in defeat.

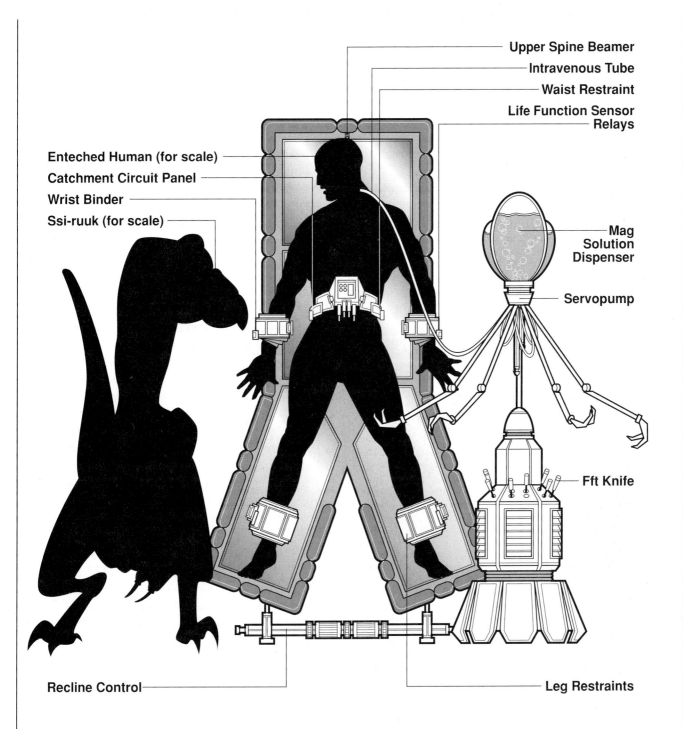

Upper Spine Beamer

Intravenous Tube

Waist Restraint

Life Function Sensor Relays

Enteched Human (for scale)

Catchment Circuit Panel

Wrist Binder

Ssi-ruuk (for scale)

Mag Solution Dispenser

Servopump

Fft Knife

Recline Control

Leg Restraints

ORGANIC GILL

MON CALAMARI ORGANIC GILL

The Mon Calamari organic gill is an engineered biotechnology symbiont that filters ocean water to provide a steady stream of breathable air to the wearer. While Mon Calamari can breathe water, they are predominantly air breathers, and this creature was developed to negate the discomfort they encounter when they switch to breathing water during long underwater journeys.

The gill is a small, transparent, gelatinous blob that fits over the user's nose and mouth. It draws breathable, gaseous oxygen from the ocean water, allowing the wearer to travel underwater for an indefinite period with no risk of drowning. While this is uncomfortable at first, most wearers quickly adapt to these creatures, which are lighter and less cumbersome than conventional air tanks and filtering systems.

The gill readily accepts physical implants such as chin protectors and clamps for goggles. Comlink transceivers, each equipped with a small microphone and earphones, slide into the gill, which fits around them and holds them permanently in place. As with standard comlinks, this unit can be tuned to any of the thousands of standard frequencies.

Most users don formfitting wet suits, and many carry waterproof backpacks containing food, an emergency comlink, and a medpac. Many Mon Calamari also carry a portable scanner that enables them to detect and avoid oceanic predators such as the krakana.

Each organic gill costs two hundred credits and lives for several weeks. Although designed for Mon Calamari and Quarren, organic gills are compatible with many oxygen-breathing species, including humans, although Sullustans are allergic to the organic gills. Organic gills are quite popular with tourists, since they allow them to explore the wonders found beneath a planet's ocean surface but eliminate the need to carry air tanks or use submersibles.

During one of her missions to the planet Mon Calamari, Princess Leia Organa donned an organic gill and was guided around the planet's oceans by the Mon Calamari named Clighal. The gills allowed Clighal and Leia to travel in secret as they searched for Admiral Ackbar, who had resigned his commission from the New Republic and had gone into hiding after a tragic piloting accident on the planet Vortex.

Clighal led Leia to a creature known as the Knowledge Bank, a primitive sentience that is aware of all the events that occur in Mon Calamari's oceans. Leia learned from it that Ackbar was living in a small sea pod near the Mkbuto Seatree Preserve. Upon finding him, she revealed that the accident had actually been sabotage engineered by the Empire. Relieved by this news, Ackbar rejoined the New Republic's navy and played a vital role in defeating Admiral Daala's fleet of Star Destroyers when they attacked Calamari.

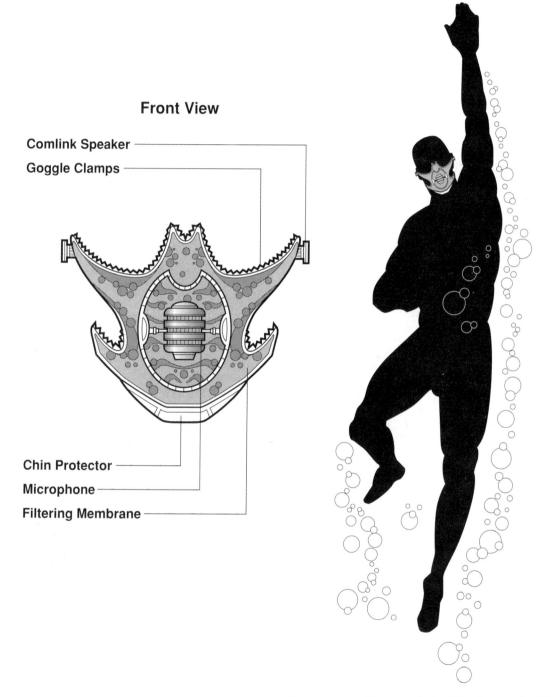

Front View

Comlink Speaker

Goggle Clamps

Chin Protector

Microphone

Filtering Membrane

Swimmer (for scale) with Organic Gill

MAGWIT'S MYSTIFYING HOOP

MAGWIT'S MYSTIFYING HOOP

The grand finale of Magwit the Magician's stage show is his Mystifying Hoop Trick. But unlike the countless performers who rely on expensive special effects trickery and misdirection, Magwit utilizes a remarkable portable teleportation machine that transports him from the stage without a trace.

Magwit's system consists of a handheld controller, two separate teleporter frames, and a boxlike teleportation generator. These frames—one is a hoop, and the other is a rectangle—incorporate a short-range matter transmitter and receptor mechanism. Each is just over two meters across, large enough to allow Magwit and his assistants to walk through without having to stoop.

Each teleporter's outer ring is insulated so that it can be grasped, held, and moved. When something passes through one of the rings, the teleportation generator instantaneously transports the object (or person) to the other frame. The system offers a maximum teleportation range of fifty meters, and its power demands are extraordinary. The teleporters drain their power cells after only one minute of use.

The transmitter receptors and matter transmitters seldom last more than three uses before burning out. It seems safe to assume that the results would be tragic if someone were in transit when the unit failed, although Magwit has been lucky enough never to experience such an incident.

The device is far more advanced than even the New Republic's best technology. Some have theorized that whatever passes through the hoop is broken down into energy and transmitted to the other teleporter. Another theory suggests that the teleporter transmits the object into hyperspace; if this is the case, the teleportation generator must cloak the object or person in a sheath of energy, as occurs with starships when they travel in hyperspace, since normal matter is vaporized instantly when it interacts with the energies of hyperspace.

The truth is that Magwit doesn't quite understand how the teleporter works. Many years ago he befriended the teleporter's original owner—a rather strange alien—all the while observing how to operate and repair the device. Magwit eventually stole the teleporter and fled, establishing his traveling magic show.

Boba Fett recruited Magwit and his teleportation system when the bounty hunter set out to capture the space pirate Bar-Kooda. Magwit had encountered Bar-Kooda several years earlier and had been forced to entertain the space pirate and his gang of cutthroats aboard the ship *Bloodstar*. This time Magwit performed his normal routine and concluded the performance with his hoop trick, but he tricked Bar-Kooda into walking through the hoop, teleporting the pirate to the receiver in the *Bloodstar*'s cargo hold, where Boba Fett was waiting. A spectacular escape ensued, and Fett claimed his bounty and freed Magwit, who continues to dazzle the backwater worlds of the galaxy with his magic show.

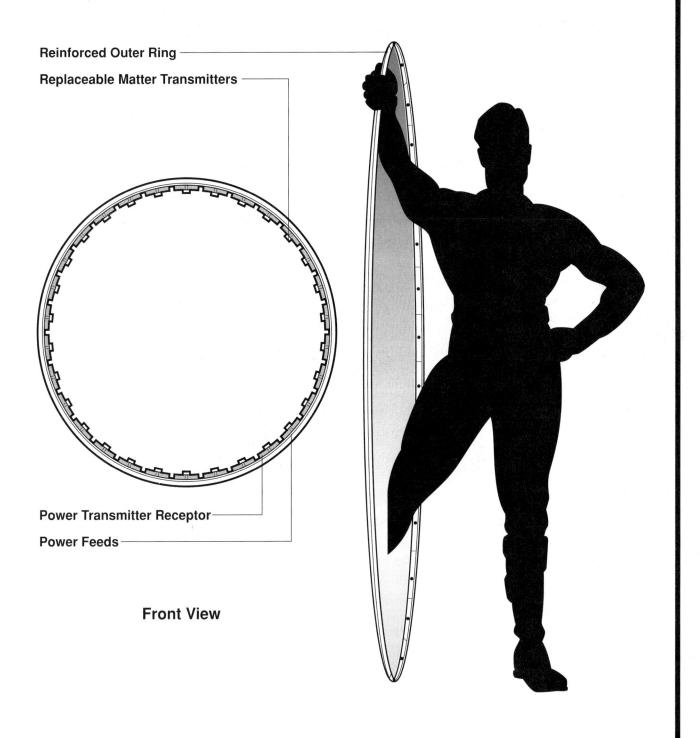

Reinforced Outer Ring

Replaceable Matter Transmitters

Power Transmitter Receptor

Power Feeds

Front View

Figure (for scale) with Hoop

INFRARED MOTION SENSOR

NEURO-SAAV NITESITE INFRARED MOTION SENSOR

Infrared motion sensors, commonly known as night scopes, detect sources of heat and motion and display them on their screens to provide users with visual assistance in darkness. They are used by scouts, big-game hunters, and soldiers and are favored by bounty hunters.

The Ubese bounty hunter Boushh wore a battle helmet that included a Neuro-Saav NiteSite infrared and motion sensor unit. The NiteSite remains a popular visual enhancement system because of its reliability and ease of use. Infrared scanners detect heat sources at ranges up to two hundred meters, while a cluster of low-illumination enhancers highlight all physical objects within ten meters, allowing the wearer to see and move in complete darkness. A flashguard filter activates in one-thirtieth of a second to negate the potentially blinding bursts of light that result from explosions, torches, flares, and flash grenades.

The unit's analysis computer can track and highlight up to fifty targets on the readout screen, while the motion sensor has up to fifty times zoom magnification and can synchronize with the user's blaster via a wireless link or a connection cable, allowing the user to display the weapon's fire vector on the screen. The NiteSite costs six hundred credits and weighs about half a kilogram. Its sturdy composite plastics protect the miniaturized optics from hard knocks, and input ports can be used to connect additional sensors.

Boushh's helmet also included a breath filter and a voice enhancer, allowing the Ubese to operate in human-standard atmospheres. Boushh added a retractable transparent display screen that could be used for viewing data files called up from the control computer. The helmet included omnidirectional sound pickups to conduct long-range eavesdropping and to detect individuals approaching from behind.

Boba Fett's battle helmet includes a similar infrared/motion sensor unit with an enhanced macrobinocular viewplate. It is linked to all his weapons, providing the infamous hunter uncanny accuracy. The Wookiee bounty hunter Snoova also uses a miniaturized infrared scanner fitted into a one-piece monocle unit that snaps over his right eye.

Imperial gunners used helmet visors that included computerized optical targeting displays. Those advanced motion sensor systems were linked directly into Imperial turbolasers, with long-range scopes that could track starships at the edge of visual sighting distance. The helmets noted the target's speed and anticipated its flight path.

There are a number of similar infrared enhancers on the market, including weapon sights such as the Neuro-Saav Sure-Sight, which enhances available light in near darkness, fog, and other low-illumination conditions. The Sure-Sight's crosshairs allow instant targeting, while readouts automatically display the distance to the target.

Standard motion sensors clip to any helmet and drop a transparent display screen in front of the user's eyes to automatically highlight all moving targets. Most of these sensors connect directly to a blaster and provide a crosshair that indicates where the blaster is aimed. Many motion sensor units include electrobinocular sensors for long-range targeting.

Front View

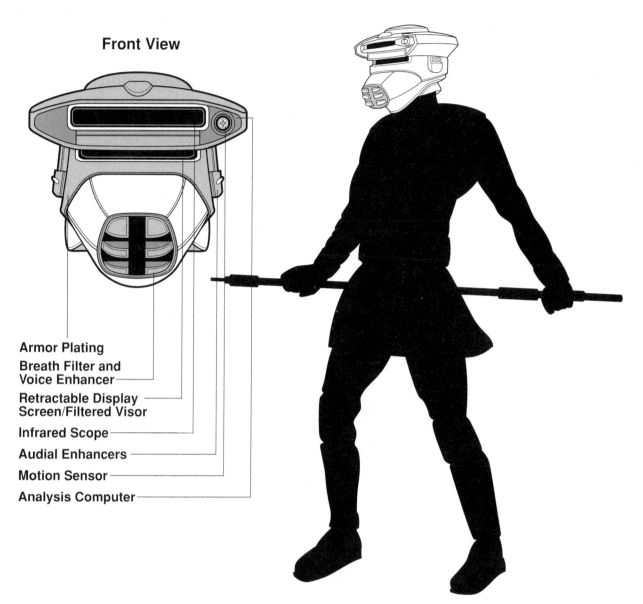

Armor Plating

Breath Filter and
Voice Enhancer

Retractable Display
Screen/Filtered Visor

Infrared Scope

Audial Enhancers

Motion Sensor

Analysis Computer

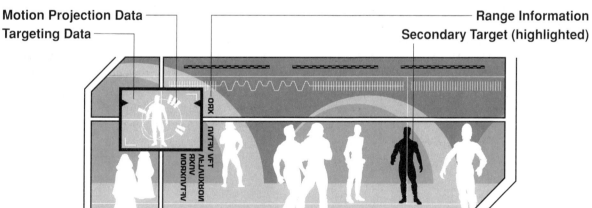

Motion Projection Data

Targeting Data

Range Information

Secondary Target (highlighted)

Scope View

About the Author

Bill Smith's writing credits include *Star Wars: The Essential Guide to Vehicles and Vessels* and numerous *Star Wars* role-playing game products for West End Games. Aside from his interest in *Star Wars* and science fiction, he is an avid stock car racing fan and spends many Saturday evenings at the local short tracks.
His wife, Amy, understands.

About the Artists

Troy Vigil began drawing at age eight and cites the *Star Wars* Trilogy and its wondrous environments as the principal factors in his decision to pursue an art career. He began his professional career in print production before becoming a freelance computer artist. His work appears in Ballantine/Del Rey's *Star Wars: The Essential Guide to Vehicles and Vessels* as well as in trading cards, magazines, calendars, posters, and studio-licensed portfolio sets. He lives in Venice Beach, California, with his partner, Stacey, and nine cats.

David Nakabayashi currently works at Industrial Light & Magic as a Visual Effects Art Director.